A Spiritual Geography of
Early Chinese Thought

Bloomsbury Studies in Philosophy of Religion

Series Editor: Stewart Goetz
Editorial Board: Thomas Flint, Robert Koons, Alexander Pruss, Charles Taliaferro, Roger Trigg, David Widerker, Mark Wynn

Titles in the Series

Freedom, Teleology, and Evil by Stewart Goetz
The Image in Mind: Theism, Naturalism, and the Imagination by Charles Taliaferro and Jil Evans
Actuality, Possibility, and Worlds by Alexander Robert Pruss
The Rainbow of Experiences, Critical Trust, and God by Kai-man Kwan
Philosophy and the Christian Worldview: Analysis, Assessment and Development edited by David Werther and Mark D. Linville
Goodness, God and Evil by David E. Alexander
Well-Being and Theism: Linking Ethics to God by William A. Lauinger
Thinking through Feeling: God, Emotion and Passibility by Anastasia Philippa Scrutton
God's Final Victory: A Comparative Philosophical Case for Universalism by John Kronen and Eric Reitan
Free Will in Philosophical Theology by Kevin Timpe
Beyond the Control of God? edited by Paul M. Gould
The Mechanics of Divine Foreknowledge and Providence edited by T. Ryan Byerly
The Kalām Cosmological Argument: Philosophical Arguments for the Finitude of the Past edited by Paul Copan with William Lane Craig
The Kalām Cosmological Argument: Scientific Evidence for the Beginning of the Universe edited by Paul Copan with William Lane Craig
Free Will and God's Universal Causality by W. Matthews Grant
Sacred Music, Religious Desire and Knowledge of God, by Julian Perlmutter
The Evolutionary Argument against Naturalism, by Jim Slagle
Why God Must Do What Is Best, by Justin J. Daeley

A Spiritual Geography of Early Chinese Thought

Gods, Ancestors, and Afterlife

Kelly James Clark and Justin Winslett

BLOOMSBURY ACADEMIC
LONDON • NEW YORK • OXFORD • NEW DELHI • SYDNEY

BLOOMSBURY ACADEMIC
Bloomsbury Publishing Plc
50 Bedford Square, London, WC1B 3DP, UK
1385 Broadway, New York, NY 10018, USA
29 Earlsfort Terrace, Dublin 2, Ireland

BLOOMSBURY, BLOOMSBURY ACADEMIC and the Diana logo
are trademarks of Bloomsbury Publishing Plc

First published in Great Britain 2023
This paperback edition published 2024

Copyright © Kelly James Clark and Justin Winslett, 2023

Kelly James Clark and Justin Winslett have asserted their right under the Copyright, Designs and Patents Act, 1988, to be identified as Authors of this work.

Series Design by Louise Dugdale
Cover image: Detail of a bronze 'fang hu' wine vessel. Late Eastern Zhou period, 4th century B.C. © GRANGER - Historical Picture Archive / Alamy Stock Photo

All rights reserved. No part of this publication may be reproduced or transmitted in any form or by any means, electronic or mechanical, including photocopying, recording, or any information storage or retrieval system, without prior permission in writing from the publishers.

Bloomsbury Publishing Plc does not have any control over, or responsibility for, any third-party websites referred to or in this book. All internet addresses given in this book were correct at the time of going to press. The author and publisher regret any inconvenience caused if addresses have changed or sites have ceased to exist, but can accept no responsibility for any such changes.

A catalogue record for this book is available from the British Library.

A catalog record for this book is available from the Library of Congress.

ISBN:	HB:	978-1-3502-6217-1
	PB:	978-1-3502-6221-8
	ePDF:	978-1-3502-6218-8
	eBook:	978-1-3502-6219-5

Series: Bloomsbury Studies in Philosophy of Religion

Typeset by Integra Software Services Pvt. Ltd.

To find out more about our authors and books visit www.bloomsbury.com and sign up for our newsletters.

Contents

List of Tables — vi

Introduction — 1

Part 1 High Gods and Their Critics

1 Heaven and the High Gods in Early China — 13
2 Heaven in the *Xunzi, Mozi*, and the *Zhuangzi* — 29
3 The Depersonalization of Heaven? — 45

Part 2 God and the Philosophers

4 Did Confucius Believe in Heaven? — 55
5 Heaven in the *Mencius* — 71

Part 3 Ancestors and Afterlife

6 Afterlife — 87
7 Sacrifice — 115

Part 4 A Deeper Dive

8 The Evolutionary Psychology of Chinese Religion — 139
9 Lesser Gods of the Pre-imperial Era — 163

Appendix: The Curious Case of Dong Zhongshu — 177
Notes — 180
Bibliography — 204
Index — 220

List of Tables

1	Instances of *Di, Shangdi,* and *Tian* in Pre-Qin texts	145
2	Instances of *Di* as a punisher and rewarder	146
3	Instances of *Shangdi* as a punisher and rewarder	146
4	Instances of *Tian* as a punisher and rewarder	147

Introduction

The Study of Religion in Early China

The study of religion in China, and in particular in early China (pre-220 CE), has been a subject of Western academic research for almost as long as modern Western academic research on China has existed. The earliest scholars of China from the West were more often than not missionaries who, owing to their calling, were deeply interested in the religiosity that they witnessed in their various missions. Though these figures provided productive insights into many local communities of their time, their missionary aims and goals also often colored descriptions of what they saw and read. In more modern academic parlance, their theoretical methodologies were sometimes based upon the religious doctrines of their own religious communities; their own religious doctrines, then, often framed how they understood and communicated religion in China. This primarily manifested as taking a broad category, "Christian religion," as the epistemological or metaphysical framework of Chinese religion. The nineteenth-century missionary and sinologist James Legge's choice of translating terms such as Heaven *Tian* 天 and *Shangdi* 上帝, China's High Deities, as "God" has given some the impression that the early Chinese worshipped the Abrahamic God.

Later scholars moved decidedly away from assuming the axiomatic status of the Abrahamic religions (or any specific religion). Chun-Fang Yu, for example, claims of Chinese religions that "there is no God transcendent and separate from the world and there is no heaven outside of the universe to which human beings would want to go for refuge" (Yu 2007: 1243–5). Frederick Mote argued that "The Chinese ... have ... no creator, god, ultimate cause, or will external to itself" (Mote 1972: 26). Sociologist Marcel Granet, in *La pensée chinoise*, claimed that the "governing ideas" of early Chinese thought included no "world of transcendent realities outside the human world" (Granet 1934: 279); Granet famously proclaimed, *"Ni Dieu, ni Loi"* (Granet 1934: 476). In his monumental *A History of Chinese Civilization,* sinologist Jacques Gernet likewise denied that the ancient Chinese were theists: "The classical formulae, 'respect' and 'fear Heaven' ....did not refer to a single, all-powerful God, the creator of heaven and earth, but instead evoked the ideas of submission to destiny, a religious respect for rituals, and serious and sincere conduct" (Gernet 1985: 193).

While such claims can and should be seen as responses to the earlier more missionary assertions of some universalist, Abrahamic God, they also seem to reflect more the concerns of the contemporary scholars asserting them than specific aspects of religiosity in China. Such non-theistic sentiments concerning Chinese religion or even "the Chinese" have tended to dominate academic work on the subject for much of the late twentieth century.

Growing and more diverse understandings of religion and religiosity have brought about a scholarly reassessment of religion in China. Notable publications by scholars such as Michael Loewe (1979), Daniel Overmeyer (1995), Poo Mu-chou (1998), Michael Puett (2002), and the large collaborative work, *Religion in early China* (Kalinowski and Lagerwey 2009), have engaged with issues such as gods, ritual, performance, and social roles—issues that fall under the rubric of "religion." They likewise have not only adopted a more narrow and focused approach to these specific topics, they have also developed their understandings of them from the diverse texts and recently discovered artefacts produced by the communities themselves. Through their methods, this scholarship has shown that religious life in early China involves a diverse panoply of religious paradigms, idioms, tropes, and practices held by diverse communities separated both geographically and temporally.

Such scholarship points to the need to approach religion in China not as some large, monolithic ideology (this is also true of "religion" as a category the world over (Boyer 2001)), and to be wary about the imposition of axiomatic concepts derived from specific doctrines of overarching religions. This scholarship requires looking at the large and emerging range of complex and intersecting concepts and issues that have in more modern times been organized under the rubric of "religion."

A Spiritual Geography

Such an approach, a "geography" of religion, takes research on a topic as not unlike visiting a location in the complex map that makes up religion and religiosity. As one "visits" a topic, one in effect travels through this geography on a "route" that reveals the structures and methods through which these concepts intersect. Akin to a real geography, these routes will be varied and complex, reflecting the varied and complex ways in which communities understand and process these topics. Furthermore, also not unlike a real geography, we should also expect complex diversity alongside changing and even new routes. Indeed, the discovery of new routes reveals the ever-shifting and dynamic ways that local communities change in their engagement with these topics. Moreover, such explorations also reveal that such a vast religious geography continually presents many new and unexplored regions. As in any real geography, this is due not only to undiscovered areas, but also to the ever-changing connections to topics that may have earlier been thought outside the purview of the broad concept of religion. As such, we believe that the rediscovered connections of religion and philosophy in the earliest Chinese texts necessitate a thorough reexamination of early Chinese thought.

When mapping the religious geography of early China, it can be seen that there are now well-charted areas that have illuminated many ancient and diverse ritual practices, prescriptive paradigms, and religious prescriptions that have become salient in understanding the religious life of the diverse communities from this time. Yet, as noted, many areas of this spiritual geography—referring to the domains of spirits—remain untrodden, including topics such as deities, ancestors, and the afterlife remain poorly understood. This more "spiritual" area of religious geography has loomed large as a relatively unexplored and ill-ventured area.

This work is hence an exploration of many different areas of this spiritual geography, and the chapters of this work will look at each of these different areas to shed light not only on (a) the various routes that connect them to each other and other more explored areas of the map, but also (b) their implications for a more complete understanding of early Chinese thought. As such, this book will bring the spiritual geography into the larger geography of religion in China.

Akin to the many and diverse scholars who intrepidly set out to explore the realms of religion in China, these chapters reflect a variety of approaches, methodologies and even scholars. The diversity of this spiritual and religious geography warrants a diversity of approaches and perspectives, for, as has already been discussed, monolithic and axiomatic approaches to the topic of "religion" militate against a deeper and richer understanding of the complex geographies before us.

Kelly James Clark is an analytically trained philosopher with interests in religion, text understanding, Chinese thought, philosophy of religion, and human cognition. Justin Winslett is an Oxford-trained sinologist who is interested in understanding the development and use of the supernatural and the extrahuman across different periods in East Asia. Their interests intersect due to (a) the highly pervasive nature of the supernatural in many of the materials from this period, and (b) the intellectual, philosophical, and cultural importance assigned to this period and for many communities in East Asia that have followed. The intersections of Clark's and Winslett's interests have proven rich and revealed a complexity and diversity in Chinese thought that have heretofore not been fully explored. Their multivocal and multivalent approach echoes the multivocal and multivalent nature of a spiritual geography of not just early China but China in general.

Winslett's work in this book both expands and deepens our understanding of the original texts, many of which are untranslated. In so doing, he locates Clark's more philosophical explorations within a richer historical and textual context. Rejections of the High Gods and the afterlife often rely on selective and tendentious readings of texts and history. Sometimes a single line from a single text by a single author (typically Confucius) is taken as representative of a thousand years of Chinese thought. Winslett's translations and in-depth discussions of a wide variety of texts ground claims about the remarkable breadth of views in early Chinese thought and resist the temptation to construct a grand narrative arranged around a single passage or text or set of texts or author.

We are not alone in this project. Michael Puett, for example, shows how Granet, who finds in Chinese thought no "world of transcendent realities outside the human world," selectively relied on just a few Han texts when making claims about Chinese thinking in general (Puett 2002: 9). Guo Moruo writes of the anthropomorphic representations of *Di-Shangdi-Tian*: "He is fully and exactly the same as a human being" (Guo 1936). While Sarah Chang discerns a variety of meanings for *tian* in the Warring States period, she notes that *tian* most commonly meant a supreme deity (Chang 2000: 15). Chen Derong (2009) argues that according to context, "*Di* referred to the earthly emperor as well as to the heavenly emperor; *Tian* referred to the physical sky as well as to a supreme personal god." Finally, in Oxford's *A Dictionary of Asian Mythology* entry on *tian*, we read: "An ancient Chinese term, *Tian* (*T'ien*), used as early as the second millennium bce by the Chou people, means both Nature and Supreme Deity. The root meaning of the word is 'sky'—the place where the gods live. In the Chou period (1111–256bce), *Tian* was a supreme god who interacted personally with the human world" (Leeming 2001).

Some contemporary philosophers have responded, as hinted, by according the *Analects* a unique authority in understanding "the Chinese mind" (paying little heed to, for example, the *Odes* or the *Documents*). But in the era of One Hundred Schools, the claim that the *Analects* represents Chinese thought would have seemed ludicrous. Moreover, "Confucianism" was a construction of the much later Song Dynasty. So prioritizing Confucianism affords Confucius an identity and authority he never had in early Chinese thought. Finally, there's the stark empirical counter-evidence; as Thomas Wilson writes: "In spite of their reputation for reticence on matters of spirits, Confucian officials nonetheless performed sacrifices to spirits throughout imperial times until the early twentieth century. The emperor, court ministers, and civil officials followed a strict calendar of rites devoted to scores of gods and spirits at altars and temples in the capital and throughout the empire" (Wilson 2014: 186).

How, one might wonder, could otherwise highly qualified scholars miss such obvious intimations of gods, ghosts, and afterlife? Paul Rakita Goldin, who likewise argues that early China clearly countenanced beliefs in gods, ghosts, ancestors, afterlife, mind-body dualism and divine creation, speculates that, when it comes to such topics, some sinologists have fallen into the trap of essentializing "the East" and "the West," with the essentialized East always standing in stark opposition to the essentialized West. In his own words: "This is because they present China as a reified foil to a reified West, an antipodal domain exemplifying antithetic mores and modes of thought. If one of the basic characteristics of Western civilization is to delineate the universe and our place in it through the heuristic of creation myths, then China, as our Radical Other, cannot possibly do the same thing. For then China would no longer be 'China'" (Goldin 2008: 3-4). Such historians, Goldin argues, are in the business of myth-making of their own—constructing myths about China's essential opposition to anything Western, including religious beliefs.

We aim in our spiritual autobiography, instead, to heed a wide variety of texts—from received texts to tomb texts to ritual—for the many kinds of spirit beings they represent, often in relation to the human.

The High Gods and Their Critics

The first section of the book directly considers the most salient extrahuman agent in this spiritual geography of early China. Chapter 1, "Heaven and the High Gods in Early China" looks specifically at how the High Gods are depicted in a variety of early Chinese texts. The High Gods sit at the top of various pantheons suggested by the texts. Chapter 2, "Heaven in the *Xunzi, Mozi* and *Zhuangzi*," explores the intersection of the High Deity Heaven within three texts—the *Xunzi*, *Mozi*, and *Zhuangzi*. Although Heaven is an active and pervasive agent in all three texts, modern scholars typically hold these three texts as arguing anti-theistic philosophies. This chapter shows that representations of Heaven transcend such differences indicating a shared construction in the spiritual geography of early China. The third chapter, "The Depersonalization of Heaven?," rejects the influential claim that early China grew increasingly rationalistic and humanistic and, as such, less concerned with the High God.

Philosophical Reflections on China's Early Spiritual Geography

The first section of the book illustrates the rich and diverse geography of the High God to be found in many early Chinese texts. Understanding the application of the High Deity to Chinese thought is the focus of sections two and three. The second section explores the spiritual geography from within the context of what we've come to call "philosophy," in general, and "philosophy of religion" and "metaphysics" and "ethics," in particular. Its chapters address a number of philosophical arguments pertaining to this geography, addressing what Clark calls the "Naturalizing Narrative."

Like the myth that China has no creation myth (Goldin 2008), the Naturalizing Narrative has taken on a life of its own. The naturalizing narrative has four central claims. As noted previously, a number of scholars assert that

(1) *The Chinese don't believe in God or the afterlife.*

We will show that early Chinese texts are replete with representations of both the High God and the afterlife. When made aware of this, it is often asserted that

(2) *Belief in God and belief in the afterlife were common among peasants and in the* Mozi, *but not in "the philosophical texts."*

Angus Graham, for example, writes that "in passing from the *Analects* to the *Mozi* one has the impression of descending to a lower stratum of society without access to the higher culture of the Zhou" (Graham 1989: 34); he claims that the Mohist belief in punishing gods and ghosts "belongs rather to folk religion" (Graham 1989: 47). The sentiment is echoed in Benjamin Schwartz who writes that Mozi's "lack of any apparently devotional element, when combined with the inability to prove that Heaven or the spirits deliver immediate rewards and punishments, probably left his upper-class hearers indifferent to his particular religious message" (Schwartz 1985: 170). However, see Chapters 1 and 2, early Chinese transmitted texts,[1] even those artificially designated "philosophical" (so not restricted to unthinking peasants) or "daoist" (so not restricted to the *Mozi*) include representations of the High Gods. As Zhongjiang Wang argues: "… when approached without secular bias, the *Analects* and the *Liji* proclaim to us that Confucius and many non-Xunzian Confucians, in fact, had not divorced themselves from the ancient religious traditions of honoring spirits and gods" (Wang 2016: 8).

When made aware of this textual evidence to the contrary, the response is often that

   (3) *The Confucians*[2] *don't believe in God or the afterlife.*

Graham, for example, writes: "The tendency throughout the classical age is to ignore the spirits of the dead and of the mountains and rivers after paying them their customary respects and to regard Heaven as an impersonal power …" (Graham 1989: 47). Such claims often rely on such slender evidence as *Analects* 3.12:

> "Sacrifice as if [they were] present" means that, when sacrificing to the spirits, you should comport yourself as if the spirits were present.
>   The Master said, "If I am not fully present at the sacrifice, it is as if I did not sacrifice at all."

Peimin Ni claims that *Analects* 3.12 means: "This position does not focus on *believing* the existence or presence of the spirits as they are in themselves; instead, it guides one's mental disposition of their 'as-if-presence' in the practice" (Ni 2017: 121). Feng Yulan concedes the Confucian insistence on funerary and sacrificial rituals yet contends that they reject the existence of spirits; such rituals have "poetic" not ontological significance (Feng 1952: 57–8). There was, I will argue, no "tendency throughout the classical age … to ignore the spirits of the dead," even among "the Confucians."

The chapters on Confucius and Mencius, as good Confucians as any, will offer evidence against the claim that the so-called Confucians don't believe in the High God. Clark argues in Chapter 4, "Was Confucius a Theist?", that the character "Confucius" in *The Analects,* the text typically attributed to Master Confucius, affirmed or assumed the existence and importance of the High God Heaven.

In Chapter 5, "Mencius on Heaven," he argues the same of Confucius' most important follower, Mencius. Clark will show, in Chapter 6, how early Chinese texts represent, assume, and ritually illuminate afterlife beliefs (and a metaphysical conception of persons that supports it).

Then it is often claimed that

(4) *God and the afterlife are morally irrelevant to Confucian moral theory.*

Clark will argue that canonical "Confucian" texts represent the High God and afterlife beliefs as morally salient to so-called "Confucian" moral theory. Chapter 7, "Sacrifice," looks at ancestor worship, a well-known aspect of the religious geography of China. Such early conceptions of ritual, which centrally involve the High God, ancestors, and the afterlife, affirm the moral salience and communal power of such beliefs.

A Deeper Dive

The final two chapters dig deeper into early Chinese thought by expanding discussion of the nature and status of gods.

Chapter 8, "The Evolutionary Psychology of Chinese Religion," co-authored by Clark and Winslett, takes insights from cognitive science to show that one should expect to find supernatural punishment—representations of a moralizing and providential high god who rewards the righteous and punishes the wicked—in early Chinese texts. Supernatural punishment theory, a recent development in the cognitive science of religion, holds that the solution to early human cooperation beyond kin-groups was widespread belief in a super-knowing, morally providential high God. Since not all divine punishment occurs ante-mortem, supernatural punishment theory, in combination with other afterlife beliefs produced by other cognitive faculties, leads us to expect to find representations of afterlife beliefs and postmortem punishment and rewards. We vindicate supernatural punishment theory in what has long been considered an outlier to standard cognitive science of religion—China; the cognitive science of religion resists verification, it's been claimed, because China is not religious.

Finally, if there are High Gods, then there are likely lesser gods. Winslett, in Chapter 9, "Lesser Deities of the Pre-Imperial Era," looks at other extrahuman agents in the spiritual geography of early China, collectively understood as Lesser Deities. It shows how these deities are pervasive across materials from this time, and further looks at the complex ways they are represented in these texts. Although these Lesser Deities exist in relation to the High Deities, they often show their own complexity and dynamics and modes of behavior independent of other deities.

Conclusion

A spiritual geography is both multifaceted and ambiguous. While "spiritual" could mean something like "religiously uplifting," here it means something more metaphysical and historical. In its metaphysical sense, it refers to something like "member of the domain of the non-human or the above-the-human or the extrahuman; member of the domain of spirit." Included herein are such entities as ancestors, ghosts, lesser gods, and, especially, the High Gods.[3] In its historical sense, this book will look at representations of such metaphysical agents in ancient texts in, as best we can, their ancient contexts. As such, a spiritual geography would involve, at a minimum, a catalogue of spiritual entities and their relations to one another in their world and in relation to humans and their world.

This book will expand our understanding of China's early spiritual geography both for its own sake and for a better understanding of the relationship of the High Gods and the afterlife to early Chinese thought. It offers a more complete spiritual geography of early China, one that both widens and deepens our understanding of Chinese religion and the roles its various forms—including the High Gods, ancestors, and afterlife—played in shaping the thought of early China.

Part One

High Gods and Their Critics

1

Heaven and the High Gods in Early China

Early Conceptions of the High Gods[1]

The received texts from early China are replete with representations of anthropomorphic High Gods. In early China, the High Gods were referred to as *Di*, *Shangdi*, and *Tian*. The earliest references are to *Di* 帝, found in Oracle Bone inscriptions and ceremonial bronzes of the Shang dynasty (ca. 1600 BC–ca. 1046 BC). From them one sees that offerings were given to *Di* who was believed to have power over various natural events such as plagues and floods and also over human affairs. *Di* also reigned supreme over a host of lesser powers and spiritual beings, including ancestors.

David Keightley divides the Shang pantheon into six groups:

> (1) *Di*, the High God; (2) Nature Powers, like Tu, the Earth Power … He, the (Yellow) River Power, Yang … the Mountain Power … and Ri, the sun; (3) Former Lords … such as Nao and Wang Hai, whom the Shang worshippers treated differently from their ancestors; (4) predynastic ancestors …. (5) the dynastic ancestors, starting with Da Yi (the first king); and (6) the dynastic ancestresses, the consorts of the kings on the main line of descent.
>
> (Keightley 1999: 253–4)[2]

The organization of these spiritual beings was often modeled on a political hierarchy.[3] The names or titles of the beings at the top of this hierarchy were either *Di* or *Shangdi*, which are often conflated as one and the same deity in many texts. Theodore de Bary offers a summary of representations of *Di* or *Shangdi* in ancient China:

> The ancestors and Nature Powers could, like *Di*, also affect harvest, weather, campaigns, and the King's health. It is clear, however, that *Di* stood at the peak of the ultra-human, ultra-natural hierarchy, giving orders, which no ancestor

could do, to the various natural hierarchies, giving orders, which no ancestor could do, to the various natural phenomena and responding to the intercessions of the Shang ancestors who were acting on behalf of their living descendants below. That *Di* was virtually the only power who could directly order (ling) rain or thunder, as well as the only power over the winds under his control, which sets him apart from all the other Powers, natural, predynastic, or ancestor, or ancestral.

(de Bary 1999: 11)

This chapter, on the nature of the High Gods, will first look at the *Shangshu* 尚書.[4] Like all transmitted texts, the received version of the *Shangshu* is an accretional, multivalent document—its texts, gathered from disparate texts over hundreds of years, speaks in many, not always consistent, voices. In 150 BCE it reached a form similar to our versions today, but it is composed of texts from both much earlier and even most likely later. In the following section, we will take a deeper dive into socio-political and anthropomorphic representations of the High Gods in a wider variety of texts.

The High Gods in the *Shangshu*

The *Shangshu* represents a pantheon of deities and their relations to one another, from the High Gods to lesser spirits/gods and ghosts down to ancestor spirits.[5] In the *Shangshu*, *Di*, *Shangdi*, and *Tian* often name the same being within the same textual context. For example, in the "Announcement to the Prince of Kang" references to *Di* and *Shangdi* shift without notice to *Tian*. So we read that King Wen's brilliant virtue—his just ministration of punishment, for example, and his care for the widow and widower—

> ascended up to the high God (*shangdi*), and God (*di*) approved. Heaven (*tian*) gave a great charge to King Wen, to exterminate the great dynasty of Yin [that is, the Shang] and received its great appointment, so that the various States belonging to it and their peoples were brought to an orderly condition.
>
> (Legge 2000b: IX.4)

The relationship between the deities—*Tian*, *Shangdi*, and *Di*—is complex and often multivocal. In many texts, the three seem to clearly refer to the same deity. Some scholars argue that during the Warring States period *Tian* becomes an impersonal, natural force (see Schwartz 1985: ch. 2; and Puett 2003: 38–79).[6] Guo Moruo, as noted in the Introduction, writes of the anthropomorphic character of

Di, Shangdi, and *Tian:* "*Shangdi* in the *Shi* and *Shujing* is a completely personal deity, and *Tian* is able to see, listen, speak, smell, eat, act, go, think, be happy, be angry, and is able to father a son. He is fully and exactly the same as a human being" (Guo 1982: 28). The *Shangshu*, in many passages, treats *Tian* as an anthropomorphic, providential deity who cares about human welfare.

"The Great Announcement (*Da Gao* 大誥)" contains arguably the earliest reference to China's central political doctrine, the Mandate of Heaven (*tianming* 天命) (Shaughnessy 1999: 314). The Zhou overthrow of the once-blessed but now-wicked Shang dynasty was justified by the removal of divine favor from the Shang king and the transfer of divine favor to the ruling house of the Zhou. This divine reappointment was considered a moral rebuke of the Shang and an affirmation of the virtue and wisdom of Kings Wen and Wu, the founders of the Zhou dynasty. Thus, the Mandate of Heaven provided a legitimation of the overthrow of the Shang and the moral establishment of the Zhou.

After the death of King Wu, his young son, King Cheng, was elevated to the throne. The youthful King Cheng,[7] unsure of his abilities to rule the kingdom, exclaims:

> Ho! I make a great announcement to you, (the princes of) the many States, and to you, the managers of my affairs.—We are unpitied, and Heaven sends down calamities on our House, without the least intermission. It greatly occupies my thoughts, that I, so very young, have inherited this illimitable patrimony, with its destiny and domains. I have not displayed wisdom, and lead the people to prosperity, and how much less should I be able to reach the knowledge of the decree of Heaven!
>
> (Legge 2000b: Bk. VII.1)

Heaven, "unpitying" (Legge 2000b) or "merciless" (Karlgren 1950), has no respect for persons yet, in accord with justice, "sends down" calamities (injuries) from on high onto the house of Zhou (perhaps referring to their travails involved in squelching the Shang revolt in the city of Yin (the Shang capital)). The young king fears he lacks the maturity and wisdom to both understand and know the commands of Heaven (*gezhi tianming* 格知天命). Heaven, then, is portrayed as transcendent, as caring for the people (commanding and moving King Cheng to lead his people away from injustice and toward prosperity), and as the epistemological and ontological source of goodness.

In what follows King Cheng claims that his father, King Wu, had augmented "the appointment (*ming* 命) which he received from Heaven." King Cheng then consults the tortoise, perhaps as a source of divination, which connects him with the wisdom of Heaven.[8] Considering himself a "servant of Heaven" (Legge 2000b: Bk. VII.P.8), he accepts the divine charge to restore tranquility (*ning* 寧 peace and prosperity) to his kingdom. However, his advisors, noting the difficulty of the mission and the troubled state of his people, recommend against squelching the revolt. Although they encourage him to act contrary to the divinations, King Cheng determines that he cannot disregard Heaven's demand:

> Yes, I, the little child, dare not disregard the Charge of God. Heaven, favourable to the Tranquillizing king, gave such prosperity to our small country of Zhou. The Tranquillizing king divined and acted accordingly, and so he calmly received his (great) appointment. Now when Heaven is (evidently) aiding the people, how much more should we follow the indications of the shell! Oh! the clearly intimated will of Heaven is to be feared: it is to help my great inheritance.
>
> (Legge 2000b: Bk. VII.9)

Heaven returned the Zhou people to prosperity by giving grace *xiu* 休 (Karlgren 1950) to King Wu. For his part, King Wu divined the voice of God and acted in accord with the Heavenly mandate. Given Heaven's care for the people, King Cheng must heed the voice of God (follow the divinations). Heaven then assists King Cheng by purging his kingdom, creating loyalty to King Cheng among the people, restoring peace and prosperity, and enlightening the country.

Within a single paragraph we find *Di*, *Shangdi*, and *Tian* used interchangeably. In this foundational document, the Mandate of Heaven (*tianming* 天命) is also the mandate of god (*Di* 帝): *Tianming* is *shangdiming* 上帝命.[9] There is no contrast between *Tian* and *Shangdi* here. *Tian* is represented in the same anthropomorphic and providential ways of *Di*.[10] We find in these texts an affirmation of a Heavenly moral standard and a caring exerciser of moral providence.[11] Divine authority and righteousness combine to create the mandate; rulers should fear losing Heaven's mandate because of the great cost that it represents to themselves and their people. As such, those who stand under Heaven's severe authority are called to revere and obey it. With respect to the exercise of providence, the source of moral authority, and the establishment of political power, *Tian* is synonymous with *Shangdi*.

Connecting the King with the intelligence of Heaven (Legge 2000b) or Heaven's bright will (Karlgren 1950), *tianming* 天明 holds that Heaven is the moral pattern for the King (themes repeated throughout early Zhou documents).[12]

Pankenier argues that the Zhou doctrine of the Mandate of Heaven assumes an earlier theology found in the Shang:

> By attributing human-like personality to Heaven, and by vigorously reviving the conception of phenomenal nature as an index of Heaven's activity, the Zhou Chinese inevitably reimbued nature with an ethical quality. This feeling for the ethical dimension comes most strongly to the fore in the early Zhou texts, but it was by no means a Zhou innovation.
>
> (Pankenier 1995: 170)

The word *Tian* had some connotations in the Zhou period which were alien to the Shang. In the Shang oracle bone inscriptions, *Tian* refers both to the astronomical heavens and to something great.[13] During the Zhou period *Tian* retained both meanings (depending on the context) while also taking on the notion of a Supreme Being (depending on the context). Historical records show that the physical and spiritual meanings of *tian* are interconnected: it is not unlikely that theological connotations of *tian* were derived in part from its original physical meaning; as heaven towers above the earth, so too *Tian*'s authority towers over the four corners of the world.[14] Finally, the ritual of the tortoise shell, through which the Mandate of Heaven could be known, connects Zhou theology to the Shang practice of divination to determine the will of god.

Shangdi and *Tian*, as names of the High God, connote a political ruler of the universe, to whom subordinate earthly kings owe reverence and obedience. *Tianming* 天命 connotes a sacred relationship between Heaven and its people; the earthly kings, as Heaven's emissaries, exercise their benevolent rule over the people, Heaven's creation. In the "The Great Announcement," the concept of deity is of an anthropomorphic and political High God.[15]

In "The Announcement to the Prince of Kang," the Duke of Zhou advises his brother, Feng, the Prince of Kang, on the occasion of his appointment to the principality of Wei. The Duke of Zhou reminds Feng of what distinguished his father (King Wen): illustrious virtue and caution in punishments. In addition, he treated widows well, employed the employable, and had proper reverence. The Duke of Zhou unites this concern for the material conditions of life with the Mandate of Heaven:

> The fame of him ascended up to the High God, and God approved.[16] Heaven gave a great charge to King Wen, to exterminate the great dynasty of Yin [that is, the Shang] and received its great appointment, so that the various States belonging to it and their peoples were brought to an orderly condition.
>
> (Legge 2000b: IX.4)

The Prince of Kang is charged to follow his father, King Wen, especially in matters of virtue and punishment. He is advised to pursue wisdom in several steps. The first step includes pursuing the wise kings of Yin to discover how to protect and govern the people. The second step involves the study of the sages of Xia—Yao, Shun, and Yu—in order to establish his heart and instruct his people. Next, he is to seek out the wisdom of the ancient kings in order to know how to bring peace to his kingdom. The final step, out of which the former steps emerge, is "to enlarge your thoughts to the comprehension of all Heavenly principles, and virtue will be richly displayed in your person, so that you will not render nugatory the king's charge" (Legge 2000b: IX.5). Heaven is the moral foundation of human society and Heaven's mandate backed by Heaven's providence ensures its success on earth.

The Mandate of Heaven seems to function in two rather different ways. First, the Mandate of Heaven is the general sense of morality and justice that is applicable to all people at all times and places; it is the Heavenly *dao* 道 that should be mirrored on earth. Second, the Mandate of Heaven is one's specific sense of calling or vocation. The Duke of Zhou had the Heavenly Mandate to be the duke to advise the king, but he lacked the mandate to be the king. Everyone has the mandate to be on the side of virtue and justice, but not everyone has the mandate to be a ruler. The role-specific rituals that developed in this period were designed to inculcate both a virtuous inner strength and the proper attitudes of superiority and inferiority necessary for people to harmoniously fulfill their vocation. Without the training to equip people for their particular mandate, people would become servile, resentful, ambitious, or power-mongers. These attitudes would militate against harmony and peace, so the ideal and justice would be threatened.

Heaven is the moral foundation of human society, and Heaven's mandate backed by Heaven's providence ensures it will find its place on earth. The decrees of Heaven are not simply matters of the creation, sustenance, and overthrow of states but extend to the whole of the moral life. For example, the Duke of Zhou tells the Prince of Kang about a younger brother who does not consider the clear will of Heaven and hence shows disrespect for his elder brother. This passage goes on to tell of the dire social consequences of the spread of wickedness, in which "the laws of our nature given by Heaven will be thrown into disorder or destroyed" (Legge 2000b: IX.16). The rulers and the people cooperate with God in bringing about an unforeseen but desired or valued kingdom. The Prince of Kang consolidates his appointment of Heaven by assisting the king. Heaven is not above using coercion to attain its ends: Heaven can be awe-full, angry, and unhappy (Legge 1865: IX.6), inflicting severe punishments on the wicked. Heaven's appointments are not permanent: Heaven's favor would be removed if Prince Kang does not pursue virtue and show care in punishment.

Grounding the right to rule in the Mandate of Heaven was revolutionary. The hereditary right to rule based on kinship is rejected in favor of divine appointment based on wisdom and virtue. Indeed, according to "Numerous Officers," the removal of Heaven's Mandate from the wicked final Shang king was due in part to his impiety. The contrast is sharp between the favored kings who humbly courted Heaven's favor, paid careful heed to the sacrifices, and reverently strove to match in their lives the goodness of Heaven, on the one hand, and the unfavored kings who ignored Heaven, on the other.

Anthropomorphism and the High Deities

This section will take a depper dive into a wider variety of texts that offer representations of the High Deities (and surrounding spirited agents). It offer this additional detail in order to (a) enrich our understanding of the spirit world that haunted early China and (b) understand anthropomorphism as one important and persistent mode of conceiving of the High Deities, amongst a range of others. Representations of the High Deities repeatedly draw upon attributes of the human person, including human persons in hierarchical and power relations within civil society.

> The next year, Xiao Weng of Qi saw the emperor about the ways of deities. The emperor had had a Lady Wang who he had favored. The Lady had died, and Xiao Wang used a method to manifest the Lady Wang in the form of a stove god in the dead of night. The Son of Heaven watched this from behind a curtain. Thereupon, he then entreated Xiao Weng and made General Wen Cheng, rewarded him in the extreme and attended to him as an honored guest. Wen Cheng said, "Your majesty wants to connect with the gods, well, unless all your palaces, rooms and clothes are in the image of the gods, then divine then will not appear." Then, when they made to paint the imperial carriage, the retainers adorned it with victorious luminaries[17] to ward off baleful spirits. They also constructed the Ganquan palace and inside made various rooms and terraces. They painted them with Heaven, Earth, the Great Unity and various deities. They then set up sacrificial implements in order to manifest the heavenly deities. After a few years a more, this method continued to fail, and gods did not appear. He then made a silk text and fed it to a cow. The details of this weren't known,

and he said that in this cow's stomach is something fantastic. He killed it and then looked inside and obtained the text. The sayings of the text were extremely strange, and the Son of Heaven recognized his handwriting. He asked others and indeed it was an apocryphal text. Thereupon, he executed General Wen Chang and hid it.

(Shiji 13:2374)

This passage comes from the *Fengshan shu* 封禪書, a treatise found in the *Shiji* 史記 (aka The Records of the Grand Historian or, more commonly, the Historical Records), a text originating from the Western Han dynasty (206 BCE–8 AD). The treatise lays out a didactic historical narrative, portraying the various rituals, sacrificial, and extrahuman activities engaged in by both ancient leaders and the contemporary rulers of the Qin and Han empires. By "extrahuman" we mean various non-physical beings ranging from ancestor spirits through lesser gods to the High Deities; in this text "extrahuman" includes the postmortem Lady Wang (ancestor spirit), the stove god, the gods, baleful spirits, and heavenly deities. The treatise was influential for its imperial and normative ritual system, commentary on contemporary politics, and attacks on various agents, and activities deemed "unorthodox" to the system portrayed.[18] In the above section, Xiao Weng dupes the emperor (Emperor Wu of the Han (156–87 BCE)) through a number of dubious methods that he claims will magically connect the Emperor with the extrahuman. Although Xiao Weng is revealed to be a charlatan and his techniques prove ineffective, he claims that the lesser gods and spirits are attracted to images of themselves. This prompts the Emperor to have his carriages and palaces decked out in such images. When building the Ganquan palace, the Emperor had the various terraces and rooms painted with images of Heaven, Earth, the Grand Unity, and other assorted deities.

Painting their images implies that deities in general and the High Deities in particular (such as Heaven, a proper name for the High Deities) have an image to be painted. The text does not explain what this image looks like; perhaps the image of Heaven was assumed to be understood by readers.[19] If an image of Heaven is possible, then as images are representations of forms, Heaven has a form as well. But again, the *Shiji* is silent when discussing Heaven's image and form.

In texts from before the *Shiji*, in the pre-imperial period, the form of Heaven is often suggested implicitly. The approximately 324 representations of Heaven in pre-imperial texts offer diverse and complex modes of representation that reveal a large spectrum of extrahuman agents.[20] Heaven is by far the most commonly named High Deity, in comparison to *Shangdi* or *Di* for which there are ninety-one and forty-four mentions, respectively. Although explicit discussion of the form of these deities is sparse, there are many implicit mentions of their form. The texts under discussion have clear patterns of representation reflecting extrahumans in many roles and facets similar to those found in human societies.

Anthropologist Stewart Guthrie points out that when dealing with the supernatural and the extrahuman, humans have a propensity to frame them in discourse and narratives comprehensible to humans (Guthrie 1993: 177–204). As such, an anthropomorphized extrahuman agent is often represented as physically similar to humans, taking on human roles and duties. The role of *Shangdi* and Heaven as the lord of other deities, as discussed by Robert Eno and Sarah Allan, is an anthropomorphization that frames *Shangdi* and Heaven in a ruler-ruled dynamic that represents the human political culture of the time. Heaven or *Shangdi* likewise takes on actions that humans act out, such as giving orders or speaking.[21]

Anthropomorphic representations are found approximately 169 times in twenty texts from the pre-imperial period for Heaven; for *Shangdi*, they are mentioned thirty-five times in nine texts; and for *Di*, they are mentioned twenty-three times in eleven texts. This accounts for a respective 55 percent, 47 percent, and 60 percent of all the mentions of these three terms as they pertain to extrahumans in pre-imperial texts (Winslett 2014: 951–2). Statistically, anthropomorphic representations account for a majority of instances in the case of Heaven and *Shangdi*.

What does anthropomorphization mean in relation to the High Deities? Anthropomorphic representations tend to involve either the casting of the High Deities into specific human roles or depicting them with various human attributes. The High Deities, perhaps not unsurprisingly, are often cast in positions of high or supreme power. This is often seen in the vocabulary, narratives, and rhetoric employed by various texts, alongside numerous explicit mentions of the High Deities in terms of human rulers. In some cases, terms of other authority figures, such as fathers and sages, are also evinced. As the example of the *Shiji* reveals, explicit descriptions of the forms of the High Deities are rare, but they are often implicitly described with human attributes, most notably involving the ability to give birth or produce things and with a range of human emotions.

As the above quotation illustrates, the High Deities are frequently equated with rulers and other positions of authority. Pre-imperial texts abound with mentions of Heaven or *Shangdi* issuing commands and blessings or receiving obeisance and respect. As will be seen, the modes of anthropomorphization strongly frame the High Deities in terms of the familiar political and social hierarchies espoused in the texts. Given that many of these texts are concerned with the establishment of patterns and governance and the construction of a larger human world, this is perhaps not surprising (Lewis 1999b).

The connection with anthropomorphized authority may initially seem unsurprising in the case of *Di/Shangdi* as the term *Di* becomes one of the many terms used for ruler in the imperial period. A number of studies have discussed the origin of this term in oracle bones and bronzes, with claims that range from it being the name of a class of extrahumans (the ancestor of the Shang Kings) to the name of the pole star (Eno 2009: 70–7). Robert Eno and Shima Kunio argue that, in the oracle bones, the term is the name of a class of extrahuman (Kunio 1967: 188–216; Eno 1990b: 1–26). Sarah Allan, on the other hand, argues that *Di/Shangdi* was a singular entity and that it is both the ancestor of the Shang *and* the pole star (since it resides in the sky, Heaven is a metonym for it) (Allan 1991: 7–9).

Whatever their origins and associations, these early iterations are associated with authority, particularly with the issuing of orders and placement in hierarchies.[22] These concepts continue into the texts from the pre-imperial period; as they are developed these further, representations of the High Deities become increasingly anthropomorphic in their understanding and application.

Zuozhuan Zhao 1:12 (Selection) (544 BCE)
When the Marquess of Jin fell ill, The Earl of Zheng sent Gongsun Qiao[23] to Jin on a mission. He was going to diagnose the illness. Shu Xiang asked him about this, "As for the sovereign's illness, the diviners say that 'Shi Shen and Tai Tai have become revenants'. The Scribes have no knowledge of these two. We dare ask you who these two *shen* are?" Zichan said, "In the past Gaoxinshi[24] had two sons. The elder was called Ye Bo. The younger was called Shi Shen. They lived in a vast forest but were not on good terms. One day they took up arms and attacked each other. *Di* was not pleased and moved Ye Bo to Shangqiu to be in charge of Antares. This is the source of the Shang and so Antares is also known as the Star of Shang. He moved Shi Shen to Daxia to be in charge of Orion.[25] This is the source of the people of Tang who submitted to the Xia and the Shang. Its last leader was Shu Yu of the Tang."[26]

At the time that Lady Yi of King Wu became pregnant with Da Shu, she dreamt that *Shangdi* was speaking to her, "I name your son as Yu. He will join the Tang, take up all of Orion in his domain and raise his descendants there." On her son's birth, he had a mark placed on his hand that said Yu and this was taken as his name. When King Cheng extinguished Tang he enfeoffed Da Shu there. Thus Orion is the star of Jin. If one looks upon this then, Shi Shen is the god of Orion. In the past Jintianshi[27] had a distant descendant known as Mei. He was made Head of the Department of Hydrology and sired Chong Ge and Tai Tai. Tai Tai was able to inherit his post. He made a route for the Fen and the Tao rivers and dammed a great swamp so as to make a large plain. The lord of the time bestowed favour on him and enfeoffed him with all of Fenchuan. Chen, Si, Run and Huang[28] tended to his sacrifices. Now, Jin controls the Fen and has abolished them. Looking upon all of this then, Tai Tai is the god of the Fen. The repression of these two has not affected the body of the sovereign. When it is the god of the mountains and rivers, and there is a calamity of pestilence and plague, flood and drought, thereupon then we sacrifice to them. If it is the god of the sun, moon and stars and snow and frost or wind and rain are unseasonable; thereupon then we carry out a *yong* sacrifice[29] for them. If it is the body of the sovereign, then it is because of the matters of entering and exiting, food and drink and joy and sorrow. What do the god of mountains and rivers and the stars also do to him?"[30]

This passage recounts a narrative explaining the illness of the Marquess of Jin. It associates extrahuman agents with illness, something seen in other materials from this time (Raphals 2013: 87–8). *Shangdi/Di* is represented in terms of authority; its actions mirror those of a strong ruler. In the first paragraph, *Di* is responsible for the adjudication of a battle between individuals and the subsequent allotting of land; as such *Di* is responsible for the social organization and framework of the resultant polity (something that parallels the construction of rulership in texts of this time (Fibiger Bang and Turner 2015: 14–26)).

In the second paragraph, *Shangdi* appears to the wife of King Wu in a dream. Dreams are inherently extrahuman territory and, in addition to representing the High Deities' ability to permeate them, it also implicitly indicates that *Shangdi* has a form. Finally, the explanation of how the Jin came to govern their territory is put forward through *Shangdi* proclaiming the name of Lady Yi's son—another sign of authority and political control.

Shijing Huangyi
August be *Shangdi* for when he looks down upon us, there is trembling.
When he views across the four directions, he seeks the people's settlement.[31]
It was these two lands, their government, he did not assist.
It was those four lands, he gradually sought and gradually considered.[32]
When *Shangdi* was to make a leader of them, he despised their largess.
He then looked to the western reaches, stopping there; it was gifted to the house.[33]

This narrative, recounted in the *Shijing*, is typical of the appearance of *Di/Shangdi* in the text. As in the example from the *Zuozhuan*, there is no explicit mention of the agent as a ruler; however, his actions imply that the agent is like an authority within the human political realm. Indeed, the narrative illustrates *Di/Shangdi* as the arbiter and selector of the ruler extolled in the narrative, which echoes earlier understandings of *Di* in the oracle bones where it issued commands *ming* 命 (maintained through associations with the Shang rulers (Eno 2009: 72–3)).

The *Shijing* maintains similar modes of representation of Heaven within its various narratives, such as in the *Daming* below where Heaven, rather than *Di/Shangdi*, is configured as the authority that imparts governance.

> *Shijing Daming*
>
> Clear and brought, it looks down below, trembling and quaking, they look up
> Heaven finds it difficult to consider this sincere for it is not easy to be king.
> Heaven appointed the heir of the Shang, but made it so he did not embrace the four directions.
> Ren, a second daughter of Zhi,[34] from that Shang,
> Came to be married to the Zhou, and it is said they wed in Jing, for then he became King Ji.[35] This was the path of virtue.
> The great Ren then held a person, and gave birth to this King Wen.
> It was this King Wen who considered mindfully and gently,
> to display his service to *Shangdi*, and so secured numerous blessings.
> And his virtue did not wane, so that he received neighbouring lands.
> When Heaven cast its gaze, it looked down upon him and the orders it gave accumulated for him.
> When King Wen was in his first years, Heaven made him a mate.
> On the south bank of the Qia and on the islets of Wei.
> King Wen delightfully stayed, and there was a person in the large land.
>
> There was a person in the large land, who resembled a sister of Heaven.
> The King decided she was blessed and personally visited her on the Wei.
> He built boats into a bridge, and did not dwell on its extravagance.
>
> There were orders from Heaven, and it order this King Wen,
> To go to Zhou, to go to Jing, this betrothed woman was from Shen.
> She raised sons as a matter of course, and blessedly gave birth to King Wu.
> He was guarded and aided, and when ordered, smote the Great Shang.
>
> The troops of the Shang, they gathered like a forest,
> Rallying in the wilds of Mu, this is where our lord came to prominence.
> *Shangdi* looked down upon you, of unparalleled heart.[36]

Again, another narrative of the Zhou conquering the Shang is presented, a common theme in the narratives of the *Shijing* and the *Shangshu*. Apart from its obvious political and triumphalist overtones, it continues to anthropomorphize Heaven in terms akin to rulership and authority. This is more actively displayed through the use of the term "command" or "mandate" and the promotion of rulership as being decided upon by Heaven. In the above narrative, Heaven is even responsible for a ruler's marriage and the subsequent selection of the heir to the throne—highly anthropomorphic activities.

Lüshi Chunqiu Zhiyue
After eight years since King Wen of Zhou's establishment of his rule, in the sixth month of the year, King Wen fell bedridden for five days and there was an earthquake. From north to south, east to west, it did not go beyond the domain of the realm. The many ministers all plead: "We have heard this earthquake is because of our lord. Now, the King lies bedridden for five days and the earth moved, in all four directions it did not leave the domain of the realm. We all are afraid and say, 'We entreat you to move.'" King Wen said, "How are we to move?" They replied "Raise an army and move the masses so as to add to the capital's walls. Can this be moving them?" King Wen said, "It cannot. As for the manifestation of Heaven, it is to punish those with guilt. I surely have guilt, and thus heaven uses this to punish me."[37]

The representation of Heaven as a moral authority is clearly implicit in the discussion of the above from the *Lüshi chunqiu*. King Wen explicitly details Heaven as one who punishes the guilty, and implicates the earthquake, and perhaps the illness itself as punishment for his guilt. In addition to rehashing familiar tropes and characters—King Wen, ministers, sagacious rulers—this passage maintains the representation of Heaven as a moral authority, while also casting it in the role of a punisher and rewarder.[38]

In the narrative of the *Daming*, from the previous section, Heaven is actively represented as an authority figure that bestows kingship. However, other modes of representation are also present; one notable statement is that the wife that Heaven had selected for King Wen and who bore King Wu "resembled the sister of Heaven." Though the text does not elaborate on what a "sister of Heaven" looks like, what is marked is the use of a familiar term in relation to Heaven— that of sister. Although it may be understood as not literally Heaven's sister, it still assigns a human-centric term to an extrahuman agent. This representation with kin is also seen in the fourth section of the "Words of Jin" in the *Guoyu* where the expression "Family has heaven" 親有天[39] is employed thrice in a discussion of the ruler of Jin's duties and obligations. This example, like that seen in the

Daming, represents Heaven in human family terms, while also reinforcing the political didactic emphasized by both texts.

Indeed, the passage in the *Daming* explicitly ties the birth of King Wu to the arrangements of Heaven. This can be suggested to implicitly tie birth to Heaven, and the verb to bear, *shēng* 生, is seen in relation to Heaven in several other texts.

Analects 8:23
The Master said, "Heaven bore virtue in me." As for Huan Tu, what is he to me?[40]

Xunzi Rongzhen
Given that Heaven bears humans, it has the means to seize them. Intent and thought manifest in cultivation. Virtuous behavior manifests in largess. Wisdom and knowledge manifest in clarity. This is the means by which the emperor seize the realm.[41]

Hanfeizi Jielao
The one that is able to staid oneself yet completely follow along the principles of everything, surely this is what Heaven has bore. As for what Heaven bears, it bears the heart.[42]

Lüshi chunqiu Qingyu
Heaven bears humans and then makes them have greed and desires.[43]

Lüshi chunqiu Zunshi
Given that Heaven bore humans, it made their ears so that they could hear. If they do not study, then when they hear, it is no better than being deaf. It made their eyes so that they could see. If they do not study, then when they see, it is no better than being blind. It made them mouths so that they could speak. If they do not study, then when they speak, it is no better than being mutilated. It made them a mind so that they could know. If they do not study, then it is no better than being mad.[44]

Although it is often claimed that China's spiritual geography doesn't include a creator, these excerpts, from a diverse range of texts, assign the action of birthing, or producing, to Heaven—representing it as the source of things.[45] The common refrain, "Heaven bears humans," is found in the *Xunzi*, *Hanfeizi*, and the *Lüshi chunqiu*. The line from the *Xunzi* parallels the *Dang* 蕩 and *Zhengming* 烝民 poems of the *Shijing*,[46] and is cited in the *Mencius*.[47]

The initial excerpt from the *Analects* represents Heaven as the progenitor of good in humanity (or at least in the Master). The final excerpt, from the *Lüshi chunqiu*, also represents Heaven as the progenitor of humankind's body parts and the reason for possessing them; this anthropomorphic representation of the production of the body also takes on a more moral and didactic dimension to extol the virtues of leaning.

Lüshi chunqiu Zhifen

Yu[48] looked up to the sky and sighed, "I have received the mandate from Heaven, and have exhausted my strength to support the people. Life is nature. Death is mandated. Why would I be saddened by a dragon here?" The dragon cocked back its ears, lowered its tail and then died. Then Yu reached to the division between life and death and the weft of benefit and harm. For all humans and animals are the transformations of yin and yang. Yin and yang are what matures and is created by Heaven. Heaven surely has the sorrow of lose and the elation of abundance. Humans also have hardships and death and plentifulness and attainment. These are all the form of Heaven and the pattern of things.[49]

Many of the previous passages, like the one above, contain rulers or mythistorical leaders in conversation with the High Deities. This mode of representation obviously plays within the narrative of the High Deities as authority figures; some of these narratives also represent the High Deities as having human emotional states. As the passage from the *Lüshi chunqiu* above attests, Heaven can feel sorrow and elation—two common human emotions. In the *Mozi*, the emotion of love is applied to Heaven, while the *Gengsangchu* from the *Zhuangzi* depicts a dialogue on the issue of hatred between humans and Heaven.

Mozi Tianzhi zhong

Further, this does not stop and exhaust the reasons I know that Heaven's love for humans is the dearest. It is said that if one kills the not guilty, Heaven will give misfortune. Who is the one that was not guilty? It is humans? Who gives them misfortune? It is Heaven. If Heaven's not loving humans were the dearest, then why would it be told that if one kills the not guilty, then Heaven will give them is fortune. This is the reason I know that Heaven's love for man is dearest.[50]

Zhuangzi Gengsangchu

Yi had skill in hitting the mark, no matter how miniscule, yet he was foolish in making men refrain from praising him. The sage has skill about Heaven, but is foolish when dealing with humans. Having skill about heaven and finesse with humans, only the complete man is able to do this. Only an insect is able to be an insect, and only an insect is able to be Heavenly. A complete man detests Heaven. Given a Heaven detested by man, then how much more am I heavenly towards man?[51]

Human emotion is the most directly anthropomorphic representation the High Deities manifest in these texts. The *Shangshu* and *Shijing* are replete with expressions of the High Deities expressing pleasure and displeasure (Clark and Winslett 2011). As in the *Lüshi chunqiu*, this pleasure and displeasure is often reflective of whether they favor certain rulers or disfavor them, again wrapping them up in roles of punishers and rewarders and providing impetus for *why* they feel this way.

2

Heaven in the *Xunzi, Mozi,* and the *Zhuangzi*

There was a cripple in Lu, Toeless Shushan, who crawled to see Confucius. Confucius said, "You have not been mindful, and as for your past, your transgressions are as this. Even though you have come to me now, what will you achieve?" Toeless replied, "I have just not understood my responsibilities and have taken lightly my body that I have therefore lost my feet. I have come before you now and that which is still more honourable than feet exists. I therefore take responsibility to preserve it. There is nothing that Heaven does not cover, and nothing that Earth does not carry. I took you, my master, to be the world, how would I know that the likeness of my master would be like this!" Confucius said, "As for me, I am wretched. Why don't you, my master, enter? I entreat a discussion of that which has been heard." Toeless went away, and Confucius said, "Work hard disciples! That Toeless is a cripple, but still takes responsibility in learning so as to rectify the ills of his prior conduct. How much more a man of complete virtue!" Toeless spoke to Lao Dan, "As for Confucius's relationship to the perfect man, he has yet to be one! Why does he treat guests and take his students for? He is probably praying for the reputation of being astonishing and fantastical, but doesn't know that this is what the perfect man considers to be one's shackles!" Lao Dan said, "Why don't you just make him one who takes life and death as one line and the acceptable and unacceptable as one chain, and free him from his shackles. Is this not acceptable?" Toeless said, "Heaven punishes him, how can I free him?" (*Zhuangzi* 1961: 202–5)

"Schools" vs. Texts

Representations of Heaven and *Shangdi* are pluralistic and diverse. This shows the highly variant and diverse nature of the texts in discussion, texts which often were compiled and edited in the imperial period and which have been analyzed by later scholars as singular units of thought. The analysis of these "units of thought" has given rise to the idea of uniform communities of masters and pupils scattered throughout the Warring States period. These are often represented in English by the term "Schools" (mirroring the Chinese use of the term *jiā* 家). But there are intrinsic problems in applying such distinctions as uniform units of thought and schools to the texts themselves from the pre-imperial period. Mark Csikszentmihalyi and Michael Nylan have pointed out the problems with understanding 家 as reflective of discrete and finite schools in the pre-imperial period (as it was in much later post-Han intellectual discourse (Csikszentmihalyi and Nylan 2003: 61–2)). Kidder Smith demonstrates that no Warring States texts put forward communities and commonalities of ideas and "isms" (Smith and Tan 2003: 130–1). Further, William Boltz points out the convoluted, accretional construction of the texts themselves, raising questions as to the notions of groups of like-minded individuals (or an individual simpliciter) producing these texts in singular and purposeful fashion (Boltz 2005: 70–2). Finally, Kern argues that construction of these texts took centuries (Kern 2005: 316).

Such historical and structural realities illustrate why the anachronistic categorization of pre-imperial texts into discrete schools prevents understanding the various and often diverse ideas put forward in the texts themselves. A cursory glance at these texts reveals that imposing all-encompassing philosophical categories onto them creates problematic understandings of the material in them. Consider the above quote from the *Zhuangzi*, which features both Confucius and Laozi: Laozi is typically categorized with the character Zhuangzi, and the text *Zhuangzi* is typically termed "Daoist"; Confucius, on the other hand, is never categorized with the character Zhuangzi, and his signature text the *Analects* is typically termed (the anti-Daoist) "Confucian." Although the character of Confucius here is depicted as simple and unaware in comparison to the man with no toes,[1] because neither is commended or esteemed, "simple and unaware" apply as well to both Laozi and Shushan.

While its irreverence for cultural heroes speaks to the literary qualities of the *Zhuangzi*, it creates difficulties when trying to squeeze this text into later categories. Calling it "Daoist" raises questions about why this text features Confucius and ridicules Laozi. Of course, later "Daoist" communities would negotiate perfectly acceptable responses to these questions. But this illustrates a mode of knowledge construction rooted in these communities and their use of the text rather than the knowledge that the text constructs itself. If asked about what the text is saying about Laozi or Confucius, a reader of just the above passage could provide insights only from the text itself. And if one had access only to the above quotation as one's sole example of pre-imperial texts, one would understand the characters of Laozi and Confucius as equally simple and unaware.

Of course, the corpus of pre-imperial texts is greater than the single passage sited above, and Laozi and Confucius, as well as other characters, feature in many of them. So, one need not restrict oneself to representations built on a single passage from a single text. Moreover, one shouldn't presume that when their discourse moves beyond the texts themselves, the representations of later communities—of say, "Confucianism" or "Daoism"—apply meaningfully and unproblematically to the much earlier time period.[2] Such anachronistic comparing of themes and noting of patterns has inspired this chapter which will explore the High Deities (Heaven and *Shangdi*) within three early texts—the *Xunzi*, *Mozi*, and *Zhuangzi*.

The selection of these three texts is intentional; these three are often held up as being representative of three different and distinct "schools," with the *Xunzi* understood as "Confucian," the *Mozi* as "Mohist," and the *Zhuangzi* as "Daoist." But by anachronistically treating these texts as representing fundamentally different ideas (schools), one misses out on the commonalities between and diversity within the texts themselves. Indeed, these three texts share many things in common from their argumentative structures to their depictions of the High Deities. All three contain sections specifically devoted to discussing Heaven— the *Tianlun* 天論 of the *Xunzi*, the *Tianzhi* 天志 of the *Mozi*, and the *Tiandi* and *Tiandao* of the *Zhuangzi*. While Heaven is mentioned in other sections of these texts, these texts, amongst early texts, are notable for sections devoted to this single subject, and, as will be seen, they often construct Heaven in similar argumentative structures.

Xunzi

As the text's name suggests, the text as transmitted is attributed to the character of Xun Kuang 荀況 generally referred to as Xunzi. Although the *Shiji* mentions the character Xunzi in a "joint biography" with Mencius, this passage also offers a mixed intellectual pedigree for Xunzi, claiming other intellectual characters such as Li Si, Mozi, and Zhuangzi as influences (*Shiji* 1963: 2348–50). Michael Nylan has discussed this text and the growth of its arguments in knowledge communities in detail, highlighting the difficulties of its assignment to various intellectual histories and the complicated role it played in early intellectual thought (Nylan 2016: 395–433), although it is widely asserted today as one of the prime "Confucian" texts. Keeping in mind these complications, the *Xunzi* depicts interesting aspects of the spiritual geography of the pre-imperial period because it contains an entire passage devoted to the discussion of the High Deity—Heaven—the *Tianlun*.

Robert Eno, in his analysis of the *Tianlun*, notes the intellectual debate over the extrahuman status of Heaven, with many scholars arguing that "nature" is a more accurate translation of the concept; Eno rightly rejects this oversimplification owing to the polysemy and anachronism of the term, though he then claims that the concept of "naturalism" runs throughout the *Xunzi* (Eno 1990a: 131). While Eno's naturalism includes Heaven, it does not define it. Indeed, as he points out, Heaven is not actively defined in the *Tianlun*; Heaven is, instead, given numerous attributes and represented as merely a part and process of what he regards as the overarching narrative of the *Xunzi* (Eno 1990a: 154–7).

While Eno's analysis is beneficial and discusses certain perspectives on Heaven, it is more concerned with aspects of ritual 禮 than with understanding Heaven in its multitudes of meanings.

The *Tianlun* is structured into a number of parts, as the argumentative strategies and directives shift. It opens with its definitive line, "The behaviour of Heaven has constancy" (*Xunzi* 1988: 309). Yet, as it goes on, the *Tianlun*'s description is more of a null-description—the passage explains what Heaven is unable to do, as opposed to what Heaven does: Heaven is not able to make one poor (or rich), bring about calamity, or make one healthy. Heaven responds to order with good fortune and responds to disorder with bad fortune.

The second part can be understood as "defining its terms," in that it is structured by arraying a number of concepts associated with Heaven and, in certain instances, Earth. This definition often relies on the construction, "This is being called." This section is followed by a series of questions between two unnamed individuals asking about the causes of various actions such as calamities or the policies of rulers. The passage then engages in the four explanations of events through the lens of Heaven's involvement in them, and concludes with a coda.

Heaven in the second section is described by a series of seven key terms: Heavenly Occupation, Heavenly Merit, Heavenly Emotion, Heavenly Office, Heavenly Sovereign, Heavenly Nourishment, and Heavenly Governance. The construction of this passage evinces a degree of parallelism with the inner statements ending equally on, "This is what is said," with one of the terms featuring Heaven.

> After the Heavenly Occupation is established and after Heavenly Merit has come to fruition, form is complete and spirit is born. Love and hatred, enjoyment and

anger, sorrow and happiness are stored in this. Thus this is called Heavenly Emotion. The ears, eyes, nose, mouth and form are each able to encounter something, but not each other. Thus this is called Heavenly Office. The heart resides in the chest so as to govern the five organs.³ Thus this is called Heavenly Sovereign. When resources and differences are to their type so as to nourish their types, thus this is called Heavenly Nourishment. That which accords with their type is called blessed. That which goes against their type is called calamitous. Thus this is called Heavenly Governance. If one is blind to Heavenly Governance, disordered in Heavenly Office, abandons Heavenly Nourishment, goes against Heavenly Governance, turns their back on Heavenly Emotion so as to sully Heavenly Merit, this is what is called the Great Malady. The Sage makes pure his Heavenly Sovereign, makes proper his Heavenly Office, makes complete his Heavenly Nourishment, is in accord with his Heavenly Governance and nourishes his Heavenly Emotion so as to make complete his Heavenly Merit. If it is like this, then one knows what one is to do, and knows what one is not to do. Then Heaven and Earth govern and the myriad things serve. When their behaviour is crooked, yet governed and they nourishment crooked yet suitable, then in their life they will not be harmed. Thus this is called knowing Heaven.

(*Xunzi* 1988: 311)

These sequences rely upon both an internal progression where the parallel sentences lead each term upon each term and an external progression where the sequence is repeated in reverse. These terms represent Heaven in multiple facets. The terms themselves are highly anthropomorphic—Heaven is associated with an occupation and merits, as well as functions seen in humans. It has an office and is a sovereign, something that illustrates human and governmental titles, something seen before in representations of the High Deities. In addition, it is represented in relation to emotion and nourishment—basic anthropomorphic concepts.

While these terms are cryptic and ambiguous, Heavenly Emotion is the result of both Heavenly Occupation being established and Heavenly Merits coming to fruition, thus leading to one's form being established and one's spirit born. A litany of emotions is then invoked before ending with the passage's standard rhetorical framing device: "This is what is called …". The Heavenly Office is likewise defined by a list of body parts, and the Heavenly Sovereign is defined as what controls Heaven's Offices. Heavenly Nourishment is defined by the things one needs, while Heavenly Governance extends to the sorts of things that bring blessings and the sorts of things that bring harm. These constructions strongly associate the human body, its emotions, and the vagaries and realities of life, with the agent of Heaven.[4]

The third part of the passages posits two questions and answers, asking if numerous effects are caused by Heaven or by Earth. These two questions are also provided with null-responses—neither Heaven nor Earth is the cause of what is asked.

> Order and Disorder, are they because of Heaven? One responds, The sun, moon and stars have their auspicious moments, this is what is shared with Yu and Shun. Yu employed order; Shun employed disorder. Order and disorder are not because of Heaven.
>
> (*Xunzi* 1988: 311)

As in the first section, activities are identified with the sage Kings, in this case Shun and Yu rather than Yao. Heaven is represented as not being the cause of such actions.

The next sections of the text are more narrative. An anecdote featuring the state of Chu is provided first, a standard argumentative technique seen in a wide variety of early Chinese texts (Els 2012b: 16–21). This anecdote puts forward the important phrases, "one who relies on Man" and "one who relies on Heaven." In such a passage, individuals who rely on themselves are always those who benefit, while those who rely on Heaven are claimed not to understand how matters function.

Although Heaven is both depicted and mentioned, the text continues to use null-arguments to point out what Heaven does not do. Heaven in this passage is represented as not being responsible for order and disorder—something that is human caused. Heaven is not able to bring about poverty or wealth, nor does it kill or make one live.

In each of these, the human-centered focus of the text represents Heaven as disengaged from human-caused actions. However, it continues to anthropomorphize Heaven through the establishment of a number of terms related to it. It represents Heaven in terms of official positions, with related activities and duties. In all, the *Xunzi* offers a complex set of representations that are *both* anthropomorphic *and* assert a large degree of disassociation of Heaven from human affairs.

Mozi

Like the *Xunzi*, the *Mozi* has a section whose title is name-referenced to Heaven—the "Will of Heaven" 天志. Like many passages in the *Mozi*, this passage is broken into three sections—triplets or triads—of *shàng* 上, *zhōng* 中, and *xià* 下. Carine DeFoort and Nicolas Standaert have looked extensively at whether they represent three different sects or some form of evolution of each text (DeFoort and Standaert 2013: 10–16). They argue that they represent an evolving text with a high degree of unity among the sections (DeFoort and Standaert 2013: 16–17). Wiebke Denecke also holds that there is a strong degree of consistency among the triplets in terms of typical arguments and rhetorical techniques (Denecke 2010: 130–1). This section shall follow their lead and look at all three sections, as they all represent Heaven in interesting ways.[5]

The framing device of the "Will of Heaven" is an exposition given by the character Master Mozi 子墨子, punctuated once by an interlocutor that poses a question. The interlocutor is nameless, described by the generic description—"the people of the realm today." Additionally, the question or comment posed by the interlocutor is equally commonplace. This sop to the "common" or "everyday" person and their "common" or "everyday" views is standard for the interlocutor in the *Mozi* who is oft-reduced to a character defined solely by their opposing viewpoint (Denecke 2010: 136–7). However, the exposition of Master Mozi is often punctuated with reflexive questions that evoke a tone of "universal knowledge" suggesting that it is "correct."

The opening lines of the exposition discuss what the gentleman *junzi* 君子 knows and does not know. In this exposition, the gentleman is argued to only understand the small 小 and not the large 大. The dialogue contrasts the gentleman with Heaven which is purported to understand everything.

> For it is the case that Heaven cannot make there be no person in the hidden depths of the forests and valleys. It is clear that it must see them. If this is the case, then when comparing the gentleman of the lands of the realm to Heaven, they suddenly do not understand how to warn each other of this. This is the means by which I know the gentleman of the lands of the realm know the small, but do not know the large.
>
> (*Mozi* 1993: 293)

Heaven is represented as an agent of greater comprehension than the gentleman. Additionally, Heaven is represented as having the ability to "see" people regardless of how secluded they may be.

The opening segment on the gentleman's knowledge of the small transitions into further explicit discussions of Heaven.

> If this is the case, then what does Heaven, for its part, desire and what does it detest? Heaven desires righteousness and detests unrighteousness. If this is the case, then when one leaves the people of the realm through service to righteousness, then I will do what Heaven desires. If I do what Heaven desires,

> then Heaven will also do what I desire. If this is the case, what do I desire and what do I detest. I desire blessings and fortune and detest calamity and balefulness. If I do not do what Heaven desires or I do what Heaven does not desire, then, this being so, when I lead the people of the realm, it will be through service in calamity and balefulness. If this is the case, then how do I know that Heaven desires righteousness and detests unrighteousness? I say that when there is righteousness in the realm, there is life and when there is no righteousness, there is death. When there is righteousness, there is wealth, and when there is no righteousness, there is poverty. When there is righteousness, there is order, and when there is no righteousness, there is disorder. If this is the case, then Heaven wants those to be alive, and detests those to be dead. It wants those to be wealthy, and detests those to be poor. It wants those to be ordered and detests those to be disordered. This is the means by which I know that Heaven desires righteousness and detests unrighteousness.
>
> (*Mozi* 1993: 293–4)

This passage explicitly represents Heaven as an agent that desires righteousness and detests unrighteousness. While "righteousness" is undefined, through the construction of parallel sequences, the reader is made to associate these concepts not only with the desire and detestation of Heaven, but also with the antonymic states of life and death, wealth and poverty, and order and disorder. This passage's parallel rhetoric also posits the speaker, again presumed to be Master Mozi, in similar action to Heaven, explicitly encouraging righteousness.

Though Heaven serves more as a segue to this discussion, Heaven does appear explicitly in the expression—"If there is Heaven, then it governs it" and "That Heaven makes governance for the Emperor, it is clearly known that the common people of the realm do not get this" (*Mozi* 1993: 294). Both of these expressions align Heaven with the concept of governance, a highly anthropomorphic endeavor, while also aligning the emperor with Heaven. Further, they explicitly depict Heaven as the ultimate source for governance.

Segueing from this through a mention of the Emperor's action, the next section discusses the issue of Heaven's Will 天意 and the realities of what this concept means.

> When presented with Heaven's will, can or can it not be followed? Those that follow Heaven's will revel in mutual love, enjoy mutual profit and should attain wealth. Those that go against Heaven's will are divided by mutual hate, enjoy mutual impoverishment and must attain misconduct. If this is the case, then who follows Heaven's will and obtains wealth? Who goes against Heaven and obtains misconduct?
>
> (*Mozi* 1993: 294–5)

The rhetorical question sets up a dichotomy in relation to this concept of Heaven's will with respect to the Emperor and the favorability of the Emperor in following it. The passage holds up a number of culture heroes and past emperors, who followed Heaven's will, an argumentative practice seen before. The passage does not define Heaven's will, but has it actively quoted twice.

> Master Mozi said, "In their service, the highest is reverence for Heaven, the second is serving the deities and the lowest is loving the people. Thus Heaven's Will says, 'That which I love, they revel and love it. That which I profit, they revel in and profit from it. Those that love people, they are expansive from this. Those that profit people, they are heady from this.'"
>
> (*Mozi* 1993: 295)

> Master Mozi said, 'In their service, the highest is to blaspheme against Heaven, the second is to blaspheme against the ghost and the lowest is to impoverish people. Thus Heaven's will say, "Those that I love, they divide and hate. Those that I benefit, they defile and impoverish. Those that hate people, they are expansive to them. Those that impoverish people, they are heady to them.
>
> (*Mozi* 1993: 295)

Again, parallel lines are presented, albeit taken out of the larger construction. The first is cited after a discussion of cultural heroes, while the second is quoted after a discussion of tyrannical, historical figures. They reinforce the earlier dictum of what happens when one follows Heaven's will and when one goes against it.

The concept of Heaven's will is cited by Master Mozi as actually speaking and thus akin to some form of dictum. The "Will of Heaven" never provides explicit definition of Heaven's will beyond these statements.

> How do we know Heaven loves the people? Because it teaches them all. How do we know it teaches them all? Because it claims them all. How do we know it claims them all? Because it accepts sacrifices from them all. How do we know it accepts sacrifices from all? Because within the four seas all who live on grains feed oxen and sheep with grass, and dogs and pigs with grains, and prepare clean cakes and wine to do sacrifice to God on High and the spirits. Claiming all the people, why will Heaven not love them? Moreover, as I have said, for the murder of one innocent individual there will be one calamity. Who is it that murders the innocent? It is man. Who is it that sends down the calamity? It is Heaven. If Heaven should be thought of as not loving the people, why should it send down calamities for the murder of man by man? So, I know Heaven loves the people.
>
> (*Mozi* 1993: 295)

This passage seems a bit of a non-sequitur between two segments that discuss Heaven's will. However, explicit representations of Heaven are apparent. The first is through the question—"How does one know of Heaven's love for the people?" The passage, though perhaps unexpected in sequence, is not unexpected in its argumentative structure (again a series of parallel, serial lines, often posed as rhetorical questions with delivered answers). Heaven is shown to have human emotions, (love), Heaven engages in enlightening the people, Heaven holds all people, and Heaven accepts sacrifice. These qualities are played up as positives in contrast to the negatives of humans, to whom Heaven also sends down calamities, an echo of Heaven as a punisher and rewarder.

The next sections shift gears to discuss the issue of righteousness 義. Though the term is not defined, Master Mozi's prompt—"from whence come righteousness"—begins the discussion. The conclusion—"Heaven is noble, and Heaven is wise and no more. As this is the case, then virtue indeed comes from Heaven" (*Mozi* 1993: 303)—provides yet another explicit representation of Heaven as the source of the desired qualities that Master Mozi encourages. This passage also assigns the qualities of nobility and wisdom to Heaven, things which are markedly anthropomorphic and social.

> Master Mozi said, "The reason why I know of Heaven's greater nobility and wisdom to the emperor exists. I say that if the emperor does good, then Heaven is able to reward him. If the emperor does ill, then Heaven is able to punish him. If the emperor is besot with illness, disease, calamities or malevolence, then he will surely purify and wash himself and prepare libations and victuals in order to sacrifice to Heaven and the ghosts. Then Heaven is able to dispel these. This being the case, I am not aware of Heaven's prayers for blessings from the Emperor. This is how I know of Heaven's greater nobility and wisdom than the emperor."
>
> (*Mozi* 1993: 303)

Further, one sees Heaven represented in relation to the emperor, a recurring motif throughout the discourse presented by the "Will of Heaven." Herein, the power relationship is depicted with Heaven being more noble and wiser than, alongside representations of Heaven as being wise and noble, something seen before.

The resultant sections continue to reemphasize the points already illustrated alongside similar representations of Heaven. So far, the "Will of Heaven" constructs its arguments primarily as a discourse put forward by Master Mozi. Master Mozi punctures his discourse with questions to which he provides answers. Answers often rely upon parallel constructions, at times antonymic, and also often harken to cultural heroes and tyrannical figures as proto-historical demonstration of the points and arguments made. Only once does a passage start with another speaker: the people of the world ask if Heaven is more noble and wise than the emperor, to which the answer is assuredly that Heaven is wiser.

The "Will of Heaven" represents Heaven as having human emotions—love being the preeminent one, but also anger and happiness. Heaven likewise is depicted as having wisdom, nobility, and righteousness, three qualities ascribed to humans. These emotions and qualities are not held out in isolation, they also serve as justifications for Heaven's behavior and actions.

Heaven is also associated with governance; indeed, a recurring theme throughout the discussion is that of the Emperor. The "Will of Heaven" constructs a hierarchy with Heaven above the emperor. Additionally, the emperor and Heaven are portrayed in combined relationship. It even refers to Heaven enacting governance early in the passage.

In the "Will of Heaven," Heaven's will is actively invoked throughout the passage, providing additional evidence for Master Mozi's statements. Heaven's will reinforces the Mozi's anthropomorphic and governmental representations of Heaven. However, the text is silent on what Heaven's will exactly is.

Zhuangzi

Even though Heaven and Earth are large, they have their changes and balances. Even though the myriad things are many, they have their order and unity. Even though the people and ranks are massive, they have their lords and sovereigns. The sovereign puts his origin in virtue and his accomplishes from Heaven. Thus it is said, the lord of the realm in the dark past when doing nothing was Heaven and Virtue and no more. If we look at what is said with the Way, the lord of the realm is proper. If he look at divisions with the Way, then the righteousness of the lord and minister is clear. If we look at ability with the Way, then officials of the realm are ordered. If we take a sweeping look with the Way, then the responses of the myriad things are as they should be. Thus the one who is connected to Heaven and Earth, is virtuous. The one who behaves in accord with the myriad things, is with the Way. The one amongst the superiors who orders the people, is service. The one who is able to seize a chance, this is skill. Skill combines with service. Service combines with Righteousness. Righteousness combines with Virtue. Virtue combines with the Way. The Way combines with Heaven. Thus it is said, "Those amongst the ancients who reared the realm, would want nothing, as the realm was enough and would do nothing as the myriad things transformed. The pools were still and the people placated."

(*Zhuangzi* 1961: 403–4)

The *Zhuangzi's* complicated rhetorical and argumentative structure has already been observed. It often rejects direct definitions of its terms in keeping with larger arguments concerning language in parts of the text (Berkson 1996: 102–3). The *Tiandi* and the *Tiandao* sections are no exception. They do not directly explain what Heaven is, as seen in both the *Mozi* and the *Xunzi*, but rather represent Heaven in a number of ways in the larger narrative of the texts. These are constructed as a series of sections that do not conform in a linear fashion. At first glance, they seem independent. Yet they share similarities such as argumentative structures, particularly with anecdotes featuring Confucius, and opening passages that provide numerous representations of Heaven.[6]

As seen in the above *Tiandi* section, Heaven is represented as parallel to Earth, something not commonly seen in the other texts discussed in this chapter, and this is placed in a series of parallel structures equating Heaven and Earth with the myriad things and the masses. Later, Heaven is said to be from what sovereigns take their accomplishments. And Heaven parallels virtue, which happens when the sovereign of the world does nothing. The section also defines being virtuous as being connected with Heaven and Earth, and following a series reaches the ultimate unit in the series, Heaven.

This reliance on serial parallels structuring key terms is an argumentative technique that is seen in the other two texts of this passage. This rhetorically "defines" the key terms by requiring the reader to understand them in relation to other terms. In this case, Heaven is represented in relation to virtue. These depictions also reinforce the depiction of Heaven as related to the notion of the sovereign.

> The Master said, "On the matter of the Dao, it covers and enfolds the myriad things and overflows into greatness. The gentleman cannot but remove his heart from it. Doing it when doing nothing is called Heaven. Saying something while doing nothing is called Virtue. Profiting things while loving humans is called humaneness. Sharing things when different is called Greatness. Not being aloof when taking action is what is called Kindness. Not sharing when one has multitudes is called wealth. Thus holding on to virtue is called principle and being successful with virtue is called the establishment, while following along in the Way is called completion. To not subdue intentions with things is called the Completion. The gentleman is clear about these ten, and then sheaths them in the greatness of the service to his heart and inundates them in the limits of his acting for the myriad things."
>
> (*Zhuangzi* 1961: 406–7)

This cryptic passage again takes the form of defining set terms, which are in serial progression. As in the *Xunzi*, the use of a serial progression ties the concepts it is introducing together and explicates each through the other. The progression begins with Heaven said to be "Doing it when doing nothing," which immediately ties Heaven into the concept of doing nothing or *wuwei*, a complex concept with a lengthy pedigree in the *Zhuangzi* and other Warring States texts (Barrett 2011: 680–2). The use of one complex and ambiguous concept such as Heaven being explained in relation to another complex and ambiguous concept is typical of the *Zhuangzi*. Perhaps the high prestige attached to each concept connects the two. Moreover the polysemy of the character of Heaven suggests both anthropomorphizing it in relation to the ideal state of a ruler and raising the idea of Heaven being a state itself.

> The Way of Heaven rotates, yet accumulates nothing. Thus the myriad things come to completion. The Way of *Di* rotates, yet accumulates nothing, thus the realm turns to him. The Way of the Sages rotates, yet accumulates nothing, thus within the seas submit to them … As for those who are completely clear upon the virtue of Heaven and Earth, this is called Ancestor of the Great Fundament and those who are given the Harmony of Heaven. This is the reason for balancing and stabilizing the realm is the one who is given the Harmony of the People. Being given the Harmony of the People is called the Happiness of the People. Being given the Harmony of Heaven is called the Happiness of Heaven.
>
> Zhuangzi says, "My master! My master! If he minces the myriad things, it will not make him cruel. If he shines out across the myriad generations, it will not make him humane. If he grows up in high antiquity, it will not make him long-lived. If he covers and embraces Heaven and Earth and carves out the forms of the masses, it will not make him corrupt. This is the Happiness of Heaven. Thus it is said that the one who knows the Happiness of Heaven, will be acted on by Heaven in life and will be transformed by things in death. When they are still, they will share virtue with Yin and when they are active they will share raucousness with Yang. Thus the one who knows the Happiness of Heaven is without Heaven's Ire, without the People's Disapproval, without the Being's Disinterest and without the Ghost's Blame. Thus it is said that when he moves, it is because of Heaven. When he is still, it is because of Earth. If he is established with a united heart, then he will rule over the realm. His ghost will not become a revenant and his soul will not be pestilent. If he is established with a united heart, then the myriad things will submit. To speak with stillness and emptiness, yet still extend to Heaven and Earth, to connect to the Myriad Things, this is called the Happiness of Heaven. As for the Happiness of Heaven it is the heart of the Sage and one rears the realm with it."
>
> (*Zhuangzi* 1961: 457–63)

These opening passages, with an excerpt from the first one, come from the *Tiandao* section of the *Zhuangzi*. They show similar construction to the *Tiandi* section, in that it is made up of a collection of units meant to be understood as a whole. Like the *Tiandi*, the opening unit serves to establish the subject matter and offer definitions of a sort. The passage is even more cryptic than those in the *Tiandao* owing to the high level of unique terms employed.

In terms of Heaven, these interrelationships once again tie Heaven to the concept of virtue, but additionally represent Heaven with a number of features through the development of unique terms involving it—the Way of Heaven, the Harmony of Heaven, the Happiness of Heaven, and the Ire of Heaven. Heaven clearly is represented with human emotional qualities, and indeed these are sequenced in relation to Harmony of People and the Happiness of People, alongside being responsible for sages and proper behavior.

Conclusion

The passage from the *Zhuangzi* at the start of this chapter introduced what might seem an odd amalgamation of characters, tropes, and concerns. However, as this chapter has shown, it displays argumentative techniques and representations that are also found in other texts. The passages from these three texts display a variety of representations of the High Deity Heaven and employ them in a variety of ways. These passages also display similarities in their representations, despite the claim that these texts are completely different in focus and form (and "school").

All three texts employ similar modes of argument. They engage in creating serial arguments that place the concepts and agents that they are discussing in direct relation to each other. They evoke anecdotes to explain and further their arguments, relying on similar cultural heroes and mythistorical narratives. And, they also rely on opening passages that establish topics of discussion and create framing devices for the subsequent sections and sub-arguments.

Heaven is represented in all of these modes of argumentation. In all three texts, Heaven is represented in anthropomorphic ways particularly in Heaven's association with governance (all three construct Heaven in governmental terms familiar to those of the human realms that these texts participate in). They likewise portray Heaven with human emotions and mental states. These qualities are seen in other texts as has been discussed in other chapters, reflecting even more widespread use of such representations and suggesting the possibility that these may not have been restricted to the communities that constructed these texts.

Despite various differences, there are many similarities particularly in the ways in which Heaven is represented between these texts. That Heaven and other deities are pervasive in pre-imperial texts has been shown in the previous chapter. These three texts play on that pervasiveness by representing Heaven in their arguments to convince their readers both of the validity of such arguments and of the representations and modes in which they are arguing.

3

The Depersonalization of Heaven?

Introduction

Heaven (*tian*), in many of early China's foundational texts, is represented as a person with a will, and a person who is superknowing and morally provident; Heaven also creates and cares for his people. Early Chinese texts overflow with representations of an anthropomorphic emperor in heaven. Some scholars claim, however, that in the later Zhou, there was a decided shift from religion to philosophy, in which Chinese thought shook off superstitious religious beliefs in favor of Confucian rational humanism. Hall and Ames, for example, claim that "there is a gradual depersonalization of *tian*, first in the relatively early identification of the will of *tian* with popular consensus, and further in a gradual redefinition of *tian* as a designation for the regular pattern discernible in the unfolding processes of existence" (Hall and Ames 1987: 203). They concede that in the *Analects*,

> *T'ien* [*Tian*] seems to have had some religious significance for the Chou [Zhou] people who conquered the Shang at the end of the second millennium B.C. Given that the Chou was a federation of militant, semi-nomadic border tribes prior to their conquest of the Shang, there is no written basis for determining whether or not, or to what extent, *t'ien* was held to be a personal deity. The fact that *t'ien* also means 'sky' might suggest that in this prehistoric period it was seen as a non-personal, unifying force of considerable dimensions at some distance from the human world.
> (Hall and Ames 1987: 202–3)

Therefore, the history of thought in ancient China, according to the narrative, is the history of the depersonification of Ultimate Reality, the depersonalization of Heaven.

Yuri Pines offers the best defense of the narrative of the historical depersonalization of Heaven, "this emancipation of the human world from the dominance of transcendental forces" (Pines 2002: 57). His case is built upon the *Zuozhuan*, which he claims offers contemporary commentary on the Spring and Autumn (*Chunqiu*) period (772–455 BCE). In this chapter, I will present and reject Pines' claim to the gradual depersonalization of Heaven in early China.

Pines and the *Zuozhuan*

Pines sifts through the historical-critical arguments regarding the dating of the *Zuozhuan* and concludes that it was compiled by a single editor-author perhaps by 360 BCE based on first-hand reflections of thinkers in the Chunqiu period. Pines, however, has not offered compelling reason to think the *Zuozhuan*'s contents are reliably pre-Confucius. Early Chinese texts were filtered through the Han so it is difficult to know what is pre-Qin and what is not. Scholarly consensus holds that the *Zuozhuan* is the product of post-Confucius polemicists. David Schaberg (2001), for example, claims the document derives from anonymous authors during the Warring States era (479–222 BCE).

Moreover, Pines claims that the *Zuozhuan* reveals to us, as his title boldly asserts, "the foundations of Confucian thought." Again, Schaberg demurs, arguing that the issues raised in the *Zuozhuan* reflect concerns of each author's own day and age, not the earlier Spring and Autumn era. Schaberg's claim would undermine Pines' chronological argument. Schaberg writes: "Given the difficulty of pinpointing a moment of composition for any of the speeches, it is impossible to write a history of the development of rhetoric during the Spring and Autumn period" (Schaberg 2001: 27).

Let us, however, grant Pines' key but controversial assumption: the *Zuozhuan* offers an authentic and authoritative picture of the pre-Confucian era it represents. Does the *Zuozhuan*, thus understood, support the gradual depersonalization of Heaven?

The Depersonalization of Heaven

Pines claims to see a secularizing trend during the Chunqiu period: formerly religious rituals performed during sacrificial rites at the ancestral temple were emptied of their religious content. He contends that there is a devolution of religious terms into their secular equivalents. Finally, he declares the ultimate emancipation of secular rulers from the gods, ghosts, and spirits of the early

Zhou tradition.[1] Pines argues that Heaven devolves in three temporal and conceptual stages, which can be traced in the *Zuozhuan*:

> *Stage 1: Heaven as the Lord-on-High.* "Early Chunqiu statesmen conceived of Heaven as a purposeful deity that was responsive to human actions, and Heaven's wishes had to be complied with" (Pines 2002: 66). Heaven is represented as the foundation of moral and political order (*tianming*) and must be consulted on affairs of state. Heaven is personal, purposeful and providential.
>
> *Stage 2: Heaven as objective but impersonal law.* During the mid-Chunqui, "Heaven as an active and sentient force began to disappear" (Pines 2002: 61). Heaven is increasingly identified with an objective but impersonal law that influences human affairs. Rituals shift from offerings to Heaven to improving one's behavior and rule.
>
> *Stage 3: Heaven as an incomprehensible natural force.* In the *Zuozhuan* we read that "Heaven's way is distant, the human way is near" so the shift to human affairs and concerns (and away from Heaven) is complete. Because Heaven's ways are inscrutable, Heaven is politically irrelevant.

Pines concludes that Xunzi (an allegedly a-theistic follower of Confucius), then, represents the culmination of the rationalistic and skeptical Chinese mind in this representative quotation:

> Rescuing the sun or moon from eclipse, praying [for rain] in time of drought, deciding great affairs only after reading cracks and casting stalks are not because one expects to get what he asks, but to manifest refined culture (*wen*). Hence, superior men consider these as refined culture, while the people consider these as dealing with deities. To consider them refined is auspicious, to consider them as dealing with deities is baleful.
>
> (Pines 2002: 54)

According to Pines, Heaven is, by the end of the Chunqiu period, morally, socially, and politically irrelevant. Confucian humanism, as represented in the *Xunzi*, reigns supreme.

Who Represents Chinese Thought?

Even granting Pines' highly speculative historical assumptions, his argument for the depersonalization of Heaven is untenable. For example, he writes: "Sima Hou's skeptical mood is representative of late Chunqiu attitudes toward

Heaven" (Pines 2002: 67). Is Sima Hou's skepticism, as Pines claims, *representative* of late Chunqiu attitudes? How does one make judgments of representativeness covering such a vast historical era and geographical area? Is Sima Hou's skepticism representative even of the *Zuozhuan* (or even the alleged later strata of the *Zuozhuan*)? How is Heaven represented in other contemporary texts (which would help us see if Sima Hou's skepticism were indeed representative of late Chunqiu attitudes)? Claims of representativeness in pre-Qin China are exceedingly difficult to establish. Likewise, in what sense is Xunzi, even taken as a-theistic, representative of Chinese thought of his time?[2]

Even if all doubts about the authenticity of the *Zuozhuan* were removed, it is a single, non-representative text.[3] While one might be inclined to treat this or that ancient Chinese text (usually the *Analects*) as representative of Chinese thought, in ancient China one finds a plethora of texts containing a plethora of ideas; no text, as far as we can tell, is any more or less representative of early China or early Chinese beliefs or the early Chinese mind or early Chinese philosophy than any other. Instead, one finds a plethora of ideas within early China's diverse, accretional, multi-authored texts.

Moreover, post-Chunqiu texts contain a wide variety of representations of Heaven, many of which see Heaven as an active, anthropomorphic deity (some, to be sure, take Heaven to be a natural force). There is no single, authoritative, or representative text which best transmitted or informed the Chinese mind. And in the plethora of non-representative pre-Qin texts, there is a plethora of views on the nature of divinity ranging widely from good, providential, and transcendent person, on the one hand, to impersonal, immanent, and amoral force, on the other. No single view—theistic or non-theistic—represents the so-called Chinese mind.

Moreover, the privileging of a single text or set of so-called representative texts for understanding the ancient Chinese mind is anachronistic. Michael Loewe, among others, cautions about asserting the pre-eminence of Confucianism to Chinese thought:

> An implicit assumption that runs through many of the accounts of China's history, whether written in East Asia or the West, and whether concerning early or modern times, has colored the view that many have taken of the basic nature of the Chinese empires. We have been nurtured on the belief that 'Confucianism' characterized imperial China; that the prominent place taken by Confucianism may be traced to the teachings and practices of the Han dynasty; that it was the example and efforts of the Han emperors and officials, whose reign and rule endured as a continuum for four hundred years, that had achieved this result in

reaction against the unethical ways of their predecessors of Qin; and that in all this process, it was the precepts and sayings ascribed to Kongzi that shaped the thoughts of philosophers, writers, historians, and servants of government until the twentieth century.

(Loewe 2012)

Even restricting ourselves to the *Zuozhuan* itself, Pines' arguments are based on just a few allegedly representative examples or statements. For example, he retells the story of the "prudent statesman" Zi Chan who distanced himself "from speculation on Heaven's will." Zi Chan, Pines tells us, was a clear-sighted reformer who expressed rational disdain for those who invoked Heaven or the lesser deities (Pines 2002: 69). In response to Pi Zao, who claimed to channel Heaven's will, Zi Chan responded:

> The Way of Heaven is distant, while the Way of Men is near; unless it can be reached, how can [Heaven] be known? How can [Pi] Zao know the Way of Heaven? This man is a great talker, so why should some of his words not be true?

Given his many claims about Heaven, Zi Chan argues, even Pi Zao was likely to be right at least some of the time. Given the paucity of true predictions over false ones, Zi Chan came to believe that Heaven was inscrutable and so those who spoke on Heaven's behalf were unworthy of consideration. Pines concludes from this example:

> Zi Chan's views, while by no means unanimously endorsed by his contemporaries, signified nevertheless the basic trend of late-Chunqiu attitudes toward Heaven .... Heaven was stripped of its sentient and interventionist attitudes and was no longer expected to actively restore political order. Future debates notwithstanding, the majority of Chinese thinkers would share Zi Chan's belief: mundane affairs are to be solved here and now.

(Pines 2002: 70)

Zi Chan represents, he claims, "the basic trend" that Heaven could not and should not be trusted.

Is Zi Chan's view, as Pines claims, representative of later Chunqiu thinkers (even in the *Zuozhuan*)? Is there a trend among late Chunqiu thinkers about the nature of divinity?

Taeko Brooks' exhaustive study of the 131 passages of the *Zuozhuan* containing the word *tian* 天 (Heaven) paints a very different picture: "I find that these passages imply different roles for Heaven in human affairs, and that the differences cannot be explained as differences in belief between states, or as evolution of ideas during the Spring and Autumn period, but are more likely compositional strata" (Brooks 2003/04). Brooks finds multiple and incompatible conceptions of Heaven throughout the *Zuozhuan*, but no temporal clustering of conceptions as Pines' evolutionary and chronological argument requires.

If Pines' argument were correct, we would expect to find representations of Heaven as active and personal clustered at the beginning (of the book, *Zuozhuan*, and the era, Chunqiu) with representations of Heaven as impersonal and irrelevant clustered at the end (of the book, *Zuozhuan*, and the era, Chunqiu). Brooks shows that 63 of the 131 *Zuo* references are to an active Heaven defined as follows: "Heaven in this category is seen not only as responding to human actions, but sometimes as acting on its own initiative, with its own agenda for history;" these sixty-three occurrences are fairly evenly distributed from beginning to end. Seven of the final ten, and sixteen of the final thirty references to Heaven are active. While Heaven as a natural force occurs twenty-five times, Heaven as natural occurs in only one in ten, and seven of thirty references in the final chapters of the *Zuozhuan*. In short, the occurrences and uses of Heaven in the *Zuozhuan* mitigate against the claim of the depersonalization of Heaven. So even if the *Zuozhuan* were representative of Chinese thought or channeled the Chinese mind, it would not support the narrative of the progressive depersonalization of Heaven.[4]

David Schaberg notes that "King Wen" from the *Shijing* is quoted in the *Zuozhuan* more often and by more authors "than any other inherited text"; speakers in the *Zuozhuan* and the *Guoyu*, moreover, "neglect *Shi* poems concerning other pre-dynastic Zhou heroes" (Schaberg, p. 74). While other Zhou heroes are worthies, the Heaven-blessed King Wen is the supreme moral exemplar, the one most worthy of imitation. In the *Zuozhuan* (as in the *Shijing*), King Wen's astonishing virtue is attributed to the Lord-on-High:

> The *Shi* says:
> There was King Wen:
> The emperor above gave him discernment in his heart.
> Concordant was the news of his virtue,
> And his virtue could shine.
> He could shine, he could be good;
> He could lead: he could rule.
> He reigned over these great states,
> And could bring compliance and unity.
> They united with King Wen,
> In whose virtue there was no cause for regret.
> Having received the blessings of the Lord,
> He bestowed them on his sons and grandsons.

The *wen* of King Wen is conceived as providing the ritually efficacious connection between Heaven and Earth.

A Summing Up

Three chapters in, we return to the master argument, "The Naturalizing Argument." The first two chapters put the lie to claims that: (1) *The Chinese don't believe in God.* We offered countless representations of the High God, in a wide variety of pre-imperial texts. The High God, as represented, is a non-physical person of power and authority. By "person," I mean that the High God has the essential attributes of persons—emotion, intellect, and will. Finally, the High God is the source and enforcer of morality and social harmony, with the realm of spirits mirroring a fully functioning earthly hierarchy.

Chapter 2 provided evidence against: (2) *Belief in God was common among peasants and in the <u>Mozi</u>, but not in "the philosophical texts."* The combination of the *Xunzi*, the *Mozi*, and the *Zhuanghzi*—each of which contains entire sections devoted to representations of Heaven—shows remarkable overlap of idioms, arguments, and claims. Anachronistically assigning them to discrete, so-called "schools"—"Confucian," say, or "Daoist"—conceals the similarities in the original texts taken in their original context.

Given the plethora of representations of the High God in such a wide variety of texts, something like Pines' "Depersonalization of Heaven" argument would be needed to show the shift from the High God to philosophical naturalism. Pines concedes that the *Zuozhuan* presents a complicated picture of late Chunqiu attitudes toward Heaven: "While no consensus concerning the role of Heaven in political life was reached, the sheer plurality of approaches indicates a significant departure from the Western Zhou-early Chunqiu mode of thought." But then he concludes, "It was no longer possible to advocate a political order based on and guarded by an unpredictable and incomprehensible Heaven." While it's true that no one would thereafter advocate a political order based on an *unpredictable* and *incomprehensible* Heaven, many texts—the *Analects*, the *Mencius*, and the *Mozi*, to name a few—would thereafter advocate a political order based on a *predictable* and *comprehensible* Heaven.

Pines is half right. He's right when he notes that "even a cursory look at Western Zhou versus Zhanguo writings reflects an enormous gap between attitudes toward divine authority." But he's wrong when he asserts that "no Zhanguo thinker, with the exception of Mozi, assigns divine forces any significant role in political and social life" (Pines 2002: 54). Zhanguo thought is richly and deeply varied in ways that Pines' narrative would preclude. The plethora of post-Chunqiu representations of divinity and the afterlife resist Pines' simplifying and falsifying narrative.

The metaphysically pluralistic, accretional text, the *Zuozhuan* represents divinity in various and sometimes incompatible ways that are not developmentally organized; in that pluralism, there is no rational progression, no skeptical evolution, of conceptions of divinity. There is no historically credible narrative that the Chinese mind or the Confucians drained Heaven of its anthropomorphic content and active influence on human affairs. Pines is right about this much: the historical narrative shows no consensus concerning the role of Heaven in political life. But the historical data likewise show that the pre-imperial era included a plurality of representations, approaches, and arguments concerning the nature of Heaven and the role of Heaven in human life. The widely repeated narrative that the Chinese mind or Confucianism canalized a depersonalized, naturalistic Heaven is historically unsustainable.

Part Two

God and the Philosophers

4

Did Confucius Believe in Heaven?

"Confucius"

Any discussion of what Confucius (551–479 BC) did or did not believe must overcome some substantial, perhaps unovercomeable, historical obstacles. Confucius died without leaving a written record of either his life or thought. We cannot, as is often done, simply abstract Confucius' biography from Confucius' *Analects* because it is not, strictly speaking, Confucius' *Analects*. Confucius did not write the *Analects*; the extant text, compiled and edited in the early Han era, is an amalgamation of sayings from a wide variety of sources from perhaps a 300-year period.[1] How much of the extant texts are the authentic words of Confucius? The traditional view—that most if not all of the *Analects* are records of the voice or teachings of the Master—is untenable. Arthur Waley, translator of the *Analects*, writes, "I think we are justified in supposing that the book does not contain many authentic sayings, and may possibly contain none at all" (Waley 1938: 25). The problem is compounded. There were thousands of "sayings of Confucius" circulating prior to the establishment of the Confucian canon, many of which are not contained in the extant text and even contradict ideas or sayings in the extant text (Hunter 2012). So we have little reason to think that the extant text contains only (or any of) the authentic sayings of Confucius.

As a character in the *Analects*, Confucius has beliefs (in much the same way that Macbeth has beliefs in Shakespeare's play *Macbeth*). But the beliefs of Confucius of the *Analects* are not necessarily the same as the beliefs of the historical Confucius.[2] From this point on, I will take the term "Confucius" to mean "the (quasi-fictional) character named 'Confucius' in the extant and composite text of the *Analects* from roughly 175 CE." When we ask, "What did Confucius believe about Heaven?," we will be discussing the metaphysical and ethical beliefs of the quasi-fictional character named "Confucius" in the *Analects*.[3]

Heaven in Confucius

One of the most famous passages in the *Analects* unites Confucius' moral journey with the decrees of Heaven (*Tianming*):

> At fifteen, I set my mind upon learning; at thirty, I took my place in society; at forty, I became free of doubts; at fifty, I understood Heaven's Mandate; at sixty, my ear was attuned; and at seventy, I could follow my heart's desires without overstepping the bounds of propriety.
>
> (*Analects* 2:4)

This passage depicts Confucius' stages on life's way, which can also be interpreted as the stages that every sage would ideally traverse. Confucius asserts that the way to achieve sageliness begins with and is driven by one's determination to learn; wisdom is then acquired through accumulated experience. After this determination to learn, the next steps involve finding one's place in the fabric of society and then driving out perplexities through the acquisition of knowledge. Only then is one in a position to understand and to obey the will of Heaven; aligning oneself with Heaven is the pivotal point between youthful maturation and human perfection. Although he did not understand the decrees of Heaven until age fifty, learning, the foundation of moral development, is aimed at understanding and according with the decrees of Heaven. In the final steps one's entire self is reoriented around the decrees of Heaven; one is fully attuned to what is right; being good, doing the right thing, becomes completely natural. One's outer actions are matched by one's inner spirit of reverence, sympathy, and respect. Or, better, one is inwardly moved spontaneously to act in accord with the decrees of Heaven. The superior person, we read later, recognizes and accedes to the imperatives of Heaven (20:3).

Zhu Xi, in his commentary, explained *Tianming*,[4] the Mandate of Heaven, as Heaven's destined plan or decree for the sage's life.[5] *Tianming*, in some contexts, is one's vocation and in others something like fate: it encompasses the sage's role in society, the sage's success and failures, and an everything that goes beyond the sage's own mortal control. Unlike fate, things beyond the sage's mortal control are ordained by Heaven. Let us consider whether "Heaven" denotes a natural and impersonal order of life (fate) or the will of a personal Supreme Being (providence).

The images, metaphors, and stories within which Confucius communicates his commitments concerning Heaven suggest Heaven's providential care for his people and Heaven as the primordial foundation of goodness. Confucius' trust in Heaven's conscious and caring intervention can be seen in his faith in Heaven's cunning and power to intervene when humans have lost the Way:

> The guardian at Yi (a border post of the state of Wei) requested to be presented to Confucius, saying: "When gentlemen come here, I have never been prevented from seeing them." Confucius' followers introduced him. When he came out from the interview, he said: "Sirs, why are you disheartened by your master's loss of office? The Way has not prevailed in the world for a long time. Heaven is going to use your master as a bell with a wooden tongue [to awaken the people]."

Legend had it that Confucius was employed by the ruler of his native state of Lu in some high and official position, perhaps as a major minister. However, because of his efficiency and uprightness, his enemies resented him and succeeded in ousting him from office. Thereafter Confucius, with neither title nor occupation, wandered from one state to another propagating rather unsuccessfully his teachings. Until his death he was never employed again by any rulers and his teaching would languish for hundreds of years before being appreciated and implemented in China.

Yet Kong Anguo from the Han dynasty would write that Confucius' loss of office was, through Heavenly providence, the world's gain: "Why being disheartened by your master's [apparent] loss of his sagacious moral [way]? The world does not have the Way for a long time already, so the lost [after reaching its extreme][6] would soon achieve its abundant fulfillment."[7] Heaven would use Confucius as the wooden tongue of a Chinese bell (*muduo*), bells used primarily to assemble the people or to announce a political decree. Zhu Xi contends that because of its nature as a political tool, *muduo* indicates Confucius' role to awaken or reprimand the public.[8] Kong Anguo explains that the use of *muduo* in this passage indicates that Heaven will work through Confucius to renew society: metaphorically portraying Confucius as a bell with a wooden clapper equates his teaching with the voice or call of Heaven itself, proclaiming reform and a return to the ancient glorious days of civilization.[9] This is one of the handful passages that explain the prophetic nature of Confucius' role in the development of Chinese culture, not as a moral teacher only, but also as a Heaven-commissioned emissary.

A political position would indeed have seemed strategic for Confucius who sought, through his ideas, to reform society. Some of his followers lamented that his loss of position doomed his mission. But Confucius assures them that Heaven would ensure that his efforts were not in vain. Zhu Xi and others have suggested that Heaven intentionally took away his office so that, as Heaven's "wooden tongue," Confucius could spread his teaching more widely through becoming an unofficial and displaced—yet Heaven-appointed—messenger who wandered without definite destination.

We can find in this a revolutionary shift toward the meritocratization of the concept of the Mandate of Heaven.[10] We learned in the tumultuous Spring and Autumn period that noble rank was not directly correlated with cultural excellence (as it had been in the early Zhou period). Kinship relations had failed as a means of equipping the ruling classes. Consequently, the notion of the Mandate of Heaven was losing its royal/aristocratic monopoly. Thus, the path toward sageliness is open to anyone willing to learn and to cultivate virtue, regardless of social status and background. In a significant departure from the aristocratic thinking of his time, Confucius said that "in education, there are no differences of any kind" (*Analects* 15:39); the task of the renewal of the world is not identified with political or aristocratic descent. Reformers and kings could be any individual who is morally qualified to receive a noble mandate from Heaven.

In Heaven's exercise of providence, we find Heaven's concern for the condition of his people; Heaven is an intervening supernatural being who works through people like Confucius to communicate Heaven's mandate. Benjamin Schwartz concurs: "Heaven, in its relations to the world of man, also still seems to manifest a mode of 'theistic' concern with human destiny for Heaven is basically 'on man's side.' Heaven supports sages and noble men in their redemptive efforts and even deliberately intervenes in the course of human history" (Schwartz 1985: 125). Heaven's concern for his people, then, is the source of Confucius' concern for people. Confucius' this-worldly ethical orientation is rooted in Heaven's compassion and justice-motivated activity within human history.

Heaven, instead of being a natural order or impersonal force, is depicted as an active and good will with strong personal fervor. Heaven is also represented in the *Analects* as supremely good. Indeed, Heaven is both the source and model of goodness. Confucius endorses the cosmogonic grounding of goodness in Heaven:[11]

> The Master said, "How great was Yao as a ruler! So majestic! It is Heaven that is great, and it was Yao who modeled himself upon it. So vast! Among the common people there were none who were able to find words to describe him. How majestic in his accomplishments, and glorious in cultural splendor!"
>
> (*Analects* 8:19)

Although the great Yao is a human moral model, his goodness is derivative; ultimately only Heaven is great. According to Schwartz, "If there is any central religious term in the *Analects*, it is the term 'Heaven,' and here again Confucius is to a degree a transmitter ... Heaven above all is the source of the moral order"

(Schwartz 1985: 22). The ultimate, primordial moral source is Heaven alone, through the modeling or imitating of which one may accomplish great things. Michael Puett comments on this analect: "Yao's rule was great because he and he alone patterned himself on Heaven. As a consequence, his 'patterned forms' (*wen zhang*) are illustrious and, the text implies, worthy of emulation. The first sage king was thus the one who brought the patterns of Heaven to the realm of humanity" (Puett 1997: 478). In short, the exemplary rulers of the Xia, Shang, and Zhou are not moral ideals because they constructed the rituals (*li*) that just happened to work to produce a harmoniously functioning society. Rather the leaders of the Xia, Shang, and Zhou were able to produce a harmoniously functioning society because their rituals embodied the fixed patterns of Heaven. They were successful leaders because they tapped into the primordial powers of Reality not because they happened upon relatively useful but ultimately optional moral practices. Puett writes: "Heaven is thus granted a normative role. The patterns of human culture (*wen*) emerged from Heaven, and it is Heaven that allows those patterns to continue" (Puett 2003: 100). Theodore de Bary concurs: "[I]f the Confucian is worldly and urbane in this respect, he, like Confucius, must heed the imperatives of Heaven as the supreme moral order in the universe, and answer to it in his conscience" (de Bary 1996: 8).

The superior person, then, stands in awe of the decrees or imperatives of Heaven, while the petty person ignores them (*Analects* 16:8). de Bary concludes that in the *Analects* Heaven is the cosmogonic grounding of the Good, one which motivates or should motivate human beings to be moral:

> It is this compelling voice of conscience and ideal standard represented by the imperatives of Heaven which serves as the ultimate criterion and court of judgment in assessing human affairs. If, according to the Confucian conception of humanity or humaneness (*ren* 仁), man can indeed be the measure of man, it is only because this high moral sense and cosmic dimension of the human mind-and-heart give it the capacity for self-transcendence. Likewise, if the Confucian, even while accepting the world, still hopes to gain the leverage on it necessary for its transformation, Heaven's imperative in the minds of men serves as the fulcrum.
>
> (de Bary 1996: 8–9)

Confucius, in spite of his belief in the transformative powers of ritual (*li*), attributed his own goodness to Heaven:

> The Master said, "It is Heaven itself that has endowed me with virtue (*Tian sheng de yu yu* 天生德于予). What have I to fear from the likes of Huan Tui?"
>
> (*Analects* 7:23)

Huan Tui, a minister in the state of Song, had attempted to take Confucius' life but Confucius claims he has nothing to fear with Heaven on his side. This passage makes little sense if Heaven is interpreted as an extension of the human community or a natural force: his appeal to Heaven is a confession of his dependence on divine assistance for his moral improvement and a recognition of the divine assistance required to persevere through life's tribulations; Confucius accepted his virtue and the inner strength it afforded him as a gift. Confucius has the inner moral strength to overcome the world through Heaven's special and favoring activity in his life.

It is clear from the preceding analect that Confucius thought it possible to incur Heaven's disapproval; consider his comment to Zilu after a meeting with Nanzi, a woman with a notorious reputation:

> The Master had an audience with Nanzi, and Zilu was not pleased. The Master swore an oath, saying, "If I have done anything wrong, may Heaven punish me! May Heaven punish me (*Tian yan zhi* 天厌之)!"
>
> (*Analects* 6:28)

The verb *yan* is suggestive of subjective disapproval or disdain; the passage may more appropriately be translated more clearly anthropomorphically as "May Heaven forsake me."

This latter passage is consonant with Confucius' general view that Heaven exercises a kind of moral providence:

> The Master was surrounded in Kuang. He said, "Now that King Wen is gone, is not culture now invested here in me? If Heaven intended this culture to perish, it would not have given it to those of us who live after King Wen's death. Since Heaven did not intend that this culture should perish, what can the people of Kuang do to me?"
>
> (*Analects* 9:5)

Given Heaven's assignment of reforming society to Confucius, how could the merely human people of Kuang prevent the realization of Heaven's plans? Heaven had given his patterns to King Wen, transmitted them through the generations, and entrusted them to Confucius. As in other contexts, we find Confucius' confidence grounded in his sense of the providential care of Heaven.

Consider a second passage in which Confucius avers to Heaven's disfavor:

> Wangsun Gu asked, "What is the meaning of this saying: 'rather than cajoling the god of the Southwest corner,[12] it is better to flatter the god of Kitchen[13]'?"
>
> The Master replied, "It is not like that. If one sins against the Heaven, then it would be nowhere to go for praying."

This is a humorous and metaphorical conversation between Confucius and Wangsun Gu, a high-ranking official from the state of Wei. Before conversing with Wangsun Gu, Confucius had an audience with Nanzi, the favorite concubine of the Duke of Wei. Wangsun Gu believed that Confucius had sought a favor from Nanzi in order to secure a high political office in Wei. Wangsun Gu, then, used a humorous metaphor to tell Confucius that rather than seeking a favor from a beautiful but useless Southwest corner (*Ao*), which stands for a pretty but powerless Nanzi, it would be more beneficial for Confucius' political career to flatter an ugly but useful furnace (*Zao*), which symbolizes an official with real function and power (like Wangsun Gu). Confucius, with equal wittiness, replied that if one committed a crime against Heaven, then and only then does one lack authority.

The message of this text primarily concerns Confucius' uprightness: he does not seek favor from any human beings but depends solely on his virtue and the Mandate of Heaven for the establishment of his legacy. Yet the metaphors reflect common contemporary representations of religious belief—Heaven or *Shangdi* is the King-on-high who presides, rules, and controls both lesser deities and human affairs. "Heaven," according to the explanation of this text in *Lunyu Zhengyi*, a classic commentary on the *Analects*, "is the great Lord of the myriad of spirits" (*bai shen zhi da jun ye*)."[14] Heaven is the supreme commander of the heavenly bureaucracy.

Confucius plays his trump card, matching metaphor for metaphor, in his reply to Wangsun Gu. The bureaucratic significance of Heaven as Arbiter of the spirits/deities means that if one violates Heaven, one violates the most powerful Power, and it would be useless to petition lesser deities or appeal to well-placed persons, no matter how powerful they are.

There is more to be said about the representations of Heaven in the *Analects*. Heaven is portrayed as widely knowing, even of our inner thoughts and motives. For example, humans cannot deceive Heaven (*Analects* 9:12).[15] Humans cannot deceive Heaven only if Heaven is some kind of superknower—with cognitive capabilities (that grant him access to our inner life) that human persons lack. While this may be a source of dismay for some (who wishes to have their inmost thoughts and desires laid bare?), for Confucius it was a source of comfort. We find this Confucian confidence in the divine knower in a variety of analects. Consider the following:

> The Master sighed, "Alas! No one understands me."
> Zigong replied, "How can you say that no one understands you, Master?"
> "I am not bitter toward Heaven, nor do I blame others. I study what is below in order to comprehend what is above. If there is anyone who could understand me, perhaps it is Heaven." (14:35)

While most humans seek this-worldly fame and fortune, Confucius did not. He was gratified by his belief that Heaven, above all, knew him and esteemed him (in spite of his apparently paltry earthly success).

Is Heaven Personal?

Philip Ivanhoe contends that in the *Analects*, Heaven is presented as "an impersonal yet concerned agent and a force for human good" (Ivanhoe 2007: 213). Ivanhoe notes that heaven is represented in the *Analects* and in the tradition that informs the *Analects* as a person with a will, as a superknower (but not necessarily omniscient), as good, as the primordial source of goodness, and as morally provident; Heaven is the creator of the people and, through the Mandate of Heaven, shows concern and even compassion for human welfare. The pre- and post-Confucian documents that are most closely associated with something like a Confucian tradition and that inform our understanding of the *Analects* are remarkably congruent in their anthropomorphic representations of Heaven. On this, Ivanhoe and I are in firm agreement (Ivanhoe 2007). Yet Ivanhoe curiously rejects the conclusion that in the *Analects* Heaven is a *person*. I say, "curiously," because an independent moral agent with a will and knowledge seems to be, paradigmatically, a person.[16]

The argument that Confucius rejects an anthropomorphic Heaven often revolves around a number of passages claiming that the Master refuses to talk about this or that. Contemporary commentators fix on these passages as evidence that Confucius never spoke about Heaven. Consider one representative passage:

> The Master never discussed strange phenomena (*guai*),[17] physical exploits (*li*),[18] disorder (*luan*), or spiritual beings (*shen*).[19]
>
> (7:20)

Based on the claim that the Master never discusses spiritual beings, it is widely asserted that the Master has no belief in Heaven.[20] Finally, claims to Confucius' agnosticism are often based on variations on the mantra, "Respect the spirits, but keep them at a distance," from *Analects* 6:22. Confucius, so it is claimed, is a kind of rationalist and skeptic, who finds expression in agnosticism about the extrahuman in this analect. Confucius, so the story goes, was perfectly willing to use widely popular beliefs in spirits to control the common person;

yet, he personally and intellectually distanced himself from them. Yi-Fu Tuan, in commenting on this passage, characteristically claims, "Confucius himself proclaimed agnosticism in otherworldly matters" (Tuan 1999: 23). Staying aloof, keeping away from, keeping one's distance from the spirits seems clear—one has to respect them and all that, but they are functionally irrelevant to his fundamentally humanist vision of "giving oneself earnestly to the duties due to men." Confucius' benevolent humanism, as manifested in this analect, is freighted with skeptical agnosticism. Hall and Ames write: "Concerning the unknown realm of gods and spirits, Confucius maintained an attitude of respectful detachment" (Hall and Ames 1987: 196).

Yet, Confucius tells his followers to *respect the spirits*. How could they (and he) *respect* the spirits all the while denying their existence or refusing to believe in them? Perhaps, in keeping with the spirit of respect, "keeping them at a distance" means something quite different from atheism or agnosticism.[21]

In *Analects* 6:22, if we take Confucius' admonition to "respect the spirits" seriously, we must understand "keeping a distance" in a manner that is consonant with respect. Surely, then, he can't have meant, "keep aloof from" or "avoid." Given the Confucian commitment to a hierarchical harmony, where everyone is in their proper place (and pleased to be so), we might understand these rituals as ones in which the participant knows his or her proper place. Herrlee Creel notes a similar use of the character *yuan* 遠 in 16:15, in which a superior person keeps his son at a distance (*yuan*). But fathers shouldn't remain aloof from or avoid their sons (and they are certainly not skeptical of their existence). In the *Analects yuan* entails sympathetically understanding one's son's needs, acting in benevolence toward one's son, and having genuine affection for one's son.

Fundamental to Confucius' social philosophy is a kind of hierarchical harmony (和 *he*) in which each person is in his or her place. The moral training of the child involves learning the proper attitudes of reverence, respect, and obedience toward those above them; fraternal goodwill to those alongside them; and paternal kindness to those beneath them. The child's learning of place will transfer from the home to society, and from society to the world. Role-specific rituals (*li*) are designed to effect the proper actions and attitudes of persons at every level. Given the social conditions of Confucius' day a premium was placed on the harmonious, peaceful, and efficient functioning of society in a time of uncertainty; individual liberty and natural rights were far from his mind. Finally, not just any harmony would do, only the harmony which unified human beings with ultimate reality: the earthly hierarchy should resemble the heavenly hierarchy. The purpose of the *li* is to effect that sort of harmony (see *Analects* 1:12).

For Confucius, hierarchical harmony reigns in the family, in society, and in the cosmos. Rituals concerning the father are designed for the father to keep his proper distance from the son (and the vice versa for the rituals for the son). The father should love and care for his son, all the while maintaining his position of authority. And religious rituals, those involving the ghosts and spirits, should create the proper distance between the superior spirits and the person doing the ritual.[22] The rituals, rooted in respect for the spirits, help the participant learn their proper place in the cosmos (which then should transfer to their place in society). This, again, would be a natural expression of both Confucius' Zhou theology and hierarchical harmony.[23]

Herlee Creel called attention to *Analects* 6:22 in his 1932 essay, "Was Confucius Agnostic?" Creel notes that while agnostic interpretations of Confucius were widespread in his day, they were scarcely considered throughout the entire commentarial tradition. He notes that the earliest post-Confucius texts which take Confucius as their authority—the *Daxue*, the *Zhongyong*, and the *Mencius*—not only fail to attest to Confucius' allegedly obvious skepticism, they

> include the most affirmatory references to the directive power of Heaven and to the spirits, the sacrifices, etc. Particularly in *Mencius* Heaven appears as a personal being, much interested in human affairs. Surely, if Confucius was agnostic, it is remarkable that his views in this respect did not make an impression upon those who came close after him in the Confucian tradition.
> (Creel 1932: 67)

Moreover, in an exhaustive study of 1,500 years of pre-Song dynasty commentaries on this and other passages alleged in support of Confucius' agnosticism, Creel claims that there is not "*a single passage of a skeptical nature*" (Creel 1932: 68, emphasis his). Not only are they not skeptical, the commentaries accept at face value the religious realities that Confucius countenances. Not a single commentator during the first 1,500 years after Confucius claimed that Confucius was an agnostic.[24]

The so-called anti-religion texts of the *Analects* offer no reason to reject Confucius' otherwise clear and forthright commitment to a personal and providential deity. In the next section I will consider the locus classicus for rejecting this view and offer a final defense of Confucius' theism.

Saying vs. Showing

In spite of the abundant evidence for Confucius' belief (Confucius, the character in the *Analects*) in the anthropomorphic and divine status of Heaven, some modern scholars continue to deny that Confucius believed in an anthropomorphic Heaven. Bryan Van Norden writes: "Most of the questions we might raise about Heaven or other aspects of Confucius' cosmology have no answers, because, based on the *Analects*, there is no evidence that Confucius had *detailed* theoretical views about cosmology" (Van Norden 2002: 22). But not having *detailed* theoretical views about cosmology is not tantamount to having no cosmological views at all. After all, Confucius does affirm that Heaven is anthropomorphic, distinct from human beings, the moral model of people, providential, etc. Granted these references to Heaven do not provide *detailed* theoretical views about cosmology, they do provide some information about Confucius' cosmological beliefs. Moreover, one might expect relatively undeveloped views if, as Roel Sterckx argues, the pre-Buddhist Chinese were "less troubled by ontological uncertainties and, instead, more preoccupied with the problem of how to deal with the spirit world in practice" (Sterckx 2007: 24).

Robert Louden argues that while Heaven is clearly not naturalistic, "Confucius ... is religious but not theistic" (Louden 2002: 79). His evidence is tucked away in a footnote: "It is true that in several of the passages cited above Heaven is said to have intentions (9:5, perhaps 3:24); and in others to possess understanding (14:35. 9:12). These uses of language seem to me to be metaphorical. However, even if one thinks they are not, they do not add up to anything close to the 'God-as-personal-being' that most mainstream believers within the major Western traditions regard as being essential to their faith"[25] (Louden 2002: 91). On what grounds are these uses of language judged to be metaphorical? Louden doesn't say. There are no internal clues in the *Analects* for making this judgment. Judged against the background of the Zhou, though, they reflect the anthropomorphic theology of the *Shujing* and the *Odes*. The question Louden raised is: "Are the references to Heaven in the *Analects* theistic, that is, personal?" If we take the references mentioned previously as non-metaphorical—and I see no reason not to—and as in line with the tradition to which Confucius adheres, Heaven is represented in the *Analects* with attributes of persons: will, intentions, beliefs, morally good, caring, etc.

The *locus classicus* informing nearly every rejection of Confucius' theism concerns a remark of his disciple Zigong. "Zigong said, 'The Master's cultural brilliance is something that is readily heard about, whereas one does not get to hear the Master expounding upon the subjects of human nature or the Way of Heaven'" (*Analects* 5:13).²⁶ He never, of course, denies the existence of Heaven in these passages, so an argument that Confucius is not a theist based on these passages would be an argument from silence. And it would be a poor argument indeed given that he does speak substantively of Heaven in many other passages²⁷ (though it is clear that on *certain* occasions to *some* people, Confucius did not speak of Heaven, spirits, etc.).²⁸

What are we to make of Confucius' not speaking of Heaven to Zigong? Should we take this as evidence of Confucius' agnosticism about heaven? First, it should be noted that the passage also says that Confucius did not speak to Zigong about human nature. But Confucius has many references, some direct but most indirect, to human nature. And although Confucius does not offer detailed theoretical views about human nature, it is clear that he has some.²⁹ And few scholars contend that he is agnostic about human nature. So Confucius' remark to Zigong should not be taken to imply agnosticism about Heaven any more than it should be taken to imply agnosticism about human nature.

Perhaps the audience is Zigong, not everyone, as this passage is typically interpreted. That is, perhaps the Master did not express his views about Heaven and human nature only to Zigong (and so was a source of frustration to Zigong).³⁰ Why might the Master not speak of Heaven and human nature to Zigong (and perhaps to others)? Zigong and many others in Confucius' audience were not morally or spiritually ready for the higher sort of knowledge of which Heaven and human nature consisted.³¹ In the passage immediately preceding Zigong's statement, we read: "Zigong said, 'What I do not wish others to do unto me, I also wish not to do unto others.' The Master said, 'Ah, Zigong! That is something quite beyond you'" (*Analects* 5:12). Given the centrality of reciprocity to Confucius' moral system (*Analects* 4:15), Zigong must be viewed as morally deficient or even defective. Sympathetic understanding is a point Zigong has not yet reached, so he is not ready to hear about heaven and human nature; Zigong may have been a clever bureaucrat (6:8) but he lacked the sympathetic understanding so essential to the Confucian moral life.³²

In several passages of the *Analects*, we learn that discussion of higher matters requires the prior attainment of moral and spiritual sensitivities. "The Master said, 'You can discuss the loftiest matters with those who are above average, but not with those who are below average'" (*Analects* 6:21). Since Zigong, as portrayed in the *Analects*, is not yet better than average, it is not surprising that Confucius would refuse to discuss superior matters with him. In another passage we read: "The Master said, 'I will not open the door for a mind that is not already striving to understand, nor will I provide words to a tongue that is not already struggling to speak. If I hold up one corner of a problem, and the student cannot come back to me with the other three, I will not attempt to instruct him again'" (*Analects* 7:8). For Confucius, knowledge was not distributed willy-nilly to whoever asked or was in his audience; knowledge was dispensed slowly depending on the receptive conditions of the listener: to those who can already supply the other three corners. Zigong is consistently portrayed as someone not yet ready to learn of the higher things. Of those who are not ready to learn of the higher things, Confucius says that he can at best control their behavior (to follow the Way), not affect their beliefs: "The common people can be made to follow it, but they cannot be made to understand it" (*Analects* 8:9). In not speaking thusly to Zigong, Confucius was following his own advice not to waste words on people of little understanding:

> If someone is open to what you have to say, but you do not speak to them, this is letting the person go to waste; if, however, someone is not open to what you have to say, but you speak to them anyway, this is letting our words go to waste. The wise person does not let people go to waste, but he does not waste his words.
> (*Analects* 15:8)

So reticent was Confucius to speak that a legend seems to have arisen that he never spoke about anything at all (*Analects* 14:13)! The *Analects* reports that Confucius seldom or never spoke of things he did in fact speak about, sometimes a great deal. For example, in Dawson's translation of *Analects* 9:1 we read: "The Master seldom spoke of profit and fate and humaneness" (Dawson 2008: 31).[33] But, as is clear in the *Analects*, the Master denigrated profit, bemoaned fate, and spoke of humaneness more than any single topic.[34] All of this supports the claim that Confucius did not speak of heaven to Zigong simpliciter on this occasion, probably for moral reasons.[35] But it does not follow that Confucius did not speak of heaven because of skepticism or agnosticism about the spirits, any more than his seldom speaking of humaneness entails agnosticism about humaneness. Finally, the passages aforementioned claim that the Master does not speak about ghosts and spirits (鬼神 *guishen*); Heaven is not mentioned at all. So even if the Master did not speak of spirits and ghosts and is thereby agnostic about them, he did speak of Heaven.

The Master's not speaking may provide an interpretive clue to much of Confucius' thought. Confucius aspired to not speaking, like Heaven. In *Analects* 17:19, we read:

> The Master sighed, "Would that I did not have to speak!"
> Zigong said, "If the Master did not speak, then how would we little ones receive guidance from you?"
> The Master replied, "What does Heaven ever say? Yet the four seasons are put in motion by it, and the myriad creatures receive their life from it. What does ever Heaven say?"

Heaven does not speak, but through Heaven the entire cosmos is ordered.[36] Heaven is silent but is the moral order of the universe. The way of Heaven may be discovered not by listening to a revelation but only by looking. One can see the Heavenly Order and the Way of Heaven: Heaven who does not speak but who orders the world. We can learn of Heaven's principle by seeing not by hearing.[37] Puett concurs: "Heaven does not speak yet it is from Heaven that the four seasons proceed and the hundred things generated. What can be transmitted, in other words, is patterned behavior: true transmission, Confucius is claiming, is not through words but rather through replicating patterns that were initially found in heaven" (Puett 1997: 479).

The Wittgensteinian distinction between saying and showing may be useful here. The early Wittgenstein believed that only factual sentences say anything about the world; if something cannot be captured in factual language, it is without sense. Ironically, in order to communicate his theory of language and logic, Wittgenstein had to rely on non-factual language, that is language which according to his own theory is without sense. He recognized his performance failure at the end of the *Tractatus* but contended that the language of the *Tractatus*, like the language of logic, while not *saying* anything can *show* us something about the world.[38]

This distinction between saying and showing would, if successful, permit Wittgenstein to show us something about the world that transcends the limits of language (see Wittgenstein 1922: 4:113–4:1212). Although the *Tractatus* enshrines factual language, Wittgenstein told Ludwig von Flicker that the book's point is an ethical one (although moral values cannot be expressed in factual language). According to Wittgenstein, the most important things—ethics, the meaning of life, God—lie beyond the limits of human language (see Wittgenstein 1922: 6:41–6:522). Wittgenstein does not deny that values or God exist, he simply denies that humans can say anything meaningful about them; but, like logic, they can show something about them. He concludes his comments on ethics, God, and the significance of the universe with the following: "There are, indeed, things that cannot be put into words. They *make themselves manifest.* They are what is mystical" (Wittgenstein 1922: 6:522).

This mystical interpretation of the *Tractatus* foils the pretensions of the positivist who sought to co-opt Wittgenstein's "argument" and makes sense of Wittgenstein's intentions and corpus which includes showings about both religion and ethics. And yet it is precisely in those silences that we can hear Confucius on Heavenly reality. As Simon Leys, translator of the *Analects*, writes:

> Confucius distrusted eloquence. He despised glib talkers, and he hated clever word games. For him, it would seem that an agile tongue must reflect a shallow mind—as reflection runs deeper, silence develops. He observed that his favourite disciple used to say so little that, at times, one could have wondered if he was not an idiot.
>
> To another disciple who had asked him about the supreme virtue of humanity, Confucius replied: "He who possesses the supreme virtue of humanity is reluctant to speak."
>
> His silences occurred essentially when his interlocutors tried to draw him on the question of the afterlife. This attitude has often led commentators to conclude that Confucius was an agnostic. Such a conclusion seems, to me, very shallow.
>
> Like the empty space in a painting, which concentrates and radiates all the inner energy, Confucius's silence is not a withdrawal or an escape—it leads to a deeper engagement into life and reality. Near the end of his career, Confucius said to his disciples: "I wish to speak no more." The disciples were perplexed: "But, Master, if you do not speak, how would little ones like us still be able to hand down any teachings?" Confucius replied: "Does Heaven speak? Yet the four seasons follow their course and the hundred creatures continue to be born. Does Heaven speak?"
>
> (Leys 1997: 3)

Showing rather than saying seems much like Confucius' strategy. The terse language, the reluctance to speak about some topics at length, the aspiration to silence, and the continual offering of models (both good and bad) indicate that Confucius wished not to say but to show us something about the self and its place in society and the cosmos. Those who would demand that Confucius say more about certain topics fail to recognize how much Confucius is showing and how little he is saying (about virtually everything).[39] Heaven does not speak but makes itself manifest.

Conclusion

Confucius, the character we encounter in the *Analects*, viewed humans as subject to a nonhuman reality, Heaven, the source of morality and social order, and providential director of human affairs. Confucius believed that most contemporary communities were in chaos and that their citizens were unjust; he maintained these views not by appealing to community standards but by appealing to Heaven, who had moral and social authority over all communities. Some communities are right (the early Zhou and the best of the Xia and the Shang) but most are woefully wrong. What was so special about the Zhou? They mirrored in their relationships the hierarchical harmony of the cosmos and so reflected the moral and bureaucratic order of Heaven. If the real, historical Confucius is or is sufficiently and relevantly like the Confucius character of the *Analects*, Confucius was a theist.

5

Heaven in the *Mencius*

Mencius

Mencius (Mengzi), the so-called "second sage," is purported to have lived in the fourth century BCE and to have written an eponomously titled monograph. Contemporary Sinologists distinguish between the character Mencius and the text, the *Mencius*. The character is either the character that appears in several texts dating to the Warring States or the creation of later scholars through interpretations that have been superimposed on a text that has been labeled "the *Mencius*" (see Denecke 2011). Philosophers often insist on such characters being the ones who "write" such texts in which they espouse their "views" but the philological evidence points to a completely different scenario. A person named "Mencius" may have had something to do with the construction of the text called "the *Mencius*" but the relation of Mencius to the *Mencius* remains unresolved. I shall set aside such critical considerations and simply refer to the text, the *Mencius*. I will demonstrate that the *Mencius* overwhelmingly represents an extrahuman agent that it refers to by the names, *Tian* (Heaven) and *Shangdi*.

Contemporary scholars argue that Mencius uses *Tian* and *Shangdi* merely as rhetorical devices to advance or reinforce his political views; Robert Eno offers the most systematic defense of this view. His reconstructed Mencius is a skeptical pragmatist who puts common religious parlance to work to achieve various political ends without regard for their truth. I argue that it is more plausible to see the *Mencius* as representing *Tian* as an anthropomorphic supreme deity. In the *Mencius*, thirty-one passages mention *Tian* (Heaven) or *Shangdi* (the Lord-on-High). The *Mencius*' representations of *Tian*/*Shangdi* are not reducible without remainder to political rhetoric. I will first outline Eno's reconstruction of Mencius and then show that the *Mencius* countenances an entirely different view.[1] I will conclude with a discussion of why it is more plausible to think of the *Mencius* as theistic. The discussion will be brief.

Eno's Theory

With respect to the role of *Tian* in Mencius' political thought, Eno argues that its use is completely pragmatic: "*T'ien* is merely a convenient rhetorical device for implantation of his populist political agenda." Eno begins by discussing Mencius' political theory. He thinks that "the heart of Mencius' political theory … [is] in his idealistic populism, and the belief that the proper function of political leaders and institutions was to serve the needs and interests of the people (Eno 1990a: 101)." Accordingly, Eno claims that Mencius uses the idea of *Tian* to achieve his political populism. Moreover, Eno argues for a dichotomy between the prescriptive and descriptive roles that were ascribed to *Tian*. He argues that "it is in the shifts between the two dimensions that the pragmatic basis of statements about *T'ien* becomes clear." By comparing passages that use these dual roles of *Tian*, Eno concludes that their uses are not equivalent and that the use of *Tian* is pragmatic:

> This distinction between two entirely different *Tians*, one *Tian* seen from the perspective of political strength, the other seen from the perspective of weakness, reveals the pragmatic nature of the role of *Tian* in Mencius' political thought. Mencius' political metaphysics recognizes political reality and does not challenge it. … He was anxious to put his programs to a crucial test in Chi.
>
> (Eno 1990a: 103)

Eno notes the different ways that Mencius talks to the king of a big state and that of a small state. He claims:

> 1B.3 and 1B.14 are the only instances where Mencius discusses *Tian* with rulers or other political actors, and this illustrate the minor role that *Tian* played in Mencius' practical political rhetoric. Judging from them, *Tian* represents political realities as Mencius saw them: prescriptive opportunities for the strong, descriptive perils for the weak. In this sense, *T'ien* is reduced to Mencius' view of practical reality.
>
> (Eno 1990a: 104)

Eno further argues:

> M:5A.5 and M:5A.6 show Mencius elaborating theories of history that rationalize his populist political theories and an acceptance of the existing institutions of hereditary privilege. Mencius' motives for doing this are not explicit in the passages, but they are not, perhaps, unimaginable … *T'ien* is not a stable concept but a chameleon-like notion that resembles nothing more than a convenient rhetorical device.
>
> (Eno 1990a: 105)

In summary, Eno claims that Mencius uses *Tian* as a rhetorical device with no metaphysical implications; *Tian* is nothing but a (powerful) tool to advance Mencius' political agenda.

Political Rhetoric?

Is the *Mencius'* theistic rhetoric little more than political expediency? Or are his undeniably political uses of *Tian* or *Shangdi* also metaphysically significant? I will argue that the *Mencius in toto* (not just the two passages Eno relies on (B3 and 1B14)) affords a realist understanding of *Tian*. First, consider how Eno constructs *Tian*. Consider the following discussion:

> *T'ien* is manifest in humane government in accord with Mencius' policies. The ruler who adopts these policies will find the people of surrounding states flocking to his domain. "He will have no enemy in the world. He who has no enemy in the world is the agent of *T'ien*. Never has there been such a one who has not ruled as true King" (*M*:2A.5). Note that in this formula, *Tian* plays no active role. The humane ruler is *T'ien*'s agent, but his political success is adequately explained by the virtue of his policies and the consequence that he ceases to have enemies. No barriers would then remain between him and the Imperial throne that would require the intervention of a transcendent power. *T'ien*'s role is passive; it adds nothing to the powers of virtue.
>
> (Eno 1990a: 103)

But why think *Tian* passive? Why think there is no divine intervention between the just ruler and the imperial throne?

The *Mencius* seems to hold that when *Tian* gives the Mandate of Heaven, he empowers his chosen with the benevolence to govern; moreover, those to whom Heaven has given his Mandate are favored and protected by Heaven. For example, we read in 5A5 that *Tian*'s favoring activity included both assisting Shun's merit and granting him the crown: "Shun assisted Yao for twenty-eight years. This is not something that could have been brought about by a human being. It was Heaven." *Tian* chose Shun and then installed him as the Son of Heaven: no passivity here. Yao offered Shun as King but Heaven had to choose and appoint him.

The *Mencius* also offers a way of assessing what was caused by humans and what was caused by heaven. In regard to conveying rich benefits on all the people during the time of Shun and Yu, in 5A6 we read: "All this was owing to Heaven and was not something that could be brought about by human beings.

What happens without anyone's causing it is owing to Heaven; what happens without comes about without anyone's accomplishing it is the mandate." This may be a Heaven of the gap, but the *Mencius* claims that there are things only *Tian* can bring about (things human beings cannot bring about): no passive *Tian* here.

In 5A3, a passage reminiscent of *Analects* 7:23, Wan Zhang speaks of Confucius' trust in Heaven's providence; in 7:23, we read: "The Master said, 'It is Heaven itself that has endowed me with virtue. What have I to fear from the likes of Huan Tui?'" (*Analects* 7:23).[2] Heaven, we are told, would not abandon those who wore his mantle. Wan Zhang asked Mencius how "Shun, upon becoming the Son of Heaven," could banish his mortal enemy (and brother!), Xiang. Why, Wan implies, did Shun not entrust himself, as Confucius did, to Heaven's care? The *Mencius* seems eager to portray Shun's trust in *Tian*'s providence, so Shun replies that he had not actually banished Xiang; instead, he manifested his trust in *Tian*'s providence by giving Xiang land and an official appointment in exchange for his allegiance. The *Mencius* explicates providence in terms of an extrahuman that wills the good fortune and protection of those who follow the Mandate and grants them power to conquer their enemies and rule the people. I will return to this later.

According to Eno, in 1B3 we find two distinct notions of *Tian* put to entirely different political uses:

> King Xuan of Qi asked, "Is there a way of conducting relations with neighboring states?"
>
> Mencius replied, "There is. But only one who is humane is able to serve a small state with a large on, as was the case when Tang served Ge and King Wen served the Kun tribes. Only the wise are able to serve a large state with a small one, as was the case when Tai Wang served the Xunyu and Goujian served Wu. One who with a large state serves a small one delights in Heaven, while one who with a small state serves a large one is in awe of Heaven. Through delighting in Heaven one preserves all-under-Heaven, and through being in awe of Heaven one preserves his state."

Eno argues, based on this passage:

> This distinction between two entirely different *Tian*s, one *Tian* seen from the perspective of political strength, the other seen from the perspective of weakness, reveals the pragmatic nature of the role of *Tian* in Mencius' political thought. Mencius' political metaphysics recognizes political reality and does not challenge it. ... He was anxious to put his programs to a crucial text in Chi.
>
> (Eno 1990a: 103)

Eno claims to find the two "different" versions of *Tian* in this passage.

Eno seems to confuse psychological reactions to *Tian* with the nature of *Tian*. There aren't "two entirely different *Tians*" in the *Mencius*, there are simply two entirely different human reactions to *Tian*—finding joy in *Tian* and acting in awe of *Tian*. Eno's claim that Mencius would shape *Tian* as he likes in order to get his political theories adopted by the King is unsupported by the *Mencius*: *Tian* is not a chameleon-like notion; *Tian* has a fixed nature which is appropriated psychologically in very different ways.

The *Mencius* does not portray Mencius as twisting the meaning of *Tian* to fit into different circumstances. When King Xuan asks Mencius for the proper way of developing good relations with neighboring states, Mencius offers different attitudes that small states should have toward big states (and vice versa). He advises the King that small states should respect the power and authority of big states and that big states should delight in serving small states. Both attitudes accord with Heaven's Mandate and the *Mencius*' broadly Confucian notion of a hierarchical harmony. Mencius' advice may be pragmatic, but that doesn't contravene the *Mencius*' representations of a fixed idea of *Tian*. One might think the attitudes reflect Heavenly realities: Heaven is like the big state and in two ways. First, Heaven, like a big state in possession of Heaven's Mandate, is authoritatively powerful so the people should awe and revere Heaven. Second, Heaven, like a big state in possession of Heaven's mandate, takes joy in the compassionate protection of Heaven's people.

Heaven's compassionate care for his people is echoed in the widely repeated statement from the "Great Declaration" in 5A5:

Heaven sees as my people see,
Heaven hears as my people hear.

Heaven does not lend a deaf ear to the plight of his people. Heaven hears and knows of injustices to the widow, the poor, and the orphan. Heaven then responds by raising up and anointing a worthy ruler to restore peace, justice, and harmony.

Eno goes on:

M:1B.3 and M:1B.14 are the only instances where Mencius discusses *Tian* with rulers or other political actors, and this illustrate the minor role that *Tian* played in Mencius' practical political rhetoric. Judging from them, *Tian* represents political realities as Mencius saw them: prescriptive opportunities for the strong, descriptive perils for the weak. In this sense, *Tian* is reduced to Mencius' view of practical reality.

(Eno 1990a: 104)

Eno claims that Mencius represents *Tian* as nothing more than political rhetoric: benefits for the strong and perils for the weak. *Tian* lacks any of the metaphysical import central to theism—a personal God who providentially cares for the world.

Other claims deserve attention, too:

> ... general relation of *Tian* to the office of Kingship ... they illustrate that even in theory Mencius was attached to no firm view of *Tian* that would distinguish it from political realities ... Clearly what he is trying to do is to identify the notion of a purposive deity with descriptive political realities, and he is willing to recast the image of *T'ien* in any way that will help him to do so. His fixed philosophical point seems to be to legitimize the will of the people through historical precedent. His 'concept' of *T'ien* must be flexible enough to allow this.
>
> (Eno 1990a: 104)

> M:5A.5 and M:5A.6 show Mencius elaborating theories of history that rationalize his populist political theories and an acceptance of the existing institutions of hereditary privilege. Mencius' motives for doing this are not explicit in the passages, but they are not, perhaps, unimaginable ... *Tian* is not a stable concept but a chameleon-like notion that resembles nothing more than a convenient rhetorical device.
>
> (Eno 1990a: 105)

But Eno's readings are tendentious. Consider the opening of 5A5:

> Wan Zhang said, "Did it happen that Yao gave the realm to Shun?"
> Mencius said, "No. The Son of Heaven cannot give the realm to someone."
> "But Shun did possess the realm? Who gave it to him?"
> "Heaven gave it to him."

Assuming that the *Mencius* is not changing the meaning of terms without clue to the reader, we are presented here with either Yao as the granter of the kingdom or Heaven as the granter of the kingdom. But no mere Son of Heaven can bestow the kingdom, only Heaven can. Bestowing, it should be noted, involves attributes of persons: the recognition of merit, the valuing of the requisite goods, the desire to give, and the conveying of a gift. Just as Yao qua person is a possible but not actual giver of the kingdom, so, too, only qua person is Heaven a possible giver of the kingdom. Without violence to our understanding of the term "give," it is used analogously with Yao and Heaven; both are persons of goodness, desire, and will. But, disanalogously, Yao lacks Heaven's power.

The passage goes on to treat Heaven as a knower with free will: "The Son of Heaven can present a man to Heaven, but he cannot cause Heaven to give him the realm. The lords can present a man to the Son of Heaven, but they cannot cause the Son of Heaven to make him lord." Just as the Son of Heaven listens to the request of the lords and then freely chooses of his own accord, so, too, *Tian* listens to the Son of Heaven but then freely chooses of *his* own accord. *Tian* has properties that Yao also has: wisdom, a will, a moral nature, and desires. And *Tian* has properties that Yao lacks: supreme moral authority and power.

Eno, however, concludes that for Mencius *Tian* is nothing but a convenient rhetorical device that is used flexibly to achieve his political agenda. I have raised reasonable doubts as to whether that is the only or even the best interpretation. The *Mencius* demands another interpretation: it represents *Tian* as a personal, providential High God. Let us consider these texts more closely.

The *Mencius* and the High God

Other scholars have demurred from interpreting *Tian* as a political metaphor or as a naturalistic force. Donald Munro argues that in claiming that human nature is derived from Heaven (6A6), Mencius is perforce claiming that moral concepts are "founded on something transcendental" (Munro 2002: 307).[3] Jeffrey Richey concurs and goes further: "Mencius thus shares with Confucius three assumptions about *Tian* as an extrahuman, absolute power in the universe: (1) its alignment with moral goodness, (2) its dependence on human agents to actualize its will, and (3) the variable, unpredictable nature of its associations with mortal actors." He goes on to state that Mencius offers a kind of theodicy: "Mencius is concerned with justifying the ways of *Tian* to humanity."[4] The *Mencius* is keen to demonstrate that, despite current skepticism and appearances to the contrary, *Tian* is the ground of human values.

The *Mencius* does not come to us in a cultural vacuum; it locates itself within a tradition, one which informs its interpretation. The *Mencius*' highly selective use of authoritative texts suggests that we locate the thought of the *Mencius* within the tradition of the Shang and the Shu. Passages that identify the *Mencius* as accountable to this authoritative tradition are employed as part of the text's argumentative strategies and not incidental asides (which would prevent one from saying: "It is the Shang and Shu that are theistic, not the *Mencius*"). While there were certainly other traditions swirling around at the time of Mencius, we must understand the *Mencius*' representations of *Tian* and *Shangdi* from within its own self-consciously selected tradition. The burden of proof then is on the one who would argue that the *Mencius* radically departs from the tradition it takes such pains to identify with.

In 1B3, for example, the *Mencius* affirms a conception of *Tian* in the *Shujing*. *Tian* is portrayed as creator of the people and as appointing teachers to help them realize peace within the kingdom. Moreover, *Tian* is equated with the Lord on High:

> Heaven, in sending down the people,
> Made a ruler for them, made them a teacher,
> Saying just that he should help the Lord-On-High,
> Bestowing grace throughout the four quarters.

Rulers and teachers are appointed by *Tian*/*Shangdi* to assist *Tian*/*Shangdi* in "bestowing grace" throughout the kingdom.[5] And, while 1B3 and 1B14 may be the only passages directed at rulers and other political actors, they are not the only passages where the *Mencius* discusses *Tian*.

With Confucius, Mencius says that "*Tian* does not speak—it simply reveals through deeds and affairs" (5A5). Let us, then, consider how other Mencian texts represent the ways that *Tian* has revealed himself through deeds and affairs.

Heaven has intentions. In 1B3, Mencius told King Xuan of Qi that it is Heaven's will that rulers should care for the people for the Lord-on-High. He quotes the *Classic of Documents* which I mentioned previously, but I will now consider the entire quotation:

> It says in the *Classic of Documents*:
>
>> Heaven, in sending down the people,
>> Made a ruler for them, made them a teacher,
>> Saying just that he should help the Lord-On-High,
>> Bestowing grace throughout the four quarters.
>> I alone am here for whoever has done wrong.
>> And for whoever has done no wrong. How dare there
>> Be under Heaven anyone with a will to transgress.

Heaven makes/develops rulers and teachers for the people, with the intention that they should help the Lord-on-High. Heaven is portrayed as maker/developer—not of the world, exactly, but at least of the people. He purposefully made/developed rulers and teachers to help the Lord-on-High, according to the *Documents*, to rectify the inferior people. They, as divine assistants, are instruments of grace bringing peace and harmony to the kingdom.

We find a similar sentiment in 5A7 where the *Mencius* quotes (and endorses) Yi Yin,

> Heaven, in giving birth to this people, causes those who are first to know to awaken those who are later to know and causes those who are first awakened to awaken those who are later to be awakened. I am one of those of Heaven's people who has awakened first; I will take this Way and use it to awaken this people. If I do not awaken them, who will do so?

Heaven both gives birth to (天生) the people and appoints and empowers teachers to enlighten the people who learn more slowly. In 5B1, the same idea in the same words appears, and we read that if he found a man or woman who "did not share in the benefits bestowed by Yao and Shun, it was as if he himself had pushed them into a ditch. So it was that he took upon himself the responsibility for the heavy weight of the world." These passages represent Heaven as giving birth to the people, as having plans (again, as having intentions), and as the bestower of grace and knowledge. Heaven's plan is that those who quickly understand the Way should assume the weighty responsibility of teaching those who are slower.

It is clear from the above passages that Heaven has intentions, and intentions are essential for personhood and necessary for divinity.[6] They are not sufficient, however, but constitute an important component of the divine nature. Next let us look at some places that suggest that Heaven has other personal attributes.

Heaven's personal attributes. In 6A16, the *Mencius* discusses nobility and honors,

> Mencius said, "There is the nobility of Heaven and the nobility of man. Humaneness, rightness, loyalty, and truthfulness—and taking pleasure in doing good, without ever wearying of it—this is the nobility of Heaven. The ranks of duke, minister, or high official—this is the nobility of man. Men of antiquity cultivated the nobility of Heaven and he nobility of man followed after it. Men of the present day cultivate Heavenly nobility out of a desire for the nobility of man, and, once having obtained the nobility of man, they cast away the nobility of Heaven. Their delusion is extreme, and, in the end, they must lose everything."

The attributes essential to the nobility of Heaven—humaneness, rightness, loyalty, and truthfulness—strongly suggest that Heaven is a person. Indeed, it is precisely those attributes that fully constitute a virtuous person's humanity. Those lacking such attributes are somehow less human, more animal-like. And only a person can delight in their virtue. Those wishing to reduce the personhood of Heaven to a natural force or the natural composition of humankind would argue that *tianjue* 天爵 is a kind of natural nobility or virtue endowed by nature. But the texts simply do not allow this interpretation. If the *Mencius* were to represent *Tian* only as natural force or the natural composition of humankind, it would be curious indeed, for example, for a natural force to take pleasure in its unwearied pursuit of goodness. And curiouser and curiouser, it would be odd if a natural force could possess the virtues of rightness and loyalty at all.

Finally, humans are to become, in a sense, god-like—possessing the attributes that constitute the nobility of Heaven.[7] Humans can but animals cannot become humane, righteous, loyal, and truthful. Humans are the right sorts of things by nature—persons—to acquire such personal attributes. It would do violence to the text to read naturalism into it. The *Mencius* clearly represents Heaven with personal attributes.

Heaven/the Lord-on-High actively influences the world. Besides having personal attributes, Heaven seems to be actively influencing the world, according to the *Mencius*. In 4A7, Mencius quoted the *Odes*,

> The descendants of Shang,
> Numbered more than hundreds of thousands,
> But when the Mandate came from the Lord on High,
> The lords submitted to the Zhou.
> The lords submitted to the Zhou,
> The Mandate of Heaven is not constant.
> The officers of Yin, admirable and earnest,
> Pour out libations at our capital.

The *Mencius* follows the classical identification of Heaven (*Tian*) with the Lord-on-High (*Shangdi*) in documents such as the *Odes* and the *Documents*. Here the *Mencius* quotes the *Odes* to make the point that when the Lord-on-High decrees something, the world and her people obey. The Lord-on-High actively influences the world by passing decrees.

Heaven is worthy of reverence. Finally, the *Mencius* represents Heaven as being worthy of reverence. The texts are neither many nor explicit, but their implication is not difficult to see. In 4B25, Mencius discusses worship of the Lord-on-High.

> Mencius said, "If Lady Xi had been covered in filth, people would have held heir noses as they passed her. But, although a person is ugly, it is possible, through fasting and purification, to become fit to perform sacrifices to the Lord-on-High."

Some may argue that Mencius is just making a point—contrasting a person's ability to sacrifice to the Lord-on-High with people stopping their noses in passing a person. But the text seems to mean that even a wicked person, if he or she morally and spiritually prepares himself or herself, can sacrifice to the Lord-on-High. Of course, the Lord-on-High can be the object of genuine sacrifice (and so requires such serious moral and spiritual preparation), only if the Lord-on-High is worthy of reverence and even of worship.

In 5A5, Mencius talks about Heaven causing a person to be in charge of the sacrifice ceremony.

> "He caused him to preside over the sacrifices, and the hundred spirits enjoyed them. This shows that Heaven accepted him. He put him in charge of affairs, and affairs were well ordered, and the hundred surnames were at peace. This shows that the people accepted him. Heaven it to him; the people gave it to him. This is why I said that 'The Son of Heaven cannot give the realm to someone.' Shun assisted Yao for twenty-eight years. This is not something that could have been brought about by a human being. It was Heaven. After Yao died, and the three years' mourning was completed, Shun withdrew from Yao's son and went south of the South River. But the lords of the realm, when they went to court, went not to Yao's son but to Shun. Litigants went not to Yao's son but to Shun. Singers sang not of Yao's son but of Shun. This is why is said, 'It was Heaven.' It was after all this that he went to the central states and ascended to the position of the Son of Heaven. If he had just taken up residence in Yao's palace and ousted Yao's son, this would have been usurpation and not Heaven's gift. The 'Great Declaration' says,
>
> > Heaven sees as my people see,
> > Heaven hears as my people hear."

Setting aside the representations of spirits in the passage, the *Mencius* represents the Lord-on-High as a being that accepts worship and also appoints leaders of that worship. To believe that, one must also believe that the Lord-on-High is a person.

Heaven is inscrutable. I averred in the opening of this section to the *Mencius'* theodicy. The *Mencius* seems concerned to reconcile Heaven's mandate and the existence of unjust rulers; moreover, he is concerned to understand how Heaven could have failed to appoint the worthy, say Confucius, as king. The *Mencius* portrays the pattern of Heaven's moral providence which is discernible from history: overthrow the wicked and then appoint the worthy. But Heaven had, for a time, supported kinship relationships in the assignation of the king and stood by as less noble kings (appointed by birthright) fell into decline. While the pattern of the Heaven who did not speak is discernible, there is a great deal that cannot be understood about Heaven's ways. For example, while Heaven is portrayed as unequivocally on the side of justice and peace, Mencius is portrayed as painfully lacking any understanding of why peace does not reign in the land;

the time seems long past due for Heaven to appoint a worthy. However, Mencius, according to the *Mencius*, resists the temptation to doubt or reject Heaven:

> As Mencius was departing from Qi, Chong Yu questioned him along the way, saying, "From your expression it would seem that you are unhappy. Yet on a former occasion I heard you [quoting Confucius] say, 'The noble person neither repines against Heaven nor reproaches men.'"
>
> That age was one time; this is another. In five hundred years a true king should appear, and in between there should be men renowned in their generation. From the beginning of the Zhou it has been more than seven hundred years. Given that number, the time is past due, and considering the circumstances, it is still possible. Heaven does not yet want to bring peace to the world. If it wanted to bring peace to the world, who is there in the present age apart from me? Why should I be unhappy?

Once again the *Mencius* seems to follow Confucius as portrayed in the *Analects*, this time in his attitude of trust in Heaven, even against appearances to the contrary. Heaven is in control and Mencius is portrayed as secure in his belief that Heaven has ordained his role in the world. Peace will come in its Heaven-ordained time. Even so, Mencius opines, the time is ripe.

Conclusion

Scholars such as Robert Eno argue that Mencius uses theistic rhetoric solely for political not metaphysical purposes. James Behuniak likewise denies that Mencius represents *Tian* as a person; he contends that "Mencius disassociates *tian* from the more anthropomorphic 'Heaven' of Mozi, which results in a more secular notion of 'forces'" (Behuniak 2005: xxiii). I have considered such arguments and found them wanting. Philip Ivanhoe partially agrees with my critique of Eno: Ivanhoe holds that Mencius represents Heaven as moral and active in the world. He writes: "Some important early Confucians ground their ethical claims by appealing to the authority of *tian* 天, 'Heaven,' insisting that Heaven endows human beings with a distinctively ethical nature and at times acts in the world." Ivanhoe claims that Mencius follows Confucius in his beliefs about Heaven—Heaven has a plan for human beings, Heaven has so created human beings that their flourishing is in keeping the Way within a just society, and Mencius has a special Heaven-appointed role to play in the realization of that plan (Ivanhoe 2007). And yet he agrees with Behuniak, Heaven is not a person; he claims that Mencius "did not regard Heaven as a personal deity, but he did conceive of it as an agent with a plan for the world and one that on occasion acts in the world to realize its will" (Ivanhoe 2007: 217).

I have argued that the *Mencius*, drawing upon the Shang and the Shu, represents *Tian*/the Lord-on-High as a personal deity: *Tian*/the Lord-on-High has intentions, other personal attributes such as knowledge, goodness, and mercy (5A1), and is worthy of worship. Eno and others would do well to heed Benjamin Schwartz's warning: "To dismiss the role which Mencius assigns to Heaven as a 'manner of speaking' again represents an arbitrary imposition of certain modern Western notions on Mencius's world view" (Schwartz 1985: 284). *Tian* acts, and so is an agent; *Tian* freely acts for reasons, and so is a person. Other than being an intentional, moral agent who knows, plans, and acts freely to realize its will, what more could there be to being a person?

I have made good on the promise to show, contra the Naturalizing Narrative, that the Confucians, at least Confucius and Mencius, believed in a High Deity: the so-called philosophical texts, surprisingly including the Xunzi and Zhuangzi (as shown in Chapter 2), represent belief in the High God. In the next two chapters, I will assess the Naturalizing claim that the Early Chinese, even the Confucians, don't believe in the afterlife.

Part Three

Ancestors and Afterlife

6

Afterlife

Since the twentieth century, it's commonplace to claim that the early Chinese did not countenance belief in the afterlife. According to A. C. Graham, "except for the Mohists, no one in ancient China much cared whether consciousness survives death" (Graham 1989: 15). Graham's claim echoes the widely cited claim of Joseph Needham:

> If one bears in mind the conception of different peoples (Indo-Iranian, Christian, Islamic, etc.) there was no such thing as an 'other world' in ancient Chinese thought at all—no heaven or hell, no creator God, and no expected end of the universe once it had emerged from primeval chaos. All was natural, and within Nature. Of course, after the permeation of Buddhism, 'the case was altered.'
> (Needham 1974: 84–5)

Graham likewise claims that afterlife beliefs entered the Chinese landscape only after the arrival of Buddhism in the third century CE.

Denials of mind-body dualism in early China are often treated as ipso facto rejections of belief in the afterlife. The belief that one's spirit lives on after the death of one's biological body typically assumes that a person's non-physical spirit or soul is ontologically distinct from a person's physical body. If the Chinese lacked a conception of a soul, they very likely lacked belief in the afterlife. Paolo Santangelo claims that the Chinese united a rejection of the soul with a rejection of the afterlife:

> There is no clear separation between spirit and matter, or soul and body ... the concept of 'mind–heart' (*xin*) is different from the idea of an exclusively human soul, endowed with reason and able to make free decisions .... Here, too, there is no place for the idea of the individual that rose in Europe from the concept of the immortality of the soul.
> (Santangelo 2007: 292)

No soul, so the argument goes, no afterlife.

Thomas Wilson, on the other hand, contends that every commentator on canonical Confucianism in imperial China understood the tradition as affirming the reality of immaterial gods, ancestors, and souls:

> At least as early as the Tang, Confucian scholars drew from classical sources to articulate a conception of spirits and the soul that provided a canonical foundation for an imperial cult system; a cult system that gave great weight to ancestors and which informed all canonical rites devoted to gods and spirits performed by generations of Confucians both at home and at imperial altars and temples. Commentaries on the *Analects*, *Record of Rites,* and *Book of Filial Piety* disclose a persistent understanding of Confucius as profoundly committed to reverent services of gods and spirits. Confucians during the imperial era propounded a detailed explanation of spirits, ghosts, and the soul largely based on statements attributed to the canonical Confucius.
>
> (Wilson 2014: 207–8)

While only the king and high-level ritual specialists aimed their cultic practices at the high gods, nearly everyone else's cultic practices centered on the spirits of their biologically deceased but still-living ancestor spirits.

Granted there is a lack of explicit discussion of the afterlife in the transmitted texts. Most of the references to ancestors in the transmitted texts involve little more than ritual advice, without any discussion of the nature of the afterlife or the metaphysics of persons. Consider the *Analects*. In 20:1, we are instructed, among a list of duties, to mourn the deceased (without defending or clarifying their postmortem existence): "He gave weight to the people, food, mourning, and sacrifice." In 1:11, the Master simply calls us to live as our fathers lived: "When someone's father is still alive, observe his intentions; after his father has passed away, observe conduct. If, for three years he does not alter the ways of his father, he may be called a filial son" (*xiao*; 孝). In 3:6 we hear that the Ji family went to make a sacrifice (to ancestors?). *Analects* 3:4 commends frugality and deep sorrow in funeral rituals. Confucius offers practical advice with no explicit discussion of the nature of ancestors or the afterlife. Just as there is very little explicit meta-ethics in the transmitted texts (but lots of practical advice to rulers about the proper treatment of their subjects), so, too, there is very little metaphysics in the transmitted texts (but lots of advice to children about the ritual treatment of their deceased parents). In general, the transmitted texts include very little second-order reflection on morality and ritual. One might, therefore, assume, as Graham and Needham assert, indifference to or even rejection of afterlife beliefs in early China.

But thousands of recently discovered tombs reveal that belief in an afterlife was widespread in early China. Within thousands of newly discovered Neolithic sites, from inscriptions on bones to paintings on silk, we have gained new insight into various Chinese conceptions of the human person, the domain of the extrahuman, and the afterlife. As Ying-Shih Yu writes: "For the first time we have unmistakable and direct evidence that testifies fully as well as vividly to the indigenous Chinese imagination of death and afterlife in pre-Buddhist antiquity. The dominant modern theory that there was no 'other world' in Chinese thought until the advent of Buddhism is thus proved to be untenable" (Yu 2016: 86). This treasure trove of information reveals that from the Shang to and through the Han, health, well-being, and morality are increasingly related to the afterlife. The relevance of tomb text and architecture to early Chinese thought cannot be exaggerated. Indeed, we have vastly more access to early Chinese beliefs and practices of people from every stripe of society from the thousands of excavated tombs than we do from the fewer than thirty transmitted texts that at best tell us about a very small intellectual or ruling elite.

The transmitted texts should be read alongside the tomb texts and pots and jars and paintings to better assess the meanings of the transmitted texts. Information gathered from tombs has opened a whole new window on the culture within which the transmitted texts emerge and breathe. In her discussion of Chinese burial patterns, Jessica Rawson writes that "the physical and the material not only reveal but also contribute to what we call 'thought'" (Rawson 1998: 107). These discoveries partially constitute the life-situation within which the transmitted text and rituals, and their represented worlds, find their meaning. The language and grammar of these texts are rooted in, as the later Wittgenstein writes, "agreement not in opinions, but in a form of life" (Wittgenstein 1953: 241). The meaning of this or that linguistic expression is a function of how humans use terms in various linguistic contexts, contexts embedded deeply within various human practices. Instead of restricting ourselves to the relatively few representations of the afterlife in the transmitted texts, we should avail ourselves of the much thicker forms of life within which these texts find their meaning. Archeologists are literally uncovering early Chinese forms of life daily.

A general picture of the afterlife during the Qin and Han, one with roots deep in China's past, has emerged. Lothar von Falkenhausen has demonstrated that early Chinese mortuary practices reveal an afterlife that is "separate and independent from the world of the living" (von Falkenhausen 2006: 300), one that it is inhabited by, among many other extrahumans, spirits of the dead (ancestors). As Guolong Lai writes:

> Dating from the fifth to the first century BCE, these tombs are not only the place where the early Chinese buried their dead but also the space onto which they projected a range of imaginings, fears, and concerns that arose in connection with the life and death of their kin, friends, and foes, people known and unknown. As such, death is not the end of one's life but entering a new relationship with both the dead and the living. The tomb is a bridge, a way station on the journey to the afterlife, and a physical message of the established conceptions of the afterworld. Consequently, the tomb is both the physical space where religious ritual and sacrifice took place and the imagined space in which people's beliefs about the invisible spiritual world unfolded.
>
> (Lai 2015: 1)

Through the increasing use of anthropomorphic images and written texts both to communicate with and describe the spirit world, we find, from the later Zhou period into the Han, increasing representations of concern for a good postmortem journey. Common elements of the geography of the afterlife focus on securing a favorable afterlife for one's deceased ancestors and increasingly elaborate documents/images/tools to aid the deceased on their postmortem journey.

I will argue that while the transmitted texts seldom address the afterlife in detail, it is nonetheless widely assumed. I will look at the evidence of tomb text and architecture in order to gain a deep and wide look at early Chinese views of the afterlife. Thus prompted by mortuary practices, I will return to the transmitted texts for evidence of afterlife beliefs.

Tomb Text, and Architecture

Because I have focused in this book on the transmitted texts, I will offer just a summary of the vast trove of information gleaned from tomb text and architecture. In the transmitted literature and artifacts and rituals concerning death, we find a wide host of representations of the afterlife. I will return soon enough to the transmitted texts.

There is, already, a great deal of invaluable, scholarly discussion of who in early China believed what and when about the afterlife (including rejecting belief in the afterlife). Some defend views of the afterlife or soul that they claim are held by nearly everyone ("the general view"), others restrict belief in the afterlife to uneducated peasants, and still others hold that there is an historical progression from widely held beliefs in the afterlife or soul to widespread rational rejection of the afterlife and soul (a progression from supernaturalism to naturalistic humanism); according to the latter view, mortuary ritual and practices are aimed at the justification and preservation of social structure—this-worldly order and harmony—not the metaphysics of spirit. Still others, as noted, claim that the early Chinese rejected beliefs both in a soul distinct from the body and the afterlife.

We can glean three things based on both tomb findings and the transmitted texts. First, there was no progressive, rationalist rejection of the afterlife and the soul in early China (though there were certainly some rationalist rejectors, such as Xunzi and his followers, of the afterlife and the soul).[1] Second, the early Chinese, at least a great many of them, believed in the afterlife and the soul. And, three, as China and Chinese thought became increasingly "Confucian," views of postmortem existence became increasingly "Confucian" as well; we don't find a decrease of belief in the afterlife in so-called "Confucianism," we find instead an increase in Confucian elements of the afterlife. This runs counter to the popular narrative that claims that as China became increasingly Confucian, it became increasingly naturalistic.

Let me note what we've argued from the very beginning of this book: there is no commonly held set of beliefs that mark out the domain of "the Chinese." While afterlife beliefs were widely held in early China, we don't know how widely and by whom. We have some textual evidence of what some literati believed and many well-preserved tombs of wealthy people, tombs richly stocked with metal and jade that survived destruction. We have considerably less evidence of what the illiterati believed; most of the poor's more modest tombs, outfitted as they were with wooden artifacts, have yielded decidedly less information than the sturdier tombs of the wealthy. So, while I will canvass likely widely held beliefs, I make no claim to universality. As Michele Pirazzoli-t'Serstevens argues, there is in early China a huge number of tombs but no unified vision of the afterlife (Pirazzoli-t'Serstevens 2009).

Nonetheless, we can infer from the art and texts of tens of thousands recently discovered tombs that already in the fourth and third centuries BCE many believed in an afterlife journey toward heaven; many likewise believed in a negative underworld called, among other things, the Yellow Springs. Some believed in two souls, *hun* 魂 and *po* 魄, one of which journeys to heaven while the other stays with the body in the tomb or descends into the Yellow Springs. Some have thought a person's spirit (*shen* 心) is confined within the tomb, others feared that spirits can re-enter the earthly realm (usually to the detriment of their relatives), and still others thought one's *shen* would and could go to heaven. Finally, a very few rejected the notion of life after death.[2]

Michael Loewe, a pioneer on early Chinese religion, analyzed artifacts in Han tombs at Mawangdui for "the underlying beliefs of the Han Chinese regarding death and the hereafter" (Loewe 1979: Preface). We find in Loewe a description of a funeral banner of the grand afterlife journey of Lady Dai, the wife of the Marquis of Dai, from death to immortality in heaven (with heaven both a place and the High God). In the painting, the deceased Lady Dai (who died about 160 BCE) can be found in the middle section, which seems to represent earth and earthly life. The lower section seems to represent an undesired and undesirable underworld. And the upper section seems to represent Lady Dai riding on a dragon for a hoped-for heaven. In short, the painting offers a guide for the successful journey of the countess' *hun* soul from death to paradise.

Since many similar paintings have been uncovered, Loewe generalizes: a wide variety of tomb text, art, and architecture represent the common belief in and wish for an afterlife in paradise. Tomb text, art, and architecture, then, were designed to help the occupant through their initial time in the tomb, to orient them toward paradise, and to provide instruction (maps, introductions to gods, etc.) to ensure their successful journey. Although contemporary scholars debate the meaning of the painting, a consensus has emerged: the picture represents the cosmos as tripartite with an undesirable underworld, earth in the middle, and heaven above, and with the human's spirit seeking postmortem fulfillment by ascending to heaven.[3]

Constance Cook analyzed the tomb of Shao Tuo, an official in the Chu court who was buried in 316 BCE. Although many contemporary philosophers claim that funerary practices are exclusively aimed at the living, Cook argues to the contrary that "once the tomb was closed and the space between the living and the dead formally distinguished, his spirit was presumed to emerge at some point from the inner coffin towards the rising sun, where he would greet ancestral spirits who would guide him on his journey" (Cook 2006: 14). Shao Tuo's tomb was replete with texts that provided testimony to his virtue and accomplishments, very likely to persuade the attending spirits of his worthiness to pass favorably into the next life. As Mark Edward Lewis writes: "The Yellow Thearch controlled the registries of life and death. There was a belief in a celestial hierarchy of deities too numerous to mention, with one serving as the Register of Deeds. A Qin or early Han text records a bureaucratic mistake in which a soul, confined to the underworld by mistake, is later restored to life" (Lewis 1999b: 60–1). Some texts likely served as talismans to protect Shao Tuo's vulnerable emerging spirit from evil spirits and to encourage other spirits to assist him. And others, labeled for travel, included maps and visas and directions to successfully negotiate the spiritual landscape on his way to heaven. Indeed, the tomb itself was likely designed to be a microcosm of the postmortem spiritual macrocosm (as aid to Shao Tuo's journey). Shao Tuo's tomb is especially valuable because it dates from the Warring States period, the time of intense philosophical speculation, the time allegedly of increasing naturalism and humanism (and rejections of the afterlife). Constance Cook concludes: "For the Chu elite, the journey to heaven seemed to begin with the movement inside the tomb—visits with familiar objects, preparation for setting off, and performance of a feast for ancestral spirits. The deceased then rides out of the tomb .... Finally he ascends ... into the astral landscape of ancestral spirits and cosmic deities" (Cook 2006: 146).

Archeologist Guolong Lai focuses on the plethora of travel items found in thousands of Warring States tombs to support his argument for the "grand journey" view of the afterlife (as the predominant but not exclusive view of the early Chinese). He writes: "I argue here that materials related to travel—daybooks, cosmographic diagrams and motifs, cartographic maps, and travel paraphernalia—were put in tombs to direct departed souls on their postmortem journeys" (Lai 2005: 31). He examines the items listed for the purpose of travel in the grave inventories of the Baoshan tomb and contends that they were intended for use by the deceased on their journey to paradise. Items for travel, "tokens of immortality," included—in addition to maps for finding the way and talismans for warding off evil spirits—caps, shoes, combs, a folding bed, and fans. Of these very mundane items, Lai writes, "[I]n the religious context of the otherworldly journey they acquired the apotropaic function of aiding and protecting the departed soul in the afterlife journey" (Lai 2005: 34). Of special religious significance is the lamp, used to guide the traveler through the very dark and dangerous terrain along the way (Lai 2002). Some items, he argues, were included to handle potential emergencies on the very arduous journey. Finally, Lai argues that road rituals (the *zu*-sacrifice), which are normal parts of funeral proceedings, suggest that biological death is the beginning of an embarkment on a long journey. In conclusion, through reflection on the religious significance of travel paraphenelia, Lai views the Warring States tomb not as the permanent residence of the deceased but as a postmortem way station on their journey to a new home.[4]

Evidence of belief in the afterlife, at least for royalty, goes far back: "The earliest textual evidence from China concerning an idea of the afterlife can be found in Shang dynasty oracle-bone inscriptions. Primarily divination records, the inscriptions mention that deceased kings dwelt in heaven together with *Di* 帝 (the Sovereign on High)" (Poo 2011: 18). I will set aside Poo's discussion of increasingly elaborate representations of the nefarious and dark underworld, the "Yellow Spring" or "Dark City," ruled by the sinister horned python, Lord Earth (Tu Bo 土伯) (Poo 2011: 18–20).[5] The hoped-for final destination for deceased souls increasingly focused on sacred Mount Tai, symbolizing a transcendent paradise. Poo sides with the journey view of the afterlife in which the tomb serves as a comfortable way-station, much needed for the transition from mortal to ancestor, on the way to paradise.

Pirazzoli-t'Serstevens, while rejecting a single vision of the early Chinese, summarizes the emerging consensus among historians of Qin-Han religion. While conceding the power and importance of various this-worldly social understandings of, say, tomb décor, she argues that it is no longer possible to deny their religious import for "the voyage to the other world and the paradise of immortality" (Pirazzoli-t'Serstevens 2009: 956). From the banners which divide the universe into three levels—the heavens, the human world, the underworld—to the bricks which serve as the gate of heaven, the tomb is carefully designed to ensure the safe voyage of the deceased to paradise.

The emerging cosmological view, then, posits a High Deity (*Tian, Shangdi*, etc.) who resides in Heaven on High, a paradaisal place where some go when they die, a middle world of humans, and a dark underworld where the souls of the dead live.

Finally, we find ritual and mortuary practices increasingly manifesting a concern and respect for the moral powers of Heaven, with especially the literati exalting their Confucian virtues in hopes of gaining paradise (Bujard 2011). While Warring States tombs typically exalt wealth and social status as qualifying the deceased for paradise, the so-called "announcements of merits" contained within the tombs became increasingly and explicitly Confucian. While the importance of merit for securing Heaven's favor was already implicit in the Mandate of Heaven (*tianming*), tomb text and architecture increasingly commend their occupants' moral character to ward off evil spirits and to ensure passage to paradise. To this end, I shall conclude this section with a discussion of grave stelae in the Han dynasty, where we find the consolidation and institutionalization of so-called Confucianism at many levels of life, including the afterlife.

While the eulogistic practice of inscribing merits and achievements on stone and metal vessels predates the Han by a millennium, "indestructible" (*jinshi*) stone stelae emerge in the Han as the preferred medium for bearing and preserving the virtue and accomplishments of the deceased into the afterlife. Drawing on such classical texts as the *Analects* and the *Odes*, each stone's inscriptions record for eternity the illustrious character of the deceased. Kenneth Brashier discusses three representative Han stelae (from a group of 700); I will discuss two. The first, that of Xianyu Huang (d. 125 AD), includes both a biographical preface and a hymn. In the biographical preface we read:

> The heaven-conferred disposition of this gentleman was a bright intelligence, and his penetrating ingenuity was excellent .... By the time he was standing upright and his milk teeth had fallen out, he followed rightness, cherishing and delighting in constant principles. He mastered the *Rites* of Dai the Younger, and within both the inner and outer apartments and the clan at large, he cultivated filial piety and friendliness. He reviewed the old and understood the pivotal. Because of his brilliant radiance and truthful sincerity, he advanced upward, his reputation climbing.
>
> (Brashier 2011: 1039–40)

The text goes on to commend Huang's filial piety and regulation of the state by means of ritual, through both exclamation and example. In the preceding passages and in what follows, the Confucian flavor is strong. As a ruler: "He bent his body's joints in humility and was pure in conduct. He honored frugality and clung to economy, favoring a government of rule by example." Little wonder this highly stylized and idealized biography concludes with lament over the premature death of this great eminence. Huang's illustrious biography issues forth in a hymn:

> Oh! How lustrous is our grandfather—
> He embosomed spotless virtue
> And forever kept filial thoughts in mind,
> Causing the magnanimous occupation to extend generation after generation ...
> ....
> (And so we) banner vast virtue and display primal merit,
> Clarifying this gentlemen's numen and informing later generations.
> While his spirit possesses consciousness, may it occupy this altar area.
>
> (Brashier 2011: 1042–3)

By manifesting Ruist-construed, Heaven-conferred virtues, the postmortem Huang has, thereby, forged links with his ancestors and connected himself to his descendants (Brashier 2011: 1042). Finally, in addition to commending Huang's virtue, the hymn notes his continued existence in the afterlife: while his spirit is conscious, it will occupy the altar area. This is, in part, a challenge to his descendants to continually offer him sacrifices to keep his name known (perhaps thereby keeping Huang conscious) forever.[6]

In the second stele that Brashier analyzes, an adult woman named Zhang Xianghang is commended/remembered for her service and respect to her (kind) mother-in-law above and her children below. She was, we read, "[b]enevolently filial and pleasantly accommodating, she heeded the rituals without misstep. She embodied the deportment of a 'young orchid' and followed in 'the footsteps of the thoughtful and reverent'" (Brashier 2011: 1050). For her good life and work, she was buried with her mother-in-law, whom she will gratefully serve postmortem, "while her *hun*-soul is still numinous" (Brashier 2011: 1050). So we hear in her hymn:

> And so she will now heed orders in such darkness,
> Continuing to uphold her intentions not to disobey.
> On this account we interred her spirit with her mother-in-law
> To serve as a support to her *hunpo*.
> Sinking into the black vastness of the dark chamber,
> She we will care for [her mother-in-law's] luminous brightness of radiant illumination.
>
> (Brashier 2011: 1052–3)

Zhang's role-specific, Confucian duties required her to respect and serve those above her, including her mother-in-law after marriage and to ritually instruct her children below her. She carries both her good character and her role with her into the next life in which her spirit will eagerly serve her mother-in-law's spirit; her flourishing, which carries on into the next life, includes fulfilling her mother-in-law's postmortem desires.

We have seen, in tomb text and architecture, varied representations of the afterlife. Scholars have converged on the view that, for example, tripartite paintings were intended to offer maps of the cosmos (underworld-thisworld-heaven) and directions and preparations for the arduous journey to a paradisal heaven, often at the side of the High God.

We also find the increasing Confucianification, if you will, of the entrance requirements for the afterlife—Confucian virtues and accomplishments increasingly become prerequisite to a good afterlife. And while there is no accepted metaphysics of the afterlife, there is, as cognitive psychology suggests, a sense or implication of mind-body dualism in representations of the body which remains in the coffin while one's spirit roams, variously, around the numinous world, within the tomb, and/or in heaven. Tomb text and architecture likewise represent an underworld in various guises, admitting of various degrees of undesirability. In short, tomb text and architecture reveal or imply metaphysically, morally, and religiously rich and suggestive representations of the postmortem existence of worthy souls and postmortem spirits with powers to, for example, appeal directly to Heaven on behalf of their living relatives or wreak havoc on the living who forego their rigorous ritual duties to their ancestors.

I have not, to be sure, divined *the* view of the afterlife of the early Chinese. We encounter in these tombs a plethora of views with little explicit theorizing about the nature of postmortem persons or the afterlife. The tombs, however, have clarified this—many early Chinese believed in the conscious postmortem existence of one's soul/spirit independent of one's body.

The Afterlife in the Transmitted Texts

To return once again to "King Wen Is On High," the most famous poem from the *Odes*, we read:

> King Wen is on high;
> Oh, he shines in Heaven!
> Zhou is an old people,
> But its charge is new.
> The land of Zhou became illustrious,
> Blessed by God's charge.
> King Wen ascends and descends
> On God's left hand, on His right.
>
> (Waley 1938: Ode 235)

This ode to King Wen was ritually spoken or sung to the postmortem King Wen who, we hear, shines in Heaven, the paradisal location in which the ascended King Wen sits at the side of the High God. While the text reveres and its pre-Qin use reveals King Wen as a model for a just and harmonious society, it likewise assumes a (likely) pre-Qin belief in the afterlife in which King Wen's spirit resides and even reigns at the side of harmony and justice (Heaven). Cognitive science of religion and mortuary texts converge on a literal and charitable reading of this text as affirming the afterlife existence of King Wen in Heaven (unless the text or times give us adequate reason to reject this interpretation).

The *Odes*, one of the most fundamental of the Confucian classics, repeatedly affirms the powers of ancestors to benefit or punish their descendants. It is partly the postmortem powers of the ancestors which ground the importance of sacrifice to ancestors—their neglect could and would bring about calamity and misfortune. So, we read repeatedly in the *Odes* that, for example, the proper feeding of ancestors brings victory, blessing, and long life (just as the betrayal of ancestors brings disaster). The calling of ancestors to draw them near through offerings of food and drink is metaphor for attracting one's ancestors with one's sincere and pure heart (by piously reflecting the ancestor's own sincerity and righteousness). And the *Odes* assumes that one's deceased ancestors can be grieved and delighted, ashamed and honored, brought near or remain distant, and attend to or ignore one's prayers and worship. In short, the *Odes* assumes the afterlife beliefs that are exemplified in many recently discovered tombs.

Moreover, virtually every one of the transmitted texts assumes the *Odes'* views of ancestors and the afterlife. I will examine a few representative and informative texts—the *Documents*, the *Liji*, the *Xiaojing*, *The Doctrine of the Mean*, the *Zhouli*, and, finally, the *Analects*.[7] Again, even if the transmitted texts do not address the postmortem status of ancestors explicitly or in great detail, their setting-in-life as revealed in the tomb-as-text assumes the postmortem existence of ancestors, who, within a much larger hierarchy of spirits with various domains and powers, demand ritual attention.

In the *Documents* we find twenty-four references to ancestor worship, ancestor temples, ancestor spirits, ancestor powers, ancestor intercession, and ancestor punishment or reward. Ancestor spirits are represented on an ontological par with anthropomorphic high gods—Heaven, *Shangdi*, *Di*—as well as various spirits of the land and sky. In Pang Geng II we hear a speech allegedly by Pan Geng, the eighteenth Shang king, famous for moving the Shang capital city to Yin. In the speech we hear of the difficulties involved in undertaking yet another move of the capital and of Pan Geng's attempts to persuade his resistant followers to acquiesce in his wise decision. At a key point, Pan Geng appeals to his ancestors:

> I think of my ancestors, (who are now) the spiritual sovereigns [*shen hou*]; when they made your forefathers toil (on similar occasions it was only for their good), and I would be enabled in the same way greatly to nourish you and cherish you. Were I to err in my government, and remain long here, my high sovereign, (the founder of our dynasty), would send down on me great punishment for my crime, and say, "Why do you oppress my people?" If you, the myriads of the people, do not attend to the perpetuation of your lives, and cherish one mind

with me, the One man, in my plans, the former kings will send down on you great punishment for your crime, and say, "Why do you not agree with our young grandson, but go on to forfeit your virtue?" When they punish you from above, you will have no way of escape.

(Legge 2000a: Pan Geng II)

Pan Geng assumes and reminds his people of his deceased ancestors, who now both serve as moral models and "rule" the earthly realm as spirits. *Shen* 神 in ancient Chinese can refer to both the deities and the spirits of the respected, deceased persons. So, depending on context, it can be translated as "gods," "deities," or "spirits." In context, *shen hou* means something like the spiritual/deified sovereign (i.e., a previous deceased kings).

These spiritual sovereigns, on the side of justice, could and would "send down" punishments on Pan Geng if he were oppressive, and "send down" punishments on his people if they refused to follow Pan Geng.

Of old, my royal predecessors made your ancestors and fathers toil (only for their good). You are equally the people whom I (wish to) cherish. But your conduct is injurious;—it is cherished in your hearts. Whereas my royal predecessors made your ancestors and fathers happy, they, your ancestors and fathers, will (now) cut you off and abandon you, and not save you from death. Here are those ministers of my government, who share with me in the offices (of the kingdom);—and yet they (only think of hoarding up) cowries and gems. Their ancestors and fathers earnestly represent (their course) to my high sovereign, saying, "Execute great punishments on our descendants." So do they advise my high sovereign to send down great calamities (on those men).

(Legge 2000a: Pan Geng II)

While alive his royal predecessors worked for the good of their followers; while biologically dead but spiritually alive they still have the power to work for the good or ill of the people. The ancestors are represented as conduits to "my high sovereign" (perhaps referring to Cheng Tang, the first king of Shang dynasty, the first ancestor) who himself can send calamities on selfish and wicked people.

In the *Liji*'s 80-plus references to ancestors, one is repeatedly admonished to care for the ancestral temple and to fastidiously attend to the rituals concerning one's ancestor spirits. We can infer the ontological status of the ancestors in the Li Yun:

Thus it is that the dark-coloured liquor is in the apartment (where the representative of the dead is entertained); that the vessel of must is near its (entrance) door; that the reddish liquor is in the hall; and the clear, in the (court) below. The victims (also) are displayed, and the tripods and stands are prepared. The lutes and citherns are put in their places, with the flutes, sonorous stones, bells, and drums. The prayers (of the principal in the sacrifice to the spirits) and the benedictions (of the representatives of the departed) are carefully framed. The object of all the ceremonies is to bring down the spirits from above, even their ancestors; serving (also) to rectify the relations between ruler and ministers; to maintain the generous feeling between father and son, and the harmony between elder and younger brother; to adjust the relations between high and low; and to give their proper places to husband and wife. The whole may be said to secure the blessing of Heaven.

(*Liji*: Liyun)

These elaborate ritual instructions reconstruct the ritual world of the deceased. Word and action, and music and wine combine, we read, "to bring down the spirits from above, even their ancestors." Ancestors, then, are represented as residing "above" in the world of spirits (presumably, heaven).[8] The aim of the ceremonies, then, is to call them down, into the mundane, middle world, to effect the rectification of relationships required to secure the blessed hierarchical harmony—ruler and ministers; father and son; elder and younger brother; high and low; and husband and wife. Again, the *Liji* mostly assumes the reality of the afterlife existence of ancestors in its many proclamations on ritual specificity. But the assumption of ancestor afterlife is the blood running through the *Liji*'s ritual heart.

Filial piety, perhaps the foundational Confucian virtue, is rooted in ritual propriety toward parents which does not cease upon the parent's death, extending as it does to the parent's postmortem spirit. While the *Xiaojing* 孝治, the Classic of Filial Piety, treats all social relationships, it focuses on the relationship between father and son, thus establishing filial piety (*xiao* 孝) as the central concept of the Confucian social system. The *Xiaojing* opens with:

When the love and reverence (of Son of Heaven) are thus carried to the utmost in the service of his parents, the lessons of his virtue affect all people and he becomes a pattern to all within the four seas: this is the filial piety of the Son of Heaven.

(Legge *Xiaojing*: 1)

The filial king, who ritually appropriates respect for those above him and compassion for those beneath, governs justly, bringing order and harmony from his family to his community to the world. When treated filially, the ministers treat their king with loyalty and those beneath them with justice and compassion.

And so on and on ("to the four seas"). The project of learning filial piety is uninterrupted by biological death: "while alive, parents reposed in (the glory of) their sons, and, when sacrificed to, their disembodied spirits enjoyed their offerings."

In the conclusion of the Xiaojing 孝治, we read of the centrality of the filial piety of the king:

> The Master said, "Anciently, the intelligent kings served their fathers with filial piety, and therefore they served Heaven with intelligence. They served their mothers with filial piety, and therefore they served Earth with discrimination. They pursued the right course with reference to their (own) seniors and juniors, and therefore they secured the regulation of the relations between superiors and inferiors (throughout the kingdom). When Heaven and Earth were served with intelligence and discrimination, the spiritual intelligences displayed (their retributive power)."
>
> "Therefore even the Son of Heaven must have some whom he honors; that is, he has his uncles of his surname. He must have some to whom he concedes the precedence; that is, he has his cousins, who bear the same surname and are older than himself. In the ancestral temple he manifests the utmost reverence, showing that he does not forget his parents. He cultivates his person and is careful of his conduct, fearing lest he should disgrace his predecessors. When in the ancestral temple he exhibits the utmost reverence, the spirits of the departed manifest themselves. Perfect filial piety and fraternal duty reach to (and move) the spiritual intelligences and diffuse their light on all within the four seas. They penetrate everywhere."
>
> (Legge Xiaojing: 15)

The Xiaojing 孝治 asserts the foundational moral importance of filial piety in serving Heaven and Earth. By cultivating and exemplifying respect for their elders and care for their juniors, "the intelligent kings" secured the hierarchical harmony and order of their kingdom—"the regulation of relations between superiors and inferiors." Since every human relationship is believed to involve superior and inferior—ruler and ministers; father and son; elder and younger brother; high and low; and husband and wife—one's role-specific duties will find harmonious expression in one's proper understanding of who is high and who is low and in the proper attitudes toward high (respect) and low (compassion). In order to ward off arrogant complacency on the part of the ruler and abject servility on the part of the ruled, the Son of Heaven must himself learn respect and honor by bowing at the feet of the worthy: "[E]ven the Son of Heaven must have some whom he honors; that is, he has his uncles of his surname. He must have some to whom he concedes the precedence; that is, he has his cousins, who bear the same surname and are older than himself." He must, in short, know his own place in the hierarchy. He humbly cultivates respect at the ancestral temple when he ritually bows down before the spirits of the departed. Only when he exhibits respect do the spirits manifest themselves to him. As a result, he departs from the temple shaped and formed in filial piety and fraternal duty, which, in turn, spread out like expanding waves to the ends of the earth: "Perfect filial piety and fraternal duty reach to (and move) the spiritual intelligences and diffuse their light on all within the four seas. They penetrate everywhere."

In *The Doctrine of the Mean* we read, without much explanation, that a person who is completely sincere is like a spirit, that the righteous ruler has no doubts about the existence of spiritual beings, and that rulers should follow King Wu and the Duke of Zhou in sacrificing to their ancestors. We can infer from the context that the passage below includes ancestors among the reference of the term "spiritual beings:"

> Confucius said: "The overabundance of the power of spiritual beings is truly amazing! Looking for them, they cannot be seen. Listening for them, they cannot be heard. There is nothing that they do not embody. They cause the people of the world to fast for purification, and wear beautiful clothes in order to participate at the sacrifices. They are overflowing, seeming to be above, seeming to be on the left and on the right. The *Book of Odes* says: 'Trying to investigate the spirits, we cannot reach them. How could we possibly grasp them with our thoughts?' The manifestation of the subtle and the inconcealability of sincerity is like this."
>
> (Mueller 2003)

While the *Zhongyong* explicitly says very little about the nature of ancestors, it repeatedly suggests, however, that sincerely extending filial piety from one's living relatives to one's living ancestors is the source of the ruler's power. Although they cannot be seen or heard (or possibly even understood), spiritual beings exist and have an abundance of subtle power for good.

If one believes, as the author of the *Zhongyong* and many in early China seem to, that one's moral community includes morally significant spirits, some of whom are deceased ancestors, then continuing to show and learn filiality after the death of one's blood relatives makes perfect sense. One's moral project is part of a continuum that begins at birth and extends through death into the afterlife. As such, the very sorts of relations and obligations toward living beings one finds in one's earthly life carry over into relations and obligations toward deceased but still living beings in the next life. Moreover, if the postmortem world is hierarchically organized in ways nearly identical to the hierarchical organization of this earthly life, then properly attending to and ritually appropriating the order and harmony of the spirit world will ipso facto engender the order and harmony one seeks for this earthly world. As one ritually reaches into the ideal world, one draws down its attendant powers for righteousness. This extension of filial piety from one's spirit and even the Spirit on High, then, would reverberate throughout the world:

> They used the Winter and Summer festival to make offerings to the Lord-on-High, and used the rituals on the ancestral temple to make offerings to the ancestors. He who could completely disclose the meaning of the Winter and Summer sacrifices, and the great Imperial sacrifice, could govern the country as easily as if he were pointing to the palm of his hand.
>
> (Mueller 2003)

The invisible spirits, whose power one ritually taps, create the kind of order and harmony in the world that laws and punishments cannot. The Ruler who properly disposes of these sacrifices to spirits can control the now rightly ordered world, "as if he were pointing to the palm of his hand."

In the *Zhouli* we find an account of the duties of "the grand minister of rites" in his court performance of official state rituals. I will excerpt its description of the other-worldly pantheon:

> The grand minister of rites supervises the rituals of the vassal states, overseeing the rites offered to heavenly spirits, human ghosts, and terrestrial divinities. He helps the king establish and protect the various states. He serves ghosts and spirits of the state with auspicious rituals, and with pure Yin sacrifices he conducts rites to Bright Heaven, the Lord on High.
>
> (from Poo 2011: 285)

According to the *Zhouli*, the spirit world includes heavenly spirits, human ghosts, and terrestrial divinities. The variously specified rituals, involving different spirits at different times, were aimed in general at the king's health and protection from natural disasters and death and defeat. The heavenly deities controlled, for example, the sun, moon, stars, and wind and rain while the terrestrial deities were masters, for example, of the land and the grain. The human ghosts, in the court rituals, likely referred to royal ancestors. Towering above the lesser deities or spirits is Bright Heaven, the Lord on High.

In the most comprehensive discussion of ancestors and afterlife in early China, *Ancestral Memory*, Kenneth Brashier rejects the view of ancestor rituals as "a simplistic and uninspired exchange of food for longevity, of prayers for prosperity" (Brashier 2011: 5). I will use his summary as our summary of the variety of views in both the transmitted and excavated texts. Brashier finds in early China five different kinds of relationships between the living and the dead:

1) When ancestor spirits are provided with the sustenance that they require through the sacrifices, they, in turn, grant the living with, among other things, a long and flourishing life and protection from enemies.
2) The sacrificer must be both sincere (*cheng* 诚) and virtuous (*de* 德) to gain the favor of their ancestor spirits.
3) The sacrificer could connect mentally and spiritually with their ancestral spirits, perhaps through dreams, in ways that positively influence their lives.
4) Various techniques such as meditation or abstinence from fine food could help one to visualize the ancestor spirits.
5) Some writers considered ancestor spirits to be fictional.[9]

Did Confucius Believe in the Afterlife?

Denials of afterlife beliefs in early China are often based on two, allegedly skeptical, texts from the *Analects*:

> Zilu asked about serving ghosts and spirits. The Master said, "You are not yet able to serve people—how could you be able to serve the ghosts and spirits?"
> "May I inquire about death?"
> "You do not yet understand life, how could you possibly understand death?" (11:12)
> "The Master did not speak of strange powers and chaotic spirits." (7:21)[10]

These widely asserted passages have served as prooftexts for Confucius'[11] (a fortiori Confucianism's[12]) this-worldly, humanistic orientation and skepticism toward the afterlife and spirits.[13] Confucius, we are assured, was concerned only with our antemortem moral comportment within the world of living human beings; he was agnostic about or even denied the afterlife. E. Bruce Brooks and Taeko Brooks claim that the former passage "represents a rejection of the belief in the unseen world on which the validity of sacrifice rests. We have here something like agnostic humanism, bent on life, not on death" (Brooks and Brooks 1998: 158). If we understand so little about antemortem life, so the claim goes, how can we presume to know anything at all about a postmortem life? Rather than concerning themselves with the unknown and even unknowable afterlife, rulers should pay more attention to this life and the this-worldly welfare of those under their care. Feng Yulan likewise claims that the humanistic Confucius rejected superstitious beliefs in gods and spirits; he argues that Confucius "displayed a rationalist attitude [toward spirits], making it probable that there were other superstitions of his time in which he did not believe" (Feng 1952, vol. 1: 58). Taken by themselves, then, these two passages constitute a prima facie anti-afterlife case.

However, a closer look at these two texts confounds this understanding of Confucius' views. Let us note three things about 7:21. First, 7:21 may be addressed solely to the person quoting the Master; perhaps the Master never spoke of spirits to *that* person or to persons *like* that person (see the Master's reluctance to speak to Zigong about certain issues in ch. 4). Second, 7:21 may be saying that the Master did not speak of *chaotic* spirits not spirits simpliciter. Perhaps the text is speaking of the early Chinese belief that the souls and energies that are released from the body when one dies can be vicious and dangerous. Such demonic forces (ghosts *gui*) can harm the living by spreading disharmony, illness, and misfortune. Perhaps the Master avoided speaking of malevolent spirits, while speaking (as he does, in other analects) of ancestor spirits. Since Confucius does speak of spirits in other passages, we should probably think 7:21 is addressed solely to the interlocutor or is restricted in scope to chaotic spirits.

Analects 11:21, as noted, has served as a prooftext of Confucius' skepticism toward the afterlife. However, as Thomas Wilson has pointed out, the skeptical interpretation would "effectively insinuate a rupture between the living and postmortem souls" (Wilson 2014: 190). Confucius' rhetorical question—"You are not yet able to serve people—how could you be able to serve the ghosts and spirits?"—betrays his commitment to this-worldly compassion toward the living. Yet it is worth noting that the question is addressed to a single person, Zilu, with paralleled assumed antecedents about Zilu—Zilu can't yet serve men and Zilu does not yet understand life. And if one cannot serve men or understand life, then one surely cannot serve the spirits and understand death. The rhetorical questions disguise several enthymemes and Confucius' implied conclusion—Zilu's moral failings preclude his understanding of the greater, spiritual things. Wilson goes on to point out that the commentarial tradition has favored just this sort of interpretation:

> Commentaries on *Analects* 11.12, moreover, often focus on serving spirits and say virtually nothing about serving the living. They stress, rather, that to serve or know the living is easier than to serve or know ghosts; learn to serve the living first, then one is prepared to undertake the more difficult task of serving one's ancestors. Chen Qun 陳群 (d. ca. 236) explains that Confucius's response was

intended to put a stop to Zilu's query since his disciple did not yet understand how to serve the living: "Because ghosts, spirits, and matters of the dead are difficult to understand, to speak of them would not benefit him, and so he didn't answer" 鬼神及死事難 明, 語之無益, 故不荅. Qing 清 (1644–1911) scholars such as Gu Yanwu 顧炎武 (1613–1682) and Liu Baonan 劉寶楠 (1791–1855) situate this passage among others concerned almost exclusively with the urgency of performing sacrifice properly and which say little about serving the living.

(Wilson 2014: 190)

According to the commentarial tradition, then, one must first learn to serve the living before one *can* serve ancestor spirits.

Let us consider several other passages where the Master speaks of spirits and sacrifice:

2:24 The Master said, "To sacrifice to spirits that are not one's own is to be presumptuous."

3:12 "Sacrificing as if [they were] present" means that, when sacrificing to the spirits, you should comport yourself as if the spirits were present. The Master said, "If I am not fully present at the sacrifice, it is as if I did not sacrifice at all."

6:22 Fan Chi asked about wisdom.

The Master said, "Working to ensure social harmony among the common people, respecting the ghosts and spirits, while keeping them at a distance, might be called wisdom."

7:35 The Master was seriously ill, and Zilu asked permission to offer a prayer.

The Master said, "Is such a thing done?"

Zilu said, "It is. The *Eulogy* reads, 'We pray for you above and below, to the spirits of Heaven and Earth.'"

The Master said, "In that case, I have already been offering up my prayers for some time now."

8:21 The Master said, "I can find no fault with [the legendary sage-king] Yu. He subsisted on meager rations, and yet was lavishly filial in his offerings to the ancestral spirits."

Although theses passages make few explicit claims about the afterlife, they do make implicit claims (see Wilson 2014). What they imply, I shall argue, is guided by two contexts. If we situate the *Analects* within the context of the thought-life of the tomb texts and architecture, then Confucius likely affirmed the existence of ancestor spirits. The commitments to the afterlife in the tomb texts should guide our understanding of the *Analects'* more implicit remarks. Second, we should expand the intellectual context, the form of life, to include all of the so-called Confucian classics, whose explicit remarks about the afterlife in the received texts should guide our understanding of the *Analects*. The very explicit commitments to the afterlife discussed above from the *Odes*, *Documents*, and *Ritual*, for example, should illuminate the text of the *Analects*.

I have just considered how to understand the afterlife views of Confucius as a character uniquely revealed in the *Analects*. If we take Confucius as the corporate character revealed within many of the received texts, then Confucius likely affirmed the existence of ancestor spirits. Hearing the Master's voice in the canonical Confucian texts makes explicit the (corporate) Master's implicit views on the afterlife.

Finally, it is simply good hermeneutic practice—a principle of hermeneutical charity—to assume that an author intends her assertions to be taken as realistic unless or until one has good reason to think they are not. Such interpretive realism would understand, for example, that worshipping the wrong spirits or worshipping them in the wrong way assumes that spirits exist.

Armed lightly with these hermeneutical tools, let us briefly examine several passages from the *Analects*. *Analects* 2:24 assumes that a variety of ancestor spirits exist, including some that one is not related to. *Analects* 3:12 assumes that while spirits may or may not be present at one's sacrifice, one should act as though they are; after all, one's rightly ordered character and rightly ordered ritual may be necessary to attract the spirits down into the ritual space. Since one cannot see spirits, one must always worship with the full sincerity that attends when one believes they are nearby. And so on with the remaining passages.

Philosopher Philip Ivanhoe demurs, arguing that Confucius had no commitment to the afterlife. He argues:

> Kongzi did not believe in any strong sense of personal survival after death. Even if one could show that he did hold some form of such a belief, it still was not part of a developed eschatology and played no role in shaping his views about how one should live one's life. That is to say, if he believed in some form of post-life survival, this was not embedded in a greater web of beliefs about a final judgment, subsequent punishment and reward, or any notion of reincarnation. I find no passages in the *Analects* to support the idea that Kongzi believed one's

individual personality survived in any form beyond death. And so, I take him as having held the view that, for all practical purposes, physical death is the end of an individual's personal consciousness.

(Ivanhoe 2011: 139)

I have offered reasons to think that Kongzi (Confucius, the character in the *Analects*) did believe in the afterlife. The best way to make sense of the repeated references to the ancestors in the *Analects* and the Confucian canon is to assume his belief in the afterlife. Even if we were to restrict ourselves to the *Analects*, its references to spirits imply deceased ancestors. Moreover, the possibility of worshipping another family's ancestors suggests that ancestor spirits can be disambiguated—that is, contra Ivanhoe, one's individual personality does survive death.

Ivanhoe's skepticism of the *Analects*' afterlife views is refuted by a realistic reading of the *Analects*. Even moreso, it is refuted within the form of life found in tomb text and architecture as well as in the transmitted texts (including the so-called Confucian canon). Within *that* form of life, Confucius' implicit can be made explicit—after death, spiritualized ancestors merit ritual attention. Thus, Confucius rejected the claim that "physical death is the end of an individual's personal consciousness."

Finally, afterlife beliefs played a role in shaping Confucius' views about how one should live one's life. Again, canonical Confucianism is more informative than the *Analects* simpliciter—the cultivation of filial piety, the root of all virtue in a Confucian hierarchical harmony, requires ritually precise actions and attitudes toward one's superior blood-kin, even ancestors; ritually cultivated filial piety, then, equips one emotionally to accept one's place in the societal hierarchy with respect and deference toward one's superiors. Hence, the *Analects* commends paying homage to spirits—respecting the spirits, mourning the spirits, and showing piety toward the spirits—with the implicit aim of the cultivation of filial piety, the root of virtue. If one were to believe that one's ancestors survive death, the ritual cultivation of piety would not end at their biological death; it would extend through death into the afterlife.

The transmitted texts represent ancestors as immaterial spirits who exhibit characteristic modes of consciousness—delight, anger, displeasure, happiness, rationality, etc. Moreover, ancestors are represented as having characteristic modes of power—to dispense harm or reward, bring fortune or misfortune, kill or increase longevity, cause wars or make peace, etc. When these texts are read within the context of the tomb texts, art and architecture, the evidence for belief in an afterlife overwhelms. Little wonder, then, that the thought-world of successive generations of Confucian officials and Confucian thinkers would be so densely populated with gods, ghosts, and spirits (Wilson 2014).

Body and Souls

As noted in the introduction, denials of the afterlife often go hand in hand with denials of mind-body dualism. According to A. C. Graham,

> [The mind-body dichotomy] never emerged in pre-Han philosophy; the word xin 心 "heart" is sometimes translated as "mind," reasonably enough in later philosophy influenced by Indian Buddhism, but in the classical period it refers only to the heart as the organ with which one thinks, approves and disapproves. (Thinking is not in traditional China located in the brain.) ... Confucius is not a victim of the post-Cartesian superstition of mind as "ghost in the machine."
>
> (Graham 1989: 15)

Yet, as Paul Goldin has noted, we find countless stories redolent of ghosts in early Chinese texts (with pre-Qin roots), "Confucian" even. Goldin's "examination of the range of attitudes about postmortem consciousness in early Chinese civilization" reveals anything but material monism about the nature of persons (Goldin 2015).[14] For example, in Tan-Gong II of the *Liji* we read that while one's flesh and bones return to the earth, one's "soul in its energy can go everywhere." Moreover, we read of the concourse of the living with the disembodied spirits of their ancestors: "The ruler and his wife take alternate parts in presenting these offerings, all being done to please the souls of the departed, and constituting a union (of the living) with the disembodied and unseen" (*Liji*, Liyun).

Let us briefly recount two stories that Goldin retells from the *Zuo Commentary to the Springs and Autumns* (*Zuozhuan* 左傳). In the first, Hu Tu is transporting the body of a deceased Crown Prince to a new grave when he encounters the Crown Prince's ghost with whom he has a conversation; we find, on the one hand, the Crown Prince's rotting body lying on the carriage and, on the other hand, the living ghost of the Crown Prince carrying on a conversation. The Crown Prince's living ghost is not identical with the Crown Prince's dead body. Goldin then tells the story of the ghost of Boyou who, though completely undetected (and likely undetectable), kills two men. As in many ghost stories of early China, Boyou was a vengeful ghost who wreaked havoc on earth until, we read, his son ritually placates his angry father and Boyou's wickedness stops. It was widely believed that the deceased, especially those who died violent deaths, can become malicious and vengeful ghosts. Mortuary rituals were designed to appease emerging malicious ghosts.[15]

How does the *Zuozhuan* conceive of the metaphysics of persons that allows for the possibility of one's deceased bodies, on the one hand, and the continuing existence of one's spirit. What is the metaphysics of persons that permits a person to be at one time a physical Crown Prince and at later time a living and active non-physical ghost of the now-deceased Crown Prince? What is the nature of spirits with postmortem powers to kill? In the *Zuozhuan* we read of Boyou:

> When people are born and begin to develop, [they have] what is called a po-soul. Once the po-soul has been born, its yang counterpart is called a hun-soul ... If one battens on things and one's essences multiply, the hun and po-souls will become strong; in this way, the luminosity of one's essence will reach the point of spiritlike perspicuity. When ordinary men and women die a violent death, their hun and po-souls are able to encroach on other people, and become licentious menaces. How much more so Liang Xiao, the progeny of our former Lord Mu [r. 627–606 B.C.], the grandson of Ziliang, the son of Zi'er!
>
> (Goldin 2015: 62)

While this passage conceives of a relationship between one's material body and the two parts of the soul—if a man flourishes physically his souls grow strong—it likewise conceives of the *hun* and *po* as capable of surviving death and going on to harm other people. Moreover, like most Western views, the soul, in this case the *hun*-soul, is associated with consciousness, spirituality, and intelligence.

Constance Cook rejects the claim that the Chinese mind is incapable of countenancing a distinction between the spiritual realm and the physical realm. She argues that the folk dualism of early Chinese thinkers permitted the conception of a nonmaterial or spiritual entity contained within a material body, which, at death, exits its material body for its postmortem journey. This immaterial entity, "his *hun*-soul" she writes, "will ascend to heaven, his form will enter the earth to dwell" (Cook 2006: 13). Cook suggests a second sort of dualism to the initial dualism of body-soul—in some Chinese texts the soul itself is represented dualistically, a composite of *hun* spirit and *po* spirit. Cook supports the idea of "the detachment of an ethereal self from the corporeal as an ancient and enduring Chinese belief" (Cook 2006: 17).

The significance of these terms is summarized by Jan de Groot:

> His *shen*, also called *hun*, immaterial, ethereal, like heaven itself from which it emanates, constitutes his intellect and the finer parts of his character, his

virtues, while his *kwei* or *po*, is thought to represent his less refined qualities, his passions, vices, they being borrowed from material earth. Birth consists of an infusion of these souls; death in their departure, the *shen* returning to the Yang or heaven, the *kwei* to the Yin or earth.

(de Groot 1910: 5)

de Groot claims that many early Chinese believed that human beings have a spirit or soul (*shen*) that consists of two parts, *hun* and *po*; upon death one's spirit separates from one's body and one's *hun* spirit flies up to heaven while one's *po* spirit goes down into the earth (or below the earth).

Textual support for *hunpo* dualism and its import for the afterlife are not restricted to a single passage from the *Zuozhuan*. Consider the following texts from the *Liji*:

- Thus they looked up to heaven (whither the spirit was gone) and buried (the body) in the earth. The body and the animal soul go downwards; and the intelligent spirit is on high. (*Liji*: Li Yun)
- Man is (the product of) the attributes of Heaven and Earth, (by) the interaction of the dual forces of nature, the union of the animal and intelligent (souls). (*Liji*: Li Yun)
- The intelligent spirit returns to heaven; the body and the animal soul return to the earth; and hence arose the idea of seeking (for the deceased) in sacrifice in the unseen darkness and in the bright region above. (*Liji*: Jiao Te Sheng)

These texts represent the afterlife as follows: the breath-soul (*hun*) returns to heaven, the bodily soul (*po*) returns to the earth.[16]

Two other ritual practices—the indwelling of the impersonator and the summoning of the soul—imply or assume a dualist view of persons. In, for example, the *Odes* and *Liji*, we hear of living persons, typically a male descendant, ritually serving as impersonators of a deceased ancestor (see Carr 2006). When song, banquet, and dance combine, the spirit of the deceased ancestor enters into and speaks through the host impersonator. In Chuci of the *Odes* we read of a grandson impersonating (representing) his ancestor. The ritual specialists then ply the ancestors, through their representatives, with food and drink and await their appearances. We repeatedly hear of the priest appealing to and involving "the filial descendent" through whom the ancestors speak:

Every form is according to rule;
Every smile and word are as they should be.
The Spirits quietly come,

And respond with great blessings; -
Myriads of years as the [fitting] reward.

(Odes Chuci)

Thus ritually appeased, and with message announced through the filial and pliant host, we read that when "the Spirits have drunk to the full" they tranquilly return to their place. The spirits have come, entered into and spoken through their host's body, and returned to their place in the other world. Again, this ritual is best understood as assuming or implying a distinction between physical body and disembodied soul.

Finally, the ritual of the summoning of the soul is likewise best explained by a commitment to body-soul dualism. This ritual was typically performed as soon as possible after a person died. There are eight references to calling back the soul in the *Liji*, including, for example:

> The uncles and elder cousins give their charges to those who are to communicate the death (to friends). The (soul of a deceased) ruler is called back in his smaller chambers, and the large chamber; in the smaller ancestral temples and in the great one: and at the gate leading to the court of the external audience, and in the suburbs all round.
>
> (*Liji*: Tan Gong I)

> Calling (the soul) back is the way in which love receives its consummation, and has in it the mind which is expressed by prayer. The looking for it to return from the dark region is a way of seeking for it among the spiritual beings. The turning the face to the north springs from the idea of its being in the dark region.
>
> (*Liji*: Tan Gong II)

> ….when one died, they went upon the housetop, and called out his name in a prolonged note, saying, "Come back, So and So." After this they filled the mouth (of the dead) with uncooked rice, and (set forth as offerings to him) packets of raw flesh. Thus they looked up to heaven (whither the spirit was gone), and buried (the body) in the earth. The body and the animal soul go downwards; and the intelligent spirit is on high. Thus (also) the dead are placed with their heads to the north, while the living look towards the south. In all these matters the earliest practice is followed.
>
> (*Liji*: Li Yun)

In the *Chuci* 楚辭 (Songs of the South), datable to the early third century BCE, we hear, in two odes, the repeated (likely ritual) mantra:

> O soul, come back! In the east you cannot abide. O soul, come back! In the south you cannot stay. O soul, go not to the west! O soul, go not to the north! O soul,

come back! Climb not to Heaven above. O soul, come back! Go not down to the Land of Darkness.

(Chu Tz'u 1962: 104–5; 110)

There might be two reasons for the ritual of the summoning of the soul. First, since the "soul in its energy can go everywhere," descendants may have sought to call souls back to their proper ritual place, the tomb, where they can grow accustomed to the afterlife and prepare for the soul's journey to heaven. Second, the widespread fear that the dead can become malevolent ghosts may have inspired the ritual to call the spirit back and, through the mortuary rituals, "tame" it so that it becomes a benevolent ancestor.

Whether one soul (*shen* or *hunpo*) or two (*hun* and *po*), the transmitted texts include passages which provide a metaphysics of the afterlife: human persons are mind-body complexes;[17] upon death, the spirit separates from the body for its new, postmortem life.

Conclusion

I have argued that early China's tomb text, and architecture manifest a form of life within which to understand the afterlife beliefs of early China. While I resisted universal generalizations—conceding difference in detail at every level and even outright rejection of the afterlife—I argued that the transmitted texts reveal a widespread commitment to the afterlife. Indeed, within that wider context, Confucius (qua character in the *Analects* or corporate character in canonical Confucianism) believes in the afterlife.

Moreover, I argued that the transmitted texts, explicitly or implicitly, represent humans as spirit-body composites. Upon death, one's spirit (variously called *shen*, *hunpo*, or *hun* and *po*) departs from one's body and either roams around one's tomb or journeys to heaven (perhaps to sit at the side of Heaven). The spirit of those who die violent deaths may become a vengeful and malevolent ghost (*shen* or *gui*). Many maladies and misfortunes were attributed to the actions of unseen but, to them, very real ghosts. The ritual of the summoning of the soul, which is aimed at calling the spirit of the recently deceased back into their body or tomb, may have sought to retrieve the deceased's ghostly spirit before it could do much harm. Finally, we hear stories of an impersonator calling down the spirit of their ancestor who fills them up and speaks through them. The most natural way of explaining these very natural and common phenomena is mind-body dualism. Moreover, some texts explicitly speak of disembodied spirits and of spirits that fly past their (former) inanimate bodies which are stuck on funeral carts or within caskets in tombs.

Explicitly and implicitly, then, from tomb to transmitted text, we find countless references to the afterlife and a metaphysics of mind-body dualism which undergirds it.

An interesting curiosity, of course, but does it make much difference?

Virtually every reference to filial piety in the *Odes* concerns the living showing ritual respect to their ancestor spirits.[18] This suggests, then, that the human moral project, as represented in the *Odes*, involves ritually cultivating the appropriate attitudes and actions toward the living spirits of deceased ancestors. Ancestors are not represented as existing only in memory or merely as examples to be followed. They are represented as living spirits under whose continuing auspices and authority humans live. As such, the cultivation of filial piety pierces the veil of death—one is not done with obeisance to one's ancestors at death or after three years of mourning. One must ritually call down one's ancestors to return to the tomb, perched as it is next door to our world, and bow down, as one does to parents in this life, to continued authority and power. By ritually bowing down to those above, one continues to learn in humility from their authority and power. As we will see in the next and final chapter, the lesson of the *Odes* generalizes—filial piety, which one cultivates in ritual devotion to one's ancestors, is the foundation of all virtue.

7

Sacrifice

Ritual and Sacrifice

It has been asserted that the Chinese don't believe in God or the afterlife. But, as we've shown, early Chinese texts are littered with representations of both the High God and the afterlife; if "text" includes funerary and tomb objects, afterlife representations overwhelm. When made aware of this, it is often asserted that the High God and afterlife beliefs are common among peasants and in the *Mozi*, but not in "the philosophical texts." However, we've shown that nearly all of the early Chinese transmitted texts, even those artificially designated "philosophical," include representations of the High God and the afterlife. When made aware of this textual evidence to the contrary, the retort is that the Confucians don't believe in God and the afterlife. And yet, as I have shown, representations of the High God and the afterlife are prevalent in the so-called Confucian canon. When made aware of this evidence to the contrary, it is often then claimed that God and afterlife beliefs are morally irrelevant to Confucian moral theory; theistic and afterlife beliefs are incidental to the moral philosophy of the Confucians; one can simply jettison such incidentals without loss to Confucian moral thought.

In this chapter I will demonstrate that in the early "Confucian texts," the High God and afterlife beliefs are, foundationally and practically, morally and socially salient. The canon to which I refer includes the Four Books—the *Analects*, *Mencius*, *The Doctrine of the Mean*, and *The Great Learning*—and the Five Classics—the *Rites*, *Documents*, *Odes*, and *Spring and Autumn Annals*; I will not be using the atypical *Changes*. I will focus primarily on *The Doctrine of the Mean* and the *Rites* but will draw upon the entire canon. Following these early "Confucian" texts, I take the terms "Heaven," "*Di*," and "*Shangdi*"—the three most typical Chinese terms for an anthropomorphic High Deity—to be virtually synonymous.

I take as data "canonical Confucianism," as found in the Four Books and Five Classics, not the *Analects* simpliciter. The exclusive and supreme authority that some scholars afford the *Analects* in framing and understanding Confucianism would have been unrecognizable in early China. Early classicism (*ru*) was based on a (shifting) set of quasi-authoritative texts with no special authority afforded the *Analects*.[1] Moreover, Confucius was a composite and complex character believed to be an influence on, a character in, or the author/editor of the entire Confucian canon. According to this tradition, Confucius "speaks" just as much in the *Documents* and *Odes* as in the *Analects*. Indeed, for over a millennium, the Five Classics were considered more important and authoritative than the *Analects*.[2]

I will reconstruct *a* canonical "Confucian" understanding of ritual sacrifice to both Heaven and ancestors.[3] I offer *a* canonical reconstruction, one of many that is consistent with at least some of the major claims of these texts; I do not offer *the* canonical Confucian view of ritual (which I believe impossible to reconstruct from these not entirely consistent, humanly constructed, accretional texts).

Students of early China are keenly aware of the importance of ritual (*li*) to Confucius, the character in the *Analects*, and in early Confucianism. In the *Analects*,[4] for example, ritual is the means to achieving benevolence (*ren* 仁), the highest virtue; every aspect of human conduct is governed by ritual. We read in *Analects* 12:1:

> Do not look unless is it in accordance with ritual; do not listen unless it is in accordance with ritual; do not speak unless it is in accordance with ritual; do not move unless it is in accordance with ritual.

Every aspect of the flourishing human life is governed by ritual; all proper human actions should be in accord with ritual.

However, contemporary students of early Chinese philosophy are not generally so aware that in the Confucian canon the most important and even foundational rituals are sacrifices first to the High God and then to ancestors. In the *Liji*, for example, we read on the very first page: "*There are five ritual constants, none is more important than sacrifice.*"

Sacrifice in the context of the *Liji* (and other early Confucian texts) includes sacrifice to Heaven (or *Di* or *Shangdi*, the terms are used interchangeably) and sacrifice to ancestors. Sacrifice to Heaven took place at ritually specified times in a temple on the outskirts of the city. To be sure, the common people did not sacrifice to Heaven and had, as far as we know, no direct or personal interactions with Heaven. We read in the *Liji* that "only the sage can sacrifice to God" (*Liji*, Ji Yi 5). Most people's most profound religiously informed and informing rituals centered on ancestral sacrifices, often at special ancestral temples or at grave sites (and at funerals).

Failure to sacrifice appropriately to the High God and to ancestors was believed to be morally and socially devastating. In "The Great Declaration" of the *Documents* we find a representative example of the importance of sacrifice, one which attributes the downfall of the Shang dynasty to King Shou's lack of reverence to Heaven and ignoring his ancestors: "I, Fa, have contemplated the government of Shang; but Shou has no repentant heart. He sits squatting on his heels, not serving God nor the spirits of heaven and earth, neglecting also the temple of his ancestors, and not sacrificing in it." The moral consequence of Shou's lack of reverence in the ritual sacrifices is a corresponding lack of benevolence (*ren* 仁). He is a wanton drunkard who oppresses his subjects:

> Abandoned to drunkenness and reckless in lust, he has dared to exercise cruel oppression. He has extended the punishment of offenders to all their relatives. He has put men into offices on the hereditary principle. He has made it his pursuit to have palaces, towers, pavilions, embankments, ponds, and all other extravagances, to the most painful injury of you, the myriads of the people. He has burned and roasted the loyal and good. He has ripped up pregnant women.

Heaven, moved to indignation, granted King Wen the right to overthrow the wicked King Shou and to establish a new and just dynastic power, the Zhou. The first order of business in the new dynasty was "special sacrifice to God." Heaven then empowered the new leader to compassionately care for his people. Sacrifice to Heaven is the first step on the dynastic path to benevolence (*ren* 仁).[5]

In this chapter, I will examine how and why the early Confucian canon supremely valued sacrifice to Heaven and ancestors. I will relate sacrifice to the canon's socio-political construction of the world as well as to its understanding of the moral life. In so doing, I will show that sacrifice is morally salient in early Confucianism and that it cannot be eliminated without loss.

Hierarchical Harmony

In the opening lines of *The Doctrine of the Mean*, we read that the Way, the moral and social path, produces harmony and even is harmonious:

> Harmonious: this is the ultimate Dao of the world.
>   Reaching centered harmony,
>   heaven and earth take their proper places
>   and the things of the world are nurtured thereby.
>
> (DM 1)[6]

In the "ultimate Dao," we find a cosmic harmony in which heaven and earth are in their proper places. We find already in this passage an allusion to the importance of hierarchy—the cosmos is harmonious when everything is in its proper place. What about earthly life, civil society?

Since Warring States China was notoriously chaotic, the Confucian search for a harmonious human society was paramount. Confucian thinkers attributed this chaos, in part, to people not being in their proper places. Unfit rulers generated oppression, starvation, and war. Of course, the ruled weren't happy with their plight and were seeking ways to displace rulers resulting in both palace intrigue and civil war. Although hierarchical, Warring States China was anything but harmonious.

According to the *Liji*, ritual reform would effect the desired harmony by getting everyone into their proper places. In the ritual sacrifices, the goal was

> to bring down the spirits from above, even their ancestors; serving (also) to rectify the relations between ruler and ministers; to maintain the generous feeling between father and son, and the harmony between elder and younger brother; to adjust the relations between high and low; and to give their proper places to husband and wife. The whole may be said to secure the blessing of Heaven.
>
> (*Liji* Bk 7)

It is noteworthy that sacrifice, the most important of the rituals, would, in all of the key human relationships (ruler-minister, father-son, elder brother-younger brother, husband-wife), create a hierarchy between the proper superiors and the proper inferiors, one marked by harmony, generosity, and reconciliation. A well-ordered human world would reflect the harmony of the cosmos, thereby securing the blessing of Heaven (where "the things of the world are nurtured thereby").

The proper alignment of the human world with the cosmic world, along with allying with one's ancestors, imparts moral power to the ruler. Gaining morally transformative power may have been viewed as essential if humans are not naturally given to benevolence. The early Confucian analysis of the human condition suggests that humans are not. Confucius[7] lamented that the world was in chaos, that the Dao was not put into action anywhere, and that he'd never met a *junzi* (a morally excellent person). In *The Doctrine of the Mean* Confucius himself says:

> There are four aspects to the Dao of the *junzi*: not one am I able to fulfill!
> To serve my father with that which I seek from my son
> To serve my ruler with that seek from my subordinates
> To serve my elders with that which I seek from my juniors
> —I cannot do it (them)!
>
> (DM 13)

Confucius confesses that he is incapable of appropriately serving those who are above him. Perhaps overcoming one's native selfishness requires tapping into the divine powers of the cosmos as well as securing the supernatural assistance of one's ancestors.

Just a few sections after lamenting his moral inability, we read, again in the voice of Confucius, of the powers of ancestral spirits:

> The Master said,
> How abundant is the virtue (*de* 德) of ghosts and spirits!
> You look at them and do not see, listen to them and do not hear,
>   yet they inhabit affairs without exception.
> They make all the people of the world fast and don ritual robes
>   in offering up sacrifices.
> Thrilling, how they seem to hover above, how they seem to be at every side.
> The *Poetry* says,
> > *The arrival of the spirits*
> > *Cannot be anticipated,*
> > *Much less may one be remiss.*
>
> The plain clarity of the subtle
>   —in just this way perfect genuineness cannot be obscured.
>
> (DM 16)

While the translator has Confucius praising the abundant virtue (*de* 德) of the ghosts and spirits, the more straightforward and natural reading might be the "abundant power" (*de* 德) of the ghosts and spirits. The original and more focal meaning of *de* 德 is, simply, "power" and, though it would come to mean something like "moral suasion" in early Confucianism, it retains its root meaning, "power," in various contexts. In this passage, the descriptions of the *de* 德 of the spirits are more redolent of power than moral suasion. Although they can't be seen or heard, "they make all the people of the world fast and don ritual robes in offering sacrifice." Although in various spirit locations, "they seem to be at every side." Given their powers, one should be constantly wary and waiting. In short, one's ancestral spirits may have just the sorts of powers to put one in one's place (contrary, perhaps, to one's native inclinations). Even if *de* 德 is best translated "virtue" in this context, it should be understood as a kind of moral, even supernatural power that transforms those beneath and around one.

Of course, being in one's proper place is not sufficient for attaining harmony. One might begrudgingly take one's place as youngest son or wife and yet find everything their superior said and did an annoyance, all the while resentfully waiting to assert themselves in various ways; perhaps they'd silently be fomenting rebellion. Moreover, one might take one's place and be lorded over by a despot, one with single-minded concern for his own needs. This is precisely the sort of precarious situation which required Heaven to shift his mandate from one ruler to another.

Being in one's place, then, is insufficient for creating the kind of harmony which secures the blessings of Heaven and by which all things are nourished. Only when those in the superior position are compassionate and those in the inferior positions are blessed and nourished are the ruled likely to be and remain content with their lot in life. Even more, only when those who are suited to rule (those who are wise and virtuous) are in ruling positions and when those underneath are pleased to be ruled by the wise and virtuous can the human world be said to have attained to harmony.

Once again, the rituals of sacrifice were believed necessary for the creation of genuine harmony. They were designed "so that all in a wider circle are harmonious with him [the ruler], and those in his narrower circle have no dissatisfactions with him" (*Liji*, Book VII, 1:1). The sacrifices at the Temple of Heaven, then, must effect hierarchical harmony, one in which the wise and just ruler is in his place and everyone else in his or hers. The sacrifices must endow the ruler with his proper sense of place and the ruled with theirs, all this *with no dissatisfactions with the ruler*; each person pleased to be in his or her proper place. Only then do we have the kind of lasting harmony that mirrors the harmony of Heaven (and secures Heaven's blessings). If there are dissatisfactions, there can be no harmony.

How, then, can the rituals effect the sort of hierarchical harmony wherein each person is in his or her proper place with no dissatisfactions with the ruler? In short, how can we attain what is commended in *The Doctrine of the Mean* (quoting the *Odes*):

> Wife and children in loving cooperation,
> It is like plucking the zither strings.
> Brothers all in unison.
> In happy harmony and joy.

(DM 15)

A Happy Harmony

How can we secure the kind of social harmony that resembles the sort of familial harmony described at the end of the previous section? How can society secure "loving harmony" like the plucking of zither strings, a "happy harmony and joy" with "all in unison"? Moreover, how can the rituals effect this sort of happy hierarchical harmony if people are indisposed to the obedience and obeisance that such a harmony would require?

One might think that the natural place to begin is with the child (the ruled), with punishments designed to ensure obeisance and obedience. It is natural, instinctive even, for the parent of the willful child to seek compliance by increasing the quantity and severity of punishments to bend the child's will to his will. And it's natural to think that such a top-down, punishment-oriented approach would secure the sort of respect for the ruler that would produce the compliance that is so essential to a successful hierarchical harmony. Such a reliance on top-down force to instill social order would require laws enforced by punishment.

Early Confucian texts such as the *Documents* have ambivalent attitudes toward punishment. At several points it endorses such punishments as whips for courts and sticks for schools; repeat offenders are to be given the death sentence. Shun's success in meting out punishments produced great effect:

> He banished the Minister of Works to You Island; confined Huan Dou on Mount Chong; drove the chief of San Miao and his people into San-wei and kept them there; held Gun till death a prisoner on Mount Yu. These four criminals being thus dealt with, *universal submission prevailed throughout the empire.*
>
> (The Canon of Shun, Legge, p. 29)

Exacting punishment on the disobedient created "universal submission"; punishment, properly meted, can even secure "sincere submission." The end game of punishment, when universal and sincere submission is achieved, is a people that no longer requires punishment: "[T]hrough punishment there may come to be no punishments, but the people accord with the path of the Mean." In the meantime, though, the ruler is advised to "continue to be strenuous" (from "The Counsels of the Great Yu," *Documents* Legge, p. 52).

And yet, according to "The Canon of Shun," as Shun contemplates the proper place of punishment, he tells himself, "Let compassion rule in punishment!" Moreover, the *Documents* counsels against excessive punishment (excessive according to their standards, not so much according to ours). The drunkard King Shou, mentioned earlier, is denounced for punishing not only criminals but their relatives (so he will be punished, by Heaven working through King Wu, for his crimes). By contrast, in "The Announcement to the Prince of Kang," a text nearly completely about punishment, young Prince Feng is repeatedly reminded to follow the example of King Wen who "was careful in the use of punishments" (though he was likewise "terrible to those who needed to be awed"). By dealing "reverently and understandingly" in the meting out of punishments, Prince Feng would "subdue men's hearts." When complete, the people will "admonish one another and strive to be obedient." However, failure to inflict appropriate punishments will have a deleterious effect: "The laws of our nature given by Heaven to our people will be thrown into great disorder and destroyed." The remedy for chaos, then, is to seek out and punish evildoers to the full extent of the law (compassionately rendered). Yet there's ambivalence: Prince Feng is warned of relying on "terror and violence" and encouraged to regulate the state with virtue (*de* 德), thus securing "the happy rule of the people."

Recalcitrant and self-seeking people seek position, power, and wealth beyond their place, thus resorting to crime and violence. No happiness there. A powerful ruler, then, must inflict punishment on transgressors of place and, by fear, maintain the regulations that keep everyone else in their places. But even if every criminal were properly punished and everyone else begrudgingly acquiescent, we have not attained to a happy harmony. While the ruler may, through threat of violence, keep people in their place, just beneath the surface of obedience is simmering resentment. According to Confucius, "If you try to guide the common people with coercive regulations and keep them in line with punishments, the common people will become evasive and will have no sense of shame" (*Analects* 2:3).

In the archaic language of Legge's translation, a happy rule won't be attained without tranquilizing and regulating the people. In the first place, in a harmonious society the people, of their own accord, follow the law (they are regulated, obedient; each is in his or her place). And, in the second place, the people are pleased to be ruled: their minds are stilled, their spirits are quiet; everyone is in their place and acting in happy accord with the ruler and the pattern of Heaven. Only by "imitat[ing] the active virtue (*de* 德) of the ancients" can Prince Feng hope to both tranquilize and regulate the people. Confucius completes the thought of his anti-punishment sentiment in the preceding paragraph with, "If, however, you guide them with Virtue, and keep them in line by means of ritual, the people will have a sense of shame and will rectify themselves" (ibid.).

Though the *Documents* itself is ambivalent about punishment, a trope emerges which is increasingly emphasized in later texts: rule by coercive power (violence and punishment) is (mostly) rejected and replaced with rule by virtue *de* 德: attractive, non-coercive, charismatic power. In short, the early Confucian remedy for chaos involves a shift from violently securing submission on the part of the ruled to ritually cultivating virtue on the part of the ruler. Ruling the state with virtue secures a happy harmony, one marked by both tranquility and regulation.

The *junzi* 君子, rather than exercising the coercive power of punishment and reward, exercises a gentle, suasive power that emanates from a benevolent disposition.

> The *junzi* persuades the people without issuing rewards;
> is without anger, yet the people are awed as if by an axe.
>
> (DM 33)

Through the attractive power (*de* 德) of the ruler, the people regulate themselves. Confucius concurs: "If you desire goodness, then the common people will be good. The Virtue of the gentleman is like the wind, and the Virtue of a petty person is like the grass—when the wind moves over the grass, the grass is sure to bend" (*Analects* 12:19).

Let us return to thinking about a happy hierarchical harmony. We have seen that the rule of laws enforced by punishment (coercion, violence, force) can instill order but such order is superficial and breeds resentment; subjects will seek ways to break laws with impunity and to overthrow arbitrary, self-serving, and vicious rulers. Hierarchy, yes; maybe even a fragile and forced truce. But there is no happiness here. The emerging Confucian vision aims at creating the conditions for a longlasting, deep, and mutually satisfying happy harmony. If a ruler cultivates virtue (*de* 德), the people will naturally and gladly take their places in civil society. We read: "The Master said, 'One who rules through the power of Virtue is analogous to the Pole Star: it simply remains in its place and receives the homage of the lesser stars'" (*Analects* 2:1). Each person is in his or her place (obedience) and yet is pleased to be ruled and so grants the ruler homage (obeisance), gladly conceding his right to rule. A happy harmony, indeed.

Confucius conceives of such a civil society as hierarchical, one that functions properly only when each person is in his or her proper place. Being in one's place is essentially hierarchical—involving positions of inferiority and superiority—and so we read Confucius' definition of good government: "Let the lord be a true lord, the ministers true ministers, the fathers true fathers, and the sons true sons" (*Analects* 12:11). Again, a happy hierarchical harmony requires willing obedience and grateful obeisance. Only then do we find "loving cooperation," with "all in unison/In happy harmony and joy."

Pride and Punishment

The emerging Confucian consensus on attaining a happy harmony shifts decidedly away from punishing subjects toward humanizing rulers. This non-coercive approach to social order requires the pursuit of righteousness and wisdom on the part of the ruler, with scant attention paid to the ruled. Confucius is more concerned about his own virtue than the obedience of the ruled (*Analects* 13:6). As noted, benevolent rulers cultivate a kind of attractive power (*de* 德), which orders (without coercive force) all of the people (even all of the surrounding states). The ruler, then, secures social order without violence—he does so, instead, through the attractive power of goodness and benevolence. As Confucius surveys the land, though, rulers seem inclined toward despotism, self-aggrandizement, and wealth. How could a ruler, then, become righteous and benevolent? His simple answer—return to the ways of old, the rituals of Yao and Shun (and of Zhou); learn from the days when people once lived in happy harmony. Only through a return to ritual can he effect a happy harmony. As we read in the *Liji*:

> *Therefore* the superior man observes these rules of propriety, so that all in a wider circle are harmonious with him, and those in his narrower circle have no dissatisfactions with him. Men acknowledge and are affected by his goodness, and spirits enjoy his virtue.
>
> (*Liji*, Book VIII, 1:1)

How can the rituals generate righteousness and benevolence in people who are naturally inclined toward self, honor, greed, and power? This is precisely the ritual problematic of, especially, the *Liji*.

Let's put the problematic in the terms of the *Liji* itself. How can a ruler create the kind of harmony where there are "no dissatisfactions with him"? We have seen the kinds of dissatisfactions that characteristically arise with laws severely enforced by punishments. The new Confucian way holds that if the *junzi* 君子 observes the proper rituals, the people "acknowledge and are affected by his goodness" (even the spirits enjoy his virtue). The rituals then effect a kind of spiritual power in the ruler in which the ruled acknowledge the ruler's goodness; in recognizing his right to rule, the people are inclined to willing, not begrudging or resentful, obedience. Additionally, the rituals effect a kind of infectious spiritual power in which goodness spreads among the people who are then self-motivated to be righteous; their right actions don't arise from an external coercive force (fear of the ruler's punishment), they arise from an internally motivating strength, *de* 德 (their own virtue). The ruled are thus both positively inclined toward the ruler and internally motivated to righteousness. Each person is in his or her place and pleased to be in it, positively respectful of and deferential toward the ruler and self-regulated. We have attained to well-regulated order without violence—in short, the kind harmony with no dissatisfactions.

Throughout the texts of canonical Confucianism, such goodness and order are unattainable apart from strict adherence to the rituals of Yao and Shun. Moreover, these rituals are considered essential to the creation of the virtues of the happy hierarchical harmony we are seeking (those that create harmony with no dissatisfactions). We read:

> The course (of duty), virtue, benevolence, and righteousness cannot be fully carried out without the rules of propriety; nor are training and oral lessons for the rectification of manners complete; nor can the clearing up of quarrels and discriminating in disputes be accomplished; nor can (the duties between) ruler and minister, high and low, father and son, elder brother and younger, be determined; nor can students for office and (other) learners, in serving their masters, have an attachment for them; nor can majesty and dignity be shown in assigning the different places at court, in the government of the armies, and in discharging the duties of office so as to secure the operation of the laws; nor can there be the (proper) sincerity and gravity in presenting the offerings to spiritual Beings on occasions of supplication, thanksgiving, and the various sacrifices. Therefore the superior man is respectful and reverent, assiduous in his duties and not going beyond them, retiring and yielding—thus illustrating (the principle of) propriety.
>
> (*Liji* Bk. I, 8)

How, then, do the rituals transform a self, honor, and money-loving ruler who relies on coercive forms of power to rein in his subjects into a virtuous ruler with attractive power? How can a self-assertive and disrespectful person become "respectful and reverent, retiring and yielding"?

We read of the antidote to self-assertion at the very beginning of the *Liji* and throughout the early Confucian canon:

> The Summary of the Rules of Propriety says: Always and in everything let there be reverence; with the deportment grave as when one is thinking (deeply), and with speech composed and definite. This will make the people tranquil. Pride should not be allowed to grow.
>
> (*Liji* I, 1:1–2:2)[8]

In the *Analects* we read that "[t]he gentleman is grand, but never arrogant; the petty person is arrogant, but never grand" (*Analects* 13:26) and the benevolent person is not motivated by arrogance or pride (*Analects* 14:1). And in the *Xiaojing* 孝治 we read of rulers and ministers: "Above others, and yet free from pride, they dwell on high, without peril" (*Xiaojing* 孝治 ch. III). The *Analects* diametrically opposes taking delight in self, pleasure, and money: "Taking joy in arrogant behavior, idle amusements, or decadent licentiousness—these are the harmful types of joy" (*Analects* 16:5). In *Analects* 11:25, we read that Confucius laughed at Yu because Yu lacked ritual propriety and humility. Finally, "The Master said: 'The gentleman takes rightness as his substance, puts it into practice by means of ritual, gives it expression through modesty, and perfects it by being trustworthy. Now that is a gentleman!'" (*Analects* 15:18). In short, the rituals are first and foremost designed to eliminate the vice of pride and to cultivate the virtue of humility.

The importance of humility to a happy harmony is evident. A prideful ruler is concerned with his own needs and desires, caring little for those beneath him. He views the people as a means to his own ends, not as valuable in their own right (hence, not deserving of his care and concern). Slights to his honor will be treated severely. A decrease in production will be seen as a threat to his comfort and well-being and dealt with harshly. He may instill order but there will be deep dissatisfactions.

The humble ruler, on the other hand, respects the people, treating them with dignity and kindness; he treats others as he himself would be treated (*Analects* 1:5, 2:20). He understands that his role is to serve the people, not to be served by them; so he does not impose upon others what he would be unwilling to accept himself (*Analects* 12:2). Finally, he treats his people with love, kindness, compassion, respect, and dignity; the humble ruler anticipates and meets the needs of his people (without them even asking). A humble ruler, then, is essential to a happy hierarchical harmony.

Ritual, Reverence, and Respect

If humility is the chief virtue of the Confucian ruler, and a humble ruler is essential to a flourishing society, how can the ruler attain humility through the ancient rituals? I will argue, in this section, that the most important rituals, the rituals of sacrifice to Heaven and to ancestors, were intended to diminish pride and increase humility. As a result, the ruler would likewise cultivate benevolence (*ren* 仁) and, as a consequence, the state would be well-ordered and the people happy. The focus here will be on reverence, the feeling, or attitude of deep respect and awe. I will argue that reverence is the ritual starting point of the diminution of pride, the increase of humility, and the development of benevolence (thus creating the foundation of a happy harmony). Ritual propriety, after all, is found in humbling one's self and giving honor to others (*Liji* Qilu 1:11).

The importance of reverence is seldom discussed in contemporary Confucian moral philosophy. And yet the call to reverence is found everywhere. In the *Liji*'s Summary of the Rules of Propriety, we read, "Always and in everything let there be reverence; … This will make the people tranquil" (*Liji* Qilu 1:1). We find in the *Liji*'s demand for reverence the hope for a happy harmony.

One philosophical approach to reverence and harmony is suggested in the previous section on pride and punishment. If, in a hierarchical society, the people are made to revere the ruler (and so are loyal), society is more likely to be well-ordered and the people tranquil. So, for example, in *Analects* 2:20 we read:

> Ji Kangzi asked: "How can I cause the common people to be respectful, dutiful, and industrious?"
>
> The Master said, "Oversee them with dignity, and the people will be respectful; oversee them with filiality and kindness, and the people will be dutiful; oversee them by raising up the accomplished and instructing those who are unable, and people will be industrious."

Ji Kang Zi selfishly asks how to *make* the people reverent and loyal so that they will work positively for *his* benefit. If they are reverent and loyal, of course, they are more likely to serve him. Confucius, however, turns the question away from the people and back on Ji Kang Zi—if *you* treat the people with dignity, they will be reverent. If *you* are filial and compassionate, they will be loyal. Moreover, if the ruler treats the people with dignity, filiality, and compassion, he will be concerned more with how he can benefit the people than himself. Thusly compassionated and cared for, the people will revere the ruler and work to their utmost (thus happily benefiting everyone, including the ruler). How can a ruler, then, learn how to treat the people with dignity, filiality, and compassion? In a word, reverence.

The *Liji*'s ritual philosophy can be summarized as follows: "Pride should not be allowed to grow; the desires should not be indulged; the will should not be gratified to the full; pleasure should not be carried to excess" (*Liji* Qilu 1:2). Ritually cultivated reverence is the Confucian antidote to pride and excessive desire, character traits of a ruler that doom society to chaos. And sacrifice to Heaven and the ancestors are the chief rituals aimed at diminishing pride and cultivating benevolence. We read:

In the sacrifice to God in the suburb, we have the utmost expression of reverence. In the sacrifices of the ancestral temple, we have the utmost expression of humanity. In the rites of mourning, we have the utmost expression of faithfulness. In the preparation of the robes and vessels for the dead, we have the utmost expression of affection. Therefore, the *junzi wants to find* the ways of *ren* 仁 and *yi* 義 *rooted in these ceremonial usages.*

(*Liji* Bk. VIII; my emphasis)

Here we find the ritual roots of all of the most important Confucian virtues: reverence in sacrifice to God, benevolence in sacrifice at the ancestral temple, and filial faithfulness in the rites of mourning. These, in turn, ground "the ways of *ren* 仁 [benevolence] and *yi* 義 [righteousness]." The root of the ritual, from which *ren* 仁 and *yi* 義 grow, is reverence and respect (*Mencius* 6A:6). The *Odes* concurs: "Reverence and goodness so mild, are the foundations of inner power" (*Odes* 256; see also 299 and 240 for a tight connection between reverence, ritual, and virtue).

We find, in *The Doctrine of the Mean*, a concise expression of the sacrifices to the High God and to ancestors along with their moral and social salience:

The Master said,
    King Wu and the Duke of Zhou, were they not of ultimate filiality!
    The filial son extends well the intentions of his father
        and carries on his father's affairs.
In spring and autumn he repairs the ancestral shrines,
   sets out the ancestral vessels,
   lays out the ancestral robes,
   and offers up the food of the season.
  The rituals of the ancestral shrines are the means of ordering the
      lines of descent, ...
The ordering of ritual ranks distinguishes the exalted from the humble. ....
  To occupy his post,
   to carry out his rituals, to perform his music,
   to respect what he honored, to love what he cherished,
   to treat the dead as one treats the living,
   to treat the departed as one treats those who remain:
     this is the ultimate of filiality.
The suburban rite of sacrifice ministers to the Lord on High;
   the rituals of the ancestral shrines minister to one's forbears.
He who comprehends the rite of the suburban sacrifice
   or the meaning of the great spring and autumn sacrifices
     can rule a state as though it lay in his palm.

(DM 19)

The ancestral rites order the present based on the ordering of the deceased ancestors. Participation in the ritual is essentially hierarchical—"The ordering of ritual ranks distinguishes the exalted from the humble." Each person sits in his or her place, high or low. Here we have the seeds of resentment and chaos. But, in carrying out the ritual the ruler takes his place as son (not as father) and, as such, sits under the authority of his deified ancestors. As he, in humility, takes his ritual place below his ancestors, he thus learns filiality.[9] In ritually effecting humility, he learns to be a filial son. He can likewise imaginatively extend the benevolence his ancestors have shown him to his "children." This is his first step on a path to a happy harmony.

In the suburban rite of sacrifice to the Lord-on-High, the ruler cultivates ritual reverence toward the source of the people, of goodness, and of history. The rites remind the ruler that he is not the Lord-on-High and so is not the source of the people, of goodness, and of history. The Lord-on-High might create virtue in him, might call him to leadership, and might use him to effect his mandate in history, but his goodness, authority, and power are derivative. We find each of these themes represented in the *Analects*:

> The Master said: "It is Heaven itself that has endowed me with virtue. What have I to fear from the likes of Huan Tui?"
>
> (*Analects* 7:23)

> A border official from the town of Yi requested an audience with the Master, saying: "I have never failed to obtain an audience with the gentlemen who have passed this way." Confucius' followers thereupon presented him.
> After emerging from the audience, the border official remarked, "You disciples, why should you be concerned about your Master's loss of office? The world has been without the Way for a long time now, and Heaven intends to use your Master like the wooden clapper for a bell."
>
> (*Analects* 3:24)

> The Master said: "How great was Yao as a ruler! So majestic! It is Heaven that is great, and it was Yao who modeled himself upon it."
>
> (*Analects* 8:19)

As great as Yao was, his goodness could not attain to the goodness of Heaven. All he could do was accord with the pattern of Heaven. The *junzi* 君子 must first and foremost stand in awe of the decree of Heaven (*Analects* 16:8).[10] Such ritually cultivated reverence is not an end in itself. In reverence, the ruler bows before the goodness and authority of the Lord-on-High, thus defeating the ruler's pride. This is but step one. Then, in humility, he is enabled to emulate the benevolent patterns of Heaven, to assume his role as a compassionate ruler, and to respect and honor his people. Bringing it full circle, he can rule a state as though it lay in his palm.

The *Liji* affirms the *Analects* 8:19 view that only Heaven is good in a basic way and that rulers are good only secondarily, derivatively, or imitatively:

> Confucius said, "It was by the rules of propriety that the ancient kings sought to represent the ways of Heaven, and to regulate the feelings of men .... Therefore those rules are rooted in Heaven, have their correspondencies in earth, and are applicable to spiritual beings."
>
> (*Liji* Bk VII.3)

Through the rituals, the ancient kings both represented the pattern of Heaven and regulated the feelings of men. The earthly pattern is rooted not in the will of the human community (perfected or not) but in the pattern of Heaven.

> Yen Yen again asked, "Are the rules of Propriety indeed of such urgent importance?"
>
> Confucius said, "It was by those rules that the ancient kings sought to represent the ways of Heaven, and to regulate the feelings of men .... Therefore those rules are rooted in heaven."
>
> (*Liji* Bk 7, sec 1)

The ruler, out of respect for Heaven, ritually brings the Heavenly pattern both into his life and down to earth.

The High God serves as more than the pattern of righteousness. *The Doctrine of the Mean* suggests that the acquisition of filiality requires a sort of divine power boost. In DM 17, after praising Shun for his filiality, the Master goes on to credit both the impartation of the virtue and the acquisition of virtue's rewards (wealth, for example, but also fame and longevity) to Heaven: "When Heaven gives birth to a thing it treats it with generosity according to its potential." The text concludes with an expression of gratitude to Heaven from the *Odes*:

> The *Poetry* says,
>> The *junzi* of great goodness,
>> How abundant his fine virtue!
>> Fit for the people, fit for all others,
>> He receives his stipend from Heaven
>> Which protects and assists him with the Mandate
>> Extended from Heaven.
>
> Thus great virtue inevitably receives the mandate.
>
> (DM 17)

Since DM 17 occurs immediately after DM 16, which affirms the powers (*de* 德) of the spirits (connecting them to the sincerity or authenticity of the *junzi* 君子), it is no stretch to think that DM 17 credits the *junzi*'s acquisition of "fine virtue!" and its "stipend" (rewards) to the transformative powers of Heaven. Heaven, in this passage, both creates the potential for virtue and develops it. Throughout life, Heaven helps and protects the *junzi* and then, in government, assists the ruler in the execution of his Heavenly vocation. Little wonder then that Heaven, thus conceived, is deserving of gratitude.[11] Gratitude is the ultimate expression of humility—graciously accepting and warmly acknowledging one's dependence on a superior person in this or that respect.

By entering into this well-ordered ritual space, with everyone in their place, the ruler recreates the pattern of well-ordered Heaven which is, unlike his contemporary society, a happy harmony. Within that space lies the possibility for the moral and spiritual transformations that are necessary for creating a happy harmony on earth. First and foremost, reverence toward Heaven generates the sort of cosmic humility necessary for glory-seeking, power-hungry, and greedy rulers; rulers are not to laws unto themselves, because they, themselves, are subject to a higher moral and spiritual authority. Secondly, the respect one shows one's deceased ancestors allows the ruler to humbly acknowledge that he is a son, dependent on the generosity of his ancestors for a good future. The ruler then gratefully accepts the gifts that his ancestors bring in response to his ritual imploring.

The music, the dance, the architecture, and the script combine to recreate the Heavenly harmony in the ritual space, allowing one a glimpse of the ultimate Dao, one that includes higher and lower beings in harmonious relationships of respect and benevolence. The music reinforces the vision—each note is in its place working together in harmony; the music speaks to the feelings of the ritual participants, each in his or her proper place, effectively transforming them from self-centered individuals into a harmonious community.

The ruler is transformed by the power of the ritual, but also by the mysterious but effective powers (*de* 德) of Heaven and the collective powers of his deified ancestors. Through reverence to Heaven he learns humility, through respect toward his ancestors he learns filiality, and taking his place among his people he treats them as his family and so learns friendship (and so will treat the people with dignity).[12]

As a ritual son of both Heaven and his spiritualized ancestors, he has ritually grasped Heavenly and fatherly benevolence.[13] Upon completion, then, the ruler leaves the ceremony as father to his people. Confucius himself claims that the sacrificial rituals would, in their turn, create a "family" that vastly exceeded kin relationships, one that extended out into the world. And just as a loving father cares for his children and a loving and respectful child cares for his aging parents, so, too, everyone will care for everyone in this newly formed family.

> When the Grand course was pursued, *all under the sky will be shared by the people*; they chose men of talents, virtue, and ability; their words were sincere, and what they cultivated was harmony. Thus men did not love their parents only, nor treat as children only their own sons. A competent provision was secured for the aged till their death, employment for the able-bodied, and the means of growing up to the young. They showed kindness and compassion to widows, orphans, childless men, and those who were disabled by disease, so that they were all sufficiently maintained. Males had their proper work, and females had their homes.
>
> (*Liji* Bk 7, sec 1; *modifications in italics*)

Of learning from one's ancestors we read:

> I think of my ancestors, (who are now) the spiritual sovereigns; when they made your forefathers toil (on similar occasions it was only for their good), and I would be enabled in the same way greatly to nourish you and cherish you. Were I to err in my government, and remain long here, my high sovereign, (the founder of our dynasty), would send down on me great punishment for my crime, and say, "Why do you oppress my people?"
>
> (*Shangshu Pan Geng* Bk. IV)

Through one's spiritual sovereigns, the ruler learns how to nourish and cherish his people (if he doesn't, his ancestors will punish him).

We find a similar sentiment in the *Liji*. Though each sits in his or her (high or low) place, the ritual music unites everyone as one (family):

> Below (in the court-yard), the flute-players played the tune of the Hsiang, while the Tâ-wei was danced, all uniting in the grand concert according to their parts, giving full development to the spirit (of the music), and stimulating the sense of virtue. The positions of ruler and minister, and the gradations of noble and mean were correctly exhibited, and the respective duties of high and low took their proper course.
>
> The officers having announced that the music was over, the king then charged the dukes, marquises, earls, counts, and barons, with all the officers, saying, "Return, and nourish the aged and the young in your eastern schools." Thus did he end (the ceremony) with (the manifestation of) benevolence.
>
> (*Liji* Bk VI, sec 30)

When the spirit of the music has taken its full, morally empowering effect, the officers leave with a spirit of benevolence, one that will manifest itself in care for the most needy in society.

As noted, the sacrifices to the High Deity and to ancestors create the virtues that constitute the roots of *ren* 仁 and *yi* 義. I have suggested *ren* 仁 and *yi* 義 are grafted onto the roots of humility, respect, friendship, and human dignity. The *Liji* connects various virtues with their respective rituals, beginning with reverence (in the sacrifice to the High Deity) leading up and into *ren* 仁 and *yi* 義.

> In the sacrifice to God in the suburb, we have the utmost expression of reverence. In the sacrifices of the ancestral temple, we have the utmost expression of humanity. In the rites of mourning, we have the utmost expression of leal-heartedness. In the preparation of the robes and vessels for the dead, we have the utmost expression of affection. In the use of gifts and offerings between host and guest, we have the utmost expression of what is right. Therefore when the superior man would see the ways of humanity (*ren* 仁) and righteousness (*yi*), he finds them rooted in these ceremonial usages.
>
> (*Liji* Bk. VIII)

Reverence and respect, benevolence and fealty, affection and righteousness are rooted in ritual. Without the elimination of pride at the outset, the entire process would be rendered worthless.

We find a version of this moral progression/transformation from self to society expressed in *The Doctrine of the Mean*:

> 'Humanity' *(ren* 仁*)* means 'human' *(ren* 人*)*:
>   cleaving to one's kin is its foremost element.
> 'Right' *(yi* 義*)* means 'appropriate' *(yi* 宜*)*,
>   honoring the worthy is its foremost element.
> The degrees that govern cleaving to one's kin
>   and the ranks that govern honoring the worthy
>   are the things that give birth to ritual...
> Hence the *junzi* cannot fail to refine his person:
>   intending to refine his person,
>   he cannot fail to minister to his parents;
>   intending to minister to his parents,
>   he cannot fail to understand others;
>   intending to understand others,
>   he cannot fail to understand Heaven.
> There are five things that extend throughout the world...
>   ruler and minister;
>   father and son;
>   husband and wife; elder and younger brother;
>   friend meeting friend.
>
> (DM 20)

The ruler ritually learns, wherever he finds himself place in society, the proper attitudes for a happy hierarchical harmony:

> When in high position, do not be arrogant towards those below.
> When in low position, do not prevail upon those above.
> Make yourself upright and do not seek what you wish in others,
> then you will encounter no resentments.
>
> (DM 14)

Neither arrogant nor presumptuous, the ruler has ritually cultivated the dispositions that ensure there will be no resentments either from those above or those below.

Thus transformed, the humble, filial, and respectful ruler will acquire extraordinary, one might think supernatural, powers of leadership, of "listening and seeing, penetration and wisdom" (DM 30).[14] He likewise becomes magnanimous, generous, gentle, and flexible, on the one hand, and vigorous, strong, firm, and resolute, on the other. In reverence, he models Heaven's pattern, with goodness spontaneously issuing forth like a flood. With their needs sensed and met, without them even speaking, the people are content and respectful. News of his benevolence spreads beyond the confines of the city to the four corners of the earth, and everyone, far and near, is attracted by his virtue; there is no one who does "not revere and cleave to him." The world itself is now happy and harmonious (and not a person was punished or a drop of blood shed). So we return to the place we started:

> Reaching centered harmony,
> > heaven and earth take their proper places
> > > and the things of the world are nurtured thereby.
>
> (DM 1)

The Moral Salience of the High God and Afterlife Beliefs

These "early Confucian" texts represent both the High God and afterlife beliefs as morally salient. Such beliefs are neither incidental nor easily discarded. Let me formalize several ways in which these texts represent the moral salience of the High God and afterlife beliefs:

- Heaven is the ultimate standard of goodness (and benevolence), which rulers are required to understand and imitate and follow. Heaven, more broadly speaking, is the ultimate standard, the Dao, of a happy harmony which societies are required to understand and imitate.[15]

- Fear of supernatural punishment, in this life and the next, motivates a life of virtue. Such punishments might be inflicted either by Heaven or by angry ancestors, through intermediaries or directly, in this life or the next.[16]
- Ritual is essential to moral transformation and the two most important rituals are the rituals of sacrifice, first to the High God and second to the ancestors.
- Sacrifices to the High God and ancestors, when done with sincerity and reverence, inculcate a proper sense of place (necessary for the creation of harmony).
- Sincere and reverential deference to Heaven and the ancestors diminishes pride (encouraging respect and benevolence toward those beneath one).
- Sincere and reverential deference to Heaven and the ancestors induces humility (encouraging respect and deference toward those above).
- The diminishing of pride and the cultivation of humility are the necessary first steps toward the cultivation of benevolence and righteousness.
- Sacrifice to Heaven (reverence), ancestors (respect), and mourning (faithfulness) are the roots of benevolence and righteousness.
- The High God and ancestors have powers to morally transform us.

There is much more to be said about each one of these. And there are more ways in which the High God and ancestors are represented as morally salient in the early Confucian texts.

The moral psychology implicit in this early Confucian conception of reality and ritual is deep and profound. Since humans flourish when bound together into an other-regarding community with shared norms and values, rituals in which individuals "lose their selves" facilitate one's sense of belonging to a community (hence, human flourishing). I'll be brief and suggestive here. While philosophers focus on beliefs, social scientists study complex systems involving both beliefs and practices. Recent social scientific research suggests that beliefs, rituals, and other aspects of religious practice, of the sort we find in the *Liji*, are/were essential means of creating and strengthening a harmonious moral community (Graham and Haidt 2010). Durkheim ([1915] 1965) argued that ecstatic group rituals engendered the sort of intense passion and joy necessary for the long-term maintenance of a cohesive group.

Recent social scientific research suggests that humans are cognitively constituted to respond morally to rituals. The experience of participating in rituals increases in-group affiliation to a greater degree than group activity alone (Wen 2016). Groups of individuals that walk, sing, or dance together show greater liking, trust, cooperation, and self-sacrifice than groups performing the same behaviors while not in synchrony (Wiltermuth and Heath 2009). Religious rituals, socio-historically, are powerful means for securing cooperation, solidarity, and success in intergroup competition (Henrich 2009). Finally, corporate religious rituals reinforce commitment to moralizing high gods which, in turn, suppresses selfishness and increases cooperation (Atran and Henrich 2010; Norenzayan and Shariff 2008; see chapter 8). Mutually reinforcing belief-ritual complexes expand community by galvanizing solidarity (maybe even as extended family) and reinforce prosocial behavior by increasing trust.

I have developed a rationally reconstructed understanding of ritual based on the early Confucian-transmitted texts. As such, it is highly speculative. As far as I know, no individual thinker, no individual canonical text, no compendium or summary of texts—authoritative or otherwise—outlines my rational reconstruction of Confucian ritual (nor, as far as I am aware, any other rational reconstruction of ritual). Yet my rational reconstruction of ritual brings together many interesting and oft-ignored texts into a unified theory that is philosophically deep and psychologically rich.

As noted throughout this book, problems abound: the early Confucian texts themselves are composite, multi-authored, ambiguous, and inconsistent. The set of texts contains a panoply of tropes, themes, advice, arguments, models, and metaphors. For example, although I claimed that early Confucianism offers a model of society based on ritual and not punishment, some canonical Confucian texts endorse rule by punishment; and though such texts temper rule by punishment with compassion and wisdom on the part of the ruler, they nonetheless endorse rule by punishment and harsh punishments at that. And while most of the texts I've cited seem to straightforwardly assume the postmortem existence of deceased ancestors, a few texts seem to suggest otherwise (so in the rituals one is not reacquainting oneself with the ancestors, one is simply recalling their memories).

Let us return to the argument of the book concerning gods, ancestors, and afterlife: there is ample textual evidence in the early Confucian canon to support belief in a morally salient High God, ancestors, and afterlife. And while I think this is also the best overall understanding of the so-called canonical Confucian texts taken as parts or wholes and in conjunction with one another, I fully concede that there may be counterexamples, even within the texts themselves, to each point that I have made. So be it. This is the best one can do with such composite and variegated texts.

Part Four

A Deeper Dive

8

The Evolutionary Psychology of Chinese Religion

Cognitive Science and Religion

Empirical support for Chinese deities can be found in the newly emerging cognitive science of religion.[1] Cognitive science rejects the assumption that cultural groups are radically different. Studies show that our common biological heritage and relatively similar environments produce both relatively similar minds and relatively similar beliefs. Evolutionary processes have shaped human cognitive faculties and, when those faculties are applied to their specific challenges (which are fairly similar across cultures), produce roughly similar beliefs. These common cognitive faculties include relatively specialized "subsystems" that structure, inform, enhance, and limit our view of the world. Rejecting the empiricist assumption of the mind as a blank slate on which experience writes, cognitive scientists hold that our minds come equipped with a set of cognitive faculties that actively processes our perceptions and shapes our conceptions of the world. Some of these faculties, in turn, have a direct influence upon the origin and development of religious beliefs. According to this model, *humans have a natural tendency to believe in gods*. Belief in gods naturally arises when certain common cognitive faculties are stimulated. A culture without gods is as much to be expected as a culture without beliefs in other persons or the external world.

In this chapter, we take inspiration from supernatural punishment theory, one expression of the cognitive science of religion, to direct an examination of ancient Chinese texts for specific conceptions of divinity and their relation to humanity. While the cognitive science of religion in general would lead us to expect to find various sorts of disembodied agents in China, supernatural punishment theory in particular would lead us to expect to find a high, moralizing god with strategic knowledge who exercises a kind of moral providence.[2]

In order to better understand China's High Deities—*Di* 帝, *Shangdi* 上帝 and *Tian* 天—we have constructed a database of instances of these three terms in texts from the Pre-Qin (Pre-221 BCE) period.[3] This database is composed of intuitively coded, representative passages from these texts where these extrahuman agents appear. By employing this database in these capacities, this chapter, guided by supernatural punishment theory, will highlight one of the common ways with which these High Deities are represented in Pre-Qin texts as punishers and rewarders. We then show how the representation of these agents as punishers and rewarders is pervasive throughout the texts of the Pre-Qin period. Though these are too diverse to be fully explained in a single paper, by taking a general survey of these representations, common idioms emerge that continue to present themselves in the passages where these agents are punishers and rewarders. Most commonly, this manifests as a moral dimension with these agents being cast as moralizing agents that punish and reward according to moral criteria, something argued for by cognitive theories of religion. This chapter will hence present and analyze some of the most salient and representative passages that show agents under such representations and idioms, showing them to be both pervasive and fundamental to the Pre-Qin understanding of the High Deities.

Supernatural Punishment Theory

Cognitive science has converged on a general picture of how our common cognitive faculties produce belief in gods.[4] Human beings are equipped with a cognitive faculty—*an agency-detecting device (ADD)*—that generates beliefs about agency. When stimulated, ADD immediately produces beliefs in an agent. The evolutionary advantages of agency detection are obvious: without such immediate beliefs/responses to certain motions (rustling bushes) or sounds (things going bump in the night), we might end up as food for a predator or the victim of an enemy. So, ADD is sensitive, prompting us to instantly respond to slightest provocation. Justin Barrett has named the disposition to form beliefs about agents given minimal stimulation the *hypersensitive agency detection device* (or HADD).

Upon the detection of agency, another cognitive faculty that cognitive scientists call the *Theory of Mind (ToM)* begins operating; ToM attributes beliefs, desires, and purposes to the postulated agent. How do HADD and ToM produce belief in gods? If ordinary, natural agents—animals and enemies—are unsuited to account for one's experiences, one might find oneself believing in extraordinary, supernatural agents, including ghosts, angels, or gods. And then HADD quickly gives way to ToM, ascribing reasons to what these agents do. Surely only a very powerful, minded agent could cause such extraordinary events (and for extraordinary reasons), so we attribute super qualities—super powers and super knowledge, for example—to the causes of super events.

There is much more to say here about the cognitive science of religion. It offers explanations of the sustainability and transmissibility of religious belief; certain sorts of beliefs seem to have an advantage because they explain a wide variety of phenomena (sustainability) and, because they are surprisingly different from most beliefs, are easy to remember and pass on to future generations (transmissibility) (Barrett 2004). It also claims to have found a cognitive faculty or set of faculties that detect the kind of design that is often alleged to support God's existence; we seem naturally disposed to treat nearly every kind of phenomena—whether human-made or natural—as designed or purposeful.[5] We may even have a natural immortality faculty and may instinctively believe that we have souls that are distinct from our bodies; for example, after people die, we continue talking with them in our minds as though they were still existing (this may partly explain widespread religious practices of ancestor worship) (Bering 2002, 2006).

Supernatural punishment theory leads us to expect that ancestral groups with high-moralizing gods will be more successful than groups without them.[6] Supernatural punishment theory helps explain the puzzling evolution of larger and larger human groups that depend on high levels of cooperation.[7] As group size increases, the ability to detect cheaters, who are a threat to the stability of the group, decreases. Because of the threat of such norm-violations to the group, detection of cheaters and their punishment is paramount but very costly. But the enforcement of moral norms, while costly, enhances cooperation and the benefits that cooperation makes possible. Belief in a supernatural punisher would transfer the "costs" of detection and punishment to (a) non-human agent(s), thereby reducing the human costs. If belief in "High Gods" that are active in human affairs and supportive of human morality can be inculcated in a group, moral defection can be diminished (and at a fairly low cost). In order to prevent cheaters, such agents must have access to strategic information—they must be superknowing about defections or cooperations that are hidden from merely human agents. And they must be believed to efficaciously exercise a kind of moral providence—to reward virtue and to punish vice. So supernatural punishment theory leads to the expectation of high-moralizing gods with strategic information who exercise moral providence. The bottom line: groups of god-fearing individuals will outcompete groups of non-believers (assuming roughly equal size and complexity).

Evidence supporting supernatural punishment theories is wide ranging. We can only here give the briefest sense of its empirical support. Studies show increased voluntary payment (when no one is watching) when a collection can has eyes drawn on it, and less cheating on computer-assisted exams when virtual eyeballs float on the screen (Bateson, Nettle, and Roberts 2006). When children are prompted with ghost-beliefs, they are less likely to give in to temptation when no one else is in the room. Religious groups with costly religious rituals show remarkably higher levels of cooperation and last vastly longer than secular groups (Sosis and Ruffle 2003). Finally, Dominic Johnson's survey of 186 people groups showed an extremely high correlation between cooperation and belief in moralizing high gods (Johnson 2005: 410–46).

Cognitive science of religion holds that religious belief is natural and will routinely take characteristic shapes and forms. The evolutionary psychology of religion suggests that religious beliefs that have been channeled into moralizing high gods can effectively overcome human selfishness necessary for the gain of cooperative benefits. Taken together, they suggest that successful human groups, including those in ancient China, will likely and repeatedly develop beliefs in high, moralizing, providential gods who exercise moral providence. Armed with this insight, what do we find when we carefully consider the ancient texts?

The High Deities of Pre-Qin Texts

Michael Loewe in the 1980s and Roel Sterckx more recently have shown that Early Chinese texts are littered with a panoply of extrahuman agents that make up diverse pantheons of figures (Loewe 2005 reprint: 17–18, Sterckx 2011). From the ritual functional agents of *shen* 神 and the ephemeral *gui* to the diverse angry spirits, forces, and malevolencies, many texts from this time reveal a rich and diverse lexicon and discourse on the extrahuman. Amongst these pantheon of figures sit two extrahuman agents who in many texts are assigned paramount or privileged roles in sacrificial rituals and discourses on the extrahuman—the High Deities of *Di* 帝 and *Shangdi* 上帝, which are understood as two different terms referring to the same agent, and *Tian* 天; these 'High Deities' rule above this panoply of lesser deities (Loewe 2005: 17).

Scholars such as K. C. Chang, Kelly James Clark, and Herrlee Glessner Creel have discussed some of the relationships between these two agents and their socio-political roles and the relationship to each other in the ancient dynasties of the Shang 商 (16th C–11th C BCE) and the Zhou 周 (11th C–475 BCE), with *Di/Shangdi* being argued to be the highest deity of the Shang with *Tian* replacing it at the top of the pantheons in the Zhou (Chang 1983: 33–34l, Clark 2005: 122, Creel 1970: 93–9). Keightley notes the strong associations with revered ancestors of the Shang royal line and *Di*'s greater, bureaucratic power when compared to other extrahumans (Keightley 1996: 253–4). Etymologically Keightley notes how the term *Di*, itself, can simply mean "sovereign," with the *Shang* of *Shangdi* indicated "superior," and was also employed in the names of the Shang kings and the mythological rulers of China and thus has a clear etymological association with socio-political power (Keightley 1996: 257).[8] Robert Eno points out how these agents are understood in high, if not pre-eminent, positions in sacrificial pantheons and are often invoked as reflecting or related to those with socio-political authority, particularly with regards to *Tian* and the Zhou Kings Eno (1990a: 23–4). In his studies on *Di*, Eno draws upon paleographic arguments to argue for earlier concepts of the term *Di* as being father, reinforcing the ancestral associations with the Shang royal line, something often argued by paleographic researchers of this term (Eno 2009: 41–102; Eno 1990[b]: 1–26). Though the realities of their prominent positions as High Deities and socio-political legitimacy are firmly established in prior research, a full analysis or survey of how these figures are represented in these texts remains to be completed, and much is still unclear about these terms. Their status as High Deities, something that transcends other deities, and their strong socio-political associations already show resonance with the arguments of supernatural punishment theory. However, for these arguments to hold, these extrahuman agents must be shown to be represented as moralizing agents possessing specialized knowledge who reward virtue and punish vice.

High Deities as Punishers and Rewarders

Despite what may seem like a very straightforward collection of twenty-eight or so texts composed by important cultural and historical figures transmitted to the modern period, these texts actually contain a vast quantity of information produced by many different hands throughout the entire Pre-Qin period. From the perspective of the religious material contained within in them, notably information on the High Deities that are the concern of this chapter, the number of representations and idioms concerning these extrahuman agents should reflect this diversity.

Indeed, when looking through the database of these passages, one does see a great diversity in terms of how these agents are represented and the capacities in which they are used in the texts. While often not provided detailed physical descriptions, in some passages these extrahuman agents are described in highly anthropomorphic form, often taking on the characteristics of rulers or sovereigns. In some passages, these agents are recipients of sacrifices while in others they are used in common curses. Hence, these texts reflect a spectrum of representations of the High Deities that were clearly of concern to these authors.

However, though there is great diversity, patterns and similarities present themselves suggesting representations that these authors divided in space and time-shared, and that what cognitive science of religion would expect. One of the most prominent ways in which these High Deities are represented is in the capacity of providing punishments or rewards to human recipients. These punishments and rewards are quite numerous, and when compared to other categories of representations seen in the database have proven to be the most variable. These agents issue forth generic punishments *fa* 罰 or calamities *huo* 禍 upon individuals or groups. Likewise, the rewards can also be generic, usually described as simply good fortune *fu* 福 or assistance *zhu* 助. More specific rewards range from these agents bestowing material rewards,[9] fecundity,[10] longevity,[11] internal powers and strengths,[12] portents and omens,[13] alleviating problems,[14] and even sagehood or transcendent states.[15] These agents also inflict specific punishments including famines, droughts and plagues,[16] disruptions to the natural world,[17] psychological problems,[18] abandonment,[19] and murder.[20]

One of the most common forms of punishment and reward is that of sociopolitical power. Given the nature of these texts as advocating good governance (Lewis 1999: 287–9), it is not surprising that such power and authority is granted and removed by these agents, as circumstances require. The sovereign is often both the intended audience of many of these texts and the subject who suffers these punishments or gains these rewards. Passages commonly show the sovereign's house or state collapsing through either unspecified means or invasion. The reward of rulers with socio-political power is also common, and resonates well with previous studies on *Di*, *Shangdi*, and *Tian* that point to their association with the legitimization of the ruling houses of the Shang and the Zhou.

Why, then, do these agents bestow these things to these subjects, most often the sovereign? In some of the passages seen, that these extrahuman agents engage in punishment and reward is simply passively stated as having occurred with no explicit explanation as to why. In several passages, however, these extrahuman agents explicitly give punishments or rewards because of reasons explained in the passage. These reasons are often of a moral dimension wherein the subjects are rewarded for proper behavior, usually for displaying virtue *de* 德, righteousness *yi* 義, and sincerity *xin* 信. Consequently, subjects who do not possess these qualities or are said to have transgressions *zui* 罪 are punished.

Statistical data on the over four hundred passages in Pre-Qin texts that represent *Di*, *Shangdi*, and *Tian* in these ways can be seen in Table 1.

These quantitative data show how in all of their occurrences punishments and rewards figure in more than a third of all passages featuring *Di* and *Tian* (though a little more than a quarter of those concerned with *Shangdi*). Additionally, in almost two-thirds of the passages where *Tian* is represented as punisher or rewarder, *Tian* is also represented in some capacity to moral providence. This is seen to be in 47 percent of the cases with *Di* and in 60 percent of the passages with *Shangdi*.

When breaking down the analysis by text, as is featured in Tables 2, 3, and 4, one begins to see greater nuances in the representations of these High Deities. One of the most marked differences evidenced by Tables 2 and 3 versus Table 4 is the greater representation of *Tian* as an extrahuman compared with *Di* and *Shangdi*. *Tian* is represented in the greatest number of Pre-Qin texts, twenty-two, in comparison to the twelve texts that feature *Di* as an extrahuman and the fourteen that feature *Shangdi*. This is also consistent with the far greater instances of *Tian* in general observed in Table 1. Furthermore, the number of texts where *Tian* is represented as punisher or rewarder is much greater—sixteen of the twenty-two texts. These texts are very diverse and represent a

Table 1 Instances of *Di*, *Shangdi*, and *Tian* in Pre-Qin texts.

	Total	Punishment and reward	P&R and morality	P&R and morality/ total punishment	P&R/total
Di	44	15	7	47%	34%
Shangdi	91	25	15	60%	27%
Tian	324	131	81	62%	40%

Table 2 Instances of *Di* as a punisher and rewarder.

Text	Total	*Di* 帝 Punishment and reward	P&R and morality	P&R and morality/ total P&R	P&R/total
Chuci	2	2	1	50%	100%
Guoyu	2	0	0		0
Laozi	1	0	0		0
Lunyu	1	0	0		0
Lüshi chunqiu	4	0	0		0
Mozi	5	0	0		0
Shangshu	7	3	2	67%	43%
Shijing	3	3	2	67%	100%
Xunzi	3	0	0		0
Yijing	3	3	0	0	100%
Yinwenzi	1	0	0		0
Zhuangzi	3	0	0		0
Zuozhuan	9	4	2	50%	44%

Table 3 Instances of *Shangdi* as a punisher and rewarder.

Text	Total	*Shangdi* 上帝 Punishment and reward	P&R and morality	P&R and morality/ total P&R	P&R/total
Chuci	2	2	0		100%
Guanzi	2	0	0		0
Guliang zhuan	1	0	0		0
Guoyu	11	1	0	9%	0
Lüshi chunqiu	9	2	1	22%	50%
Mengzi	3	0	0		0
Mozi	13	4	3	31%	75%
Shangshu	20	8	7	40%	87.5%
Shijing	13	8	4	62%	50%
Xiaojing	1	0	0		0
Xunzi	1	0	0		0
Yanzi chunqiu	4	0	0		0
Yijing	2	0	0		0
Zhouli	3	0	0		0
Zuozhuan	6	0	0		0

Table 4 Instances of *Tian* as a punisher and rewarder.

Text	Total	Tian 天 Punishment and reward	P&R and morality	P&R and morality/ total P&R	P&R/total
Chuci	3	0	0		0
Gongyang zhuan	4	1	1	100%	25%
Guanzi	5	2	2	100%	40%
Guliang zhuan	5	3	0	0	60%
Guoyu	40	25	13	52%	63%
Hanfeizi	10	0	0		0
Laozi	7	0	0		0
Lunyu	8	1	0	0	13%
Lüshi chunqiu	18	8	4	50%	44%
Mengzi	8	6	5	83%	75%
Mozi	8	2	2	100%	25%
Shangshu	36	22	13	59%	61%
Shijing	46	14	7	50%	30%
Sunzi bingfa	2	0	0		0
Wuzi	1	0	0		0
Xiaojing	1	0	0		0
Xunzi	18	3	3	100%	17%
Yanzi chunqiu	9	3	2	67%	33%
Yijing	14	1	0	0	7%
Zhouli	4	1	1	100%	25%
Zhuangzi	20	7	5	71%	35%
Zuozhuan	57	32	23	62%	40%

large swath of the textual corpus transmitted from the Pre-Qin; statistically, the instances of *Tian* being a punisher or rewarder in comparison to the total number of passages where the extrahuman *Tian* is represented vary by text, as seen in the final column, being 75 percent of all cases in the *Mengzi* to only 7 percent in the *Yijing*.

Table 4 also shows a strong association between representations of *Tian* as a moralizing agent alongside punishment and reward. In the sixteen texts that represent *Tian* as a punisher or rewarder, only three—the *Guliang zhuan*, *Analects* (*Lunyu*), and *Yijing*—do not show any additional representations as a moralizing agent.[21] In the remaining thirteen, the *Lüshi chunqiu* and *Shijing* have the lowest number of passages where both representations are seen—at

50 percent. Several passages always represent the two together, while it occurs in most passages in most texts, reinforcing that the two are most definitely seen as strongly associated.

When looking only at Tables 2 and 3, one sees a greater restriction of *Di* and *Shangdi* as punishers and rewarders in texts, only five and six of the texts in each respective case. In both cases, they are the *Chuci*, *Lüshi chunqiu*, *Mozi*, *Shangshu*, and *Shijing* with the *Guoyu* also representing *Shangdi* as a punisher or rewarder. The passages in these texts, too, generally represent *Di* and *Shangdi* in the capacity of moral providence. As seen in column four of these tables, this is observed in almost all cases, save for the *Guoyu* which never represents *Shangdi* in terms of punishment and reward and moral providence in the same passage. When looking at this limited corpus as a whole, one observes that these texts share little in common in terms of providence and authorship and represent texts from the entire breadth of the Pre-Qin period. Furthermore when compared with Table 4, save for the *Chuci*, all represent *Tian* as an extrahuman and a punisher and rewarder in addition.

This statistical information strongly supports the presence of idioms and paradigms related to supernatural punishment theory in Pre-Qin texts. As cognitive science would hold, these representations seem to be relatively widespread throughout the corpus of Pre-Qin texts. These High Deities are clearly being represented as higher agents possessed of some moralizing characteristic who engage in issuing punishments and rewards. However, these quantitative data can only provide some clues and highlight the larger trends to how these idioms actually function in these texts, particularly if, as supernatural punishment theory holds, these High Deities punish vice and reward virtue. Furthermore, though it seems Gernet and Yü are wrong in asserting a paradigm of non-theism to religion in Pre-Qin China, can it be argued that these idioms and paradigms are isolated to specific periods or thinkers in Pre-Qin China, or, as cognitive science would hold, they are universal?

The Case of the *Mozi*

Scholars of Chinese philosophy have long claimed the *Mozi* as an "uncharacteristic" text for its highly anthropomorphized, extrahuman agents. A. C. Graham has noted that these extrahuman agents, *Tian*, amongst them, can be understood as punishers and rewarders. Graham points to the Understanding Ghosts III *Minggui xia* 明鬼下, Will of Heaven I, II, III *Tianzhi shang, zhong, xia*

天志上, 中, 下, and Antifatalism I, II, III *Feiming shang, zhong xia* 非命上, 中, 下 sections as best exemplifying this view, stating that the *Mozi* argues "that men will act morally only if they cease to regard changes of fortune as their destiny, and come to recognize that Heaven [*Tian*] and the spirits reward the good and punish the wicked."[38]

Graham's interest in extrahuman agents in the *Mozi* is motivated by his constant contrasting of the ideas of the text to those found in the "Confucian" texts. "Confucian" texts, he claims, question whether these extrahuman agents exist and adhere to a more secular philosophy in line with Gernet and Yü. The *Mozi*, then, is unique in its assertion of extrahuman agents like *Tian* as divine punishers and rewarders (Graham 1978: 13–14). However, such a dichotomy between "the Confucians" and "the Mohists" is problematic if, as seems likely, no such cohesive group as "Confucians" existed in the Pre-Qin period, and no people from that time would identify themselves as such.[22]

Graham is not operating entirely from misconceptions about the philosophical discourse of this time; the *Mozi* itself is full of criticisms of ideas put forward by characters identified with the philosophical figure of Confucius such as Mencius. For example, in a dialogue between he and Mozi, Mencius raises ideas about the lack of deities in ritual only to be refuted by Mozi (*Mozi* 2006: 48.690). But to assume that this is a discourse against all things "Confucian" is misleading—no such distinction is present in this specific passage nor are texts labeled as "Confucian" bereft of extrahumans.

Indeed, the representation of *Tian* as punisher is found in the texts considered paramount in understanding Confucius, such as in the *Analects* 6:28 where Confucius asks Heaven to punish him if he has committed any wrongdoing:

> The master had an audience with Nanzi, and Zilu was not pleased. The Master swore an oath, saying, "If I have done anything wrong, may Heaven [*Tian*] punish me! May Heaven [*Tian*] punish me!"

And in *Mengzi* VA:5, where Wan Zhang 萬章 asks Mencius how it was that the King Shun came to be given the throne. Expecting that the answer is to be that Yao, bestowed it upon him, Mencius asserts that such is not the case, and rather it was bestowed by Heaven who, along with the people, were to have accepted Shun because:

> [w]hen he was put in charge of sacrifices, the hundred gods enjoyed them. This showed that Heaven accepted him. When he was put in charge of affairs, they were kept in order and the people were content. This showed that the people accepted him. Heaven gave it to him, and the people gave it to him. Hence I said,

"The Emperor cannot give the Empire to another." Shun assisted Yao for twenty-eight years. This is something which could not be brought about by man, but by Heaven alone.

(Lau 1970: 143–4)

Or consider the *Xunzi's Youzuo* 宥坐 where the disciple of Confucius, Zilu, asks Confucius why he and his followers must endure hardship when *Tian* is meant to reward the good:

Zilu went before him and asked, "From what I have heard, as for those who do good, Heaven [*Tian*] repays them with good fortune. As for those who do bad, Heaven [*Tian*] repays them with calamities. Now, you have accumulated virtue, gathered righteousness and held close the beautiful, yet we have been walking for many days. Why do we dwell like hermits?".

(*Xunzi* 1988: 28:516)

Zilu's claim assumes a certain and expected relationship between *Tian* and the good. The theistic aspects of the *Analects* are further discussed in Edward Slingerland's translation (Slingerland 2003: 62) and by Kelly James Clark (Clark 2005). Furthermore, Robert Eno has noted numerous, what he argues to be rhetorical rather than theoretical, uses of *Tian*, among which punishment and moral qualities are found, in his study of the *Tian* in the *Mengzi* and *Xunzi* (Eno 1990a: 102–4, 167–8).

It is clear, then, that an understanding of the High Deities as punishers and rewarders is not peculiar to the *Mozi* nor does it seem to accord with any "Mohist"—"Confucian" difference. Indeed, cognitive science would argue that such idioms are quite common, and representations of the High Deities have already been shown to be statistically present in a variety of texts. The representations in these three passages certainly accord well with the ideas of supernatural punishment theory, but are these idioms of punishment for the wicked and reward for the good as widespread through the time of Pre-Qin China as they seem to be philosophically?

Earliest Writings

The understanding of extrahuman agents as punishers and rewarders originating in the *Mozi* can easily be overturned by the wide distribution of these representations in Pre-Qin texts and in texts that pre-date the *Mozi*. Indeed, these representations are found in the earliest strata of Pre-Qin texts, the *Shangshu* 尚書 and *Shijing* 詩經 where they are widely articulated (as seen in

Table 2). Both of these texts are composed of material, probably both orally and textually transmitted, that originates over a large span of time from the Western Zhou (11th C BCE–771 BCE) and Spring and Autumn (770–475 BCE) periods, though the *Shangshu* contains some material composed after this and into the Han (Shaughnessy 1993: 377–80).

Of the sections of the *Shangshu* composed prior to the Qin, one sees High Deities issuing punishments and rewards in all strata of the text—from passages like the *Duofang* 多方 and *Duoshi* 多士 dated to the Western Zhou to passages like the *Gaoyaomo* 皋陶謨, *Tangshi* 湯誓, *Tanggao* 湯告, and *Yixun* 伊訓 which are dated to the Spring and Autumn period, that all three of these terms appear in terms of punishment and rewards is temporally well-distributed, even appearing in the passages dated to the Warring and States and the Han such as the *Taishi* 泰誓 and *Xianyouyide* 鹹有一德.

In the previous chapter, we read about many of the aspects of punishment and rewards related to these extrahuman agents in this text, and so it need not be restated here. However, it is worth looking at the example of the *Duofang* to understand some of the typical ways in which this representation of the gods as punisher is articulated in the passages in the Shangshu:

Shangshu 尚書 *Duofang* 多方[23]

The Duke of Zhou said, 'The king speaks to the following effect: "Ho! I make an announcement to you of the four states, and the numerous (other) regions. Ye who were the officers and people of the prince of Yin, I have dealt very leniently as regards your lives, as ye all know. You kept reckoning greatly on (some) decree of Heaven [*Tian*], and did not keep with perpetual awe before your thoughts (the preservation of) your sacrifices. '"God [*Di*] sent down correction on Xia, but the sovereign (only) increased his luxury and sloth, and would not speak kindly to the people. He showed himself dissolute and dark, and would not yield for a single day to the leadings of God [*Di*]- this is what you have heard. He kept reckoning on the decree of God [*Di*] (in his favour), and did not cultivate the means for the people's support. By great inflictions of punishment also he increased the disorder of the states of Xia. The first cause (of his evil course) was the internal misrule, which made him unfit to deal well with the multitudes. Nor did he endeavour to find and employ men whom he could respect, and who might display a generous kindness to the people; but where any of the people of Xia were covetous and fierce, he daily honoured them, and they practised cruel tortures in the cities. Heaven [*Tian*] on this sought a (true) lord for the people, and made its distinguished and favouring decree light on Tang the Successful, who punished and destroyed the sovereign of Xia.

(Legge 2000b: 214–15)

Betraying the *Shangshu*'s constant concern with socio-political authority, this passage is an excerpt from a speech purportedly given by the Duke of Zhou 周公, a legendary culture-hero who served as regent to the young King Wen at the start of the Zhou dynasty. In the above excerpt, he is expounding to the defeated vassals of the state of Shang and explaining how their defeat by the hands of the Zhou mirrors the defeat of the Xia by the Shang centuries before. His explanation for the causes of this is couched in the metaphysical and assigned as the actions of *Tian* and *Di*, the latter of whom is said to have "sent correction on Xia." The last king of the Xia ignored this correction and continued to behave wantonly and cruelly. The duke explains then that this internal misrule translated to misrule throughout the land, until his transgressions were such that *Tian* is said to have "sought a (true) lord for the people" and chose Tang, the first ruler of the Shang, to punish and destroy the Xia.

On the rhetorical level, this story serves as an explication of what has happened to the Shang and justification of the overthrow of them by the Zhou. The earlier Shang overthrow of the Xia in the same manner was due to the choice of the extrahuman agents *Di* and *Tian*. The highly moralistic language of the passage couched the last king of Xia as morally bankrupt while Tang, the first king of Shang, is morally superior. This moral behavior prompts both *Di* and *Tian* to take action. In this first instance, by sending down a correction, meant to be a warning, to the last king of the Xia who, instead of mending his licentious ways, continues them. This prompts the second action, the searching for a virtuous ruler by *Tian* who upon finding him is said to have favored him to overthrow the Tang.

In this passage one sees that these extrahuman agents are identified with proper moral behavior and also search for it in others. Furthermore, they are observed to operate as agents, of their own accord, and to select rulers that show proper moral conduct and to attempt to rectify the behavior of those of ill repute by issuing them warnings. Should these rulers not heed these warning, they are punished with the loss of socio-political power and its transference to the one whom the extrahuman agent selects.

This idiom of an extrahuman agent identifying the moral and rewarding them with socio-political power, while punishing the wicked by taking that power away, often through invasion by those who have been rewarded, is typical in the *Shangshu* and consistent with supernatural punishment theory. From the perspective of extrahuman agents, it shows how the High Deities are understood in the texts. In keeping with what has been statistically argued, and what Graham has noted as a common idiom in the *Mozi*, *Di*, and *Tian*, in this passage, the High Deities are clearly portrayed as punishers and rewarders who do so in accordance with the respective moral character of those being punished or rewarded.

These representations and idiom are common in the other passages of the *Shangshu* and can be found in one of the other earliest texts of the Pre-Qin period—the *Shijing*.

Shijing Tianbao 天保 (Excerpt)

Heaven [*Tian*] protects and establishes thee,
With the greatest security;
Makes thee entirely virtuous,
That thou mayest enjoy every happiness;
Grants thee much increase,
So that thou hast all in abundance.
Heaven [*Tian*] protects and establishes thee,
It grants thee all excellence,
So that thine every matter is right,
And thou receivest every Heavenly [*Tian*]favour.
It sends down to thee long-during happiness,
Which the days are not sufficient to enjoy.
Heaven [*Tian*] protects and establishes thee,
So that in every thing thou dost prosper,
Like the high hills, and the mountain masses,
Like the topmost ridges, and the greatest bulks;
That, as the stream ever coming on,
Such is thine increase.

(Legge 2000b: 255–6)

The *Shijing* is a collection of about three hundred poems that are believed to have emerged in the Western and Eastern Zhou and have come to serve various intellectual, ritual, and socio-political purposes (Loewe 1993: 415). *Tian*, in the passage above, blesses the one with virtue and excellence, and is ultimately responsible for one's prosperity (through *Tian*'s protection and establishment of the individual). Using poetic rhetoric of verse repetition and organic imagery to reinforce this point regarding *Tian*, it also elucidates some of the more common modes of representation of *Tian* (and indeed the other High Deities throughout the poems of the *Shijing*) and shows how these agents can be understood as punishers and rewarders in much the same way as was observed in the *Shangshu*. *Tian* bestows moral qualities upon those under its protection, and this protection evokes an air of the socio-political observed in the *Shangshu* (although the idiom of morally good behavior being rewarded with socio-political power is not present, nor is there any explanation as to why *Tian* is rewarding the individual in this poem).

However, in other poems of the *Shijing*, notably *Ban* 板, *Huangyi* 皇矣, and *Sangrou* 桑柔, elements of such idioms do present themselves. *Ban* follows a similar rhetorical structure to *Tianbao*, by stating what *Tian*, or in the opening stanza *Shangdi*, does in the opening line of each stanza, describing how *Shangdi* "has reversed [His usual course of procedure]" and *Tian* is "now sending down calamities," "now exercising oppression," and "is now displaying its anger," amongst others (Legge 2000b reprint[b]: 499). These stanzas then proceed to describe how and why these agents are doing such things. This is mainly explained as due to the moral impropriety of the people and the nation. The people are then encouraged to amend their ways by engaging in unspecified proper behavior and supporting a just state. The closing stanza of the passage, as seen below, provides explicit representation of *Tian*, pointing to it having mental and emotional capacities, something that the last, warning line explains as allowing it to understand the behavior of individuals.

Shijing 詩經 *Ban* 板 (Excerpt)

Revere the anger of Heaven [*Tian*],
And presume not to make sport or be idle.
Revere the changing moods of Heaven [*Tian*],
And presume not to drive about [at your pleasure].
Great Heaven [*Tian*] is intelligent,
And is with you in all your goings.
Great Heaven [*Tian*] is clear-seeing,
And is with you in your wandering and indulgences.

(Legge 2000b: 499)

As expected from supernatural punishment theory, *Tian* is portrayed as possessing strategic information—an awareness of morally significant behaviors (which may or may not be visible to human agents). Based on the gathering of this strategic information, punishment and reward are justly distributed.

In the opening lines of the *Huangyi* below, a highly anthropomorphized *Shangdi* is recounted to have sojourned through the world in search of a person of proper moral conduct to be made sovereign. *Shangdi*'s choice of the legendary King Da once again reinforces the idiom of the High Deities rewarding the moral with socio-political power. In turn, the passage proceeds to describe these actions of *Shangdi* in bestowing socio-political power to moral rulers, while punishing the immoral rulers by taking it away. Couched in much more socio-political terms than the previous two passages from the *Shijing*, this passage shows a great deal in common with those sections of the *Shangshu* providing justifications for the overthrow of the *Shang* (though this poem in the *Shijing* performs it with a far more lyrical and metaphoric rhetoric).

Shijing Huangyi 皇矣

    Great is God [*Shangdi*],
Beholding this lower world in majesty.
He surveyed the four quarters [of the kingdom],
Seeking for someone to give settlement to the people.
Those two [earlier] dynasties,
Had failed to satisfy Him with their government;
So throughout the various States,
He sought and considered,
For one on which he might confer the rule.
Hating all the great [States],
He turned His kind regards on the west,
And there gave a settlement [to king Da].
    [King Da] raised up and removed,
The dead trunks, and the fallen trees.
He dressed and regulated,
The bushy clumps, and the [tangled] rows.
He opened up and cleared,
The tamarix trees, and the stave-trees.
He hewed and thinned,
The mountain-mulberry trees.

(Legge 2000b: 448–57)

Throughout these two texts, the idea that these extrahuman agents can be understood as punishers and rewarders is clear. Numerous passages in both attest to such a representation, though the dynamics of that representation can be somewhat fluid. In some instances, they are simply passive statements, admonishments, or arguments that things have been given or taken by one of the High Deities. However, idioms of the moralizing nature of the subject being punished or rewarded are also consistent. In keeping with the socio-political readings of these texts, socio-political power awarded to or taken from a ruler on account of that ruler's moral state, good for reward and bad for punishment, is consistent with the statements made regarding idioms of extrahumans Graham noticed in the *Mozi*. As such, the earliest strata of texts in the Pre-Qin period clearly configure these agents as punishers and rewarders, and certainly conform to what is expected in regards to supernatural punishment theory.

Warring States

Most transmitted texts from the Pre-Qin period are dated from the fourth and third centuries BCE, with the traditional explanation for this being the massive social upheavals that the societies and the populations underwent at this time that inspired many thinkers to espouse their ideas. However, the prestige placed on many of the writings from this time that later generations, such as the Han, placed upon them has also contributed to their transmission, including the transmission of their ideas on religion, to the modern day (Graham 1989: 2–4).

Some of the earliest texts from this period, and most likely containing material before the fourth century, are the *Guoyu* 國語 and the *Zuozhuan* 左傳, two texts of very similar provenance and content. Both are chronicles of the Spring and Autumn period (770–476 BCE), recounting events from that time with narrative and dialogue. In some instances, this takes the form of proto-historiography, but, like many texts from this time, prescriptive socio-political discourse, alongside prescriptive religious discourse, sits alongside the descriptive characteristics of these texts, much like what has been seen in the *Mozi*, *Mencius*, *Xunzi*, *Shangshu*, and *Shijing*.[24]

Guoyu Jin 晉 2:3

The Duke of Guo dreamt that he was in the ancestral temple where there was a *shen* with a man's face, white fur and the claws of a tiger. It grasped a battle-axe and stood on the western eaves of the veranda. The lord was scared and ran, the deity said, 'Do not run! The Thearch [*Di*] has issued a command, "I have sent Jin to enter[25] through your gate."' The lord showed respect by kowtowing. He awoke, and summoned Shi Yin to divine this. He replied, 'If it is as your majesty says, then it was Rushou.[26] He is Heaven [*Tian*]'s *shen* of Punishment. Heaven [*Tian*] employs appropriate officials.' The lord had him imprisoned and further sent for the important people of the state to applaud the dream. Zhou Zhiqiao[27] told all of his clan, 'The masses say that Guo will perish before long. Now I believe it as well. The sovereign has not thought things out and applauds the entrance of a larger state.[28] In our case, how will we recover? I have heard this, "When a large state is with the Way, a small state entering it is called submission. When a small state is arrogant, a large state entering it is called punishment." When the people are hard pressed by the sovereign's extravagance, they will thus succeed in disobeying his orders. Now in praising his dream, the extravagance has surely been extended. This is Heaven [*Tian*] capturing him and holding him to a mirror through increasing his illness. The people are sick of his attitude and Heaven [*Tian*] also deceives him. A large state comes to execute him, and when issuing commands, they are overturned. His ancestral lands have already fallen.

The Feudal Lords have grown distant from him and the inner and outer are without close relation. Who is there in this that will save him? I do not bear to wait! I will go.' He then went to Jin with his family. In six years, the state of Guo had then perished.[29]

This passage concerns a *shen* that it identifies as Rushou and the warning that it makes to the lord of the state of Guo. This *shen* is apparently sent by *Di* and *Tian*, which the passage seems to treat as the same thing, in a dream to provide this warning that is quoted from *Di*. The use of dreams as a medium through which *Di* and *Tian* speak to rulers is not uncommon in the *Zuozhuan* and *Guoyu*. Such a thing speaks to the abilities that these texts represent these extrahumans as having, but it also touches upon the socio-political dimension of representation seen in all earlier texts discussed. In the *Guoyu*'s Jin 2:3 passage, this dimension manifests in the extrahuman's communication with the lord, the socio-political nature of the punishment the lord suffers from in not heeding the warning of *Di* and *Tian* to mend his ways and the relationship between the *shen* Rushou and *Di* and *Tian*, in which Rushou is identified as the punisher of *Tian* and is said to be employed by *Tian* for this purpose.

The text's overall didactic matches the idiom observed in the previous examples from Pre-Qin texts concerning the High Deities—improper rulers will be punished for their improprieties, usually through the loss of their state. This passage in the *Guoyu*, however, is interesting in providing narrative descriptions of both the *shen* and its relationship to *Di* and *Tian* that offer greater detail to the process of punishment that these extrahumans carry out and clearly shows these High Deities can certainly be understood in these texts within the framework of supernatural punishment theory-moralizing agents who punish vice and reward virtue.

Zuozhuan Xuan 3:3

The Prince of Chu attacked Luhun Zhirong[30] and then reached the Luo river where he displayed his army in full view on the borders of Zhou. King Ding sent Wangsun Man[31] to work things out with the Prince of Chu. The Prince of Chu heard about the size and weight of the cauldrons from him.[32] He replied, "I rely on virtue, not on cauldrons. In the past, just when the Xia had virtue, distant lands painted things and tribute money came from the nine shepherds. They cast cauldrons with the images of things, and when the hundred things were put onto them, they were complete. This made the people understand the divine and the wicked. Thus when the people entered the rivers, swamps, mountains and forests, they did not encounter the improper. And as for the demons, monsters and beasties, none were able to encounter them. Then they were able to bring harmony between the upper and the lower so as to inherit the gift of Heaven [*Tian*]. When Jie had sullied virtue, the cauldrons moved to Shang for six hundred years. When Zhou of Shang terrorized and brutalized, the cauldrons moved to Zhou. When virtue is beautiful and clear, although they are small, they are important. When their wickedness turns round to sullied confusion, although they are large, they are unimportant. Heaven [*Tian*] blesses clear virtue on those who have steadfastness. King Cheng established the cauldrons in Jiaru. Divinations have proceeded for thirty generations and seven hundred years because this is what is commanded by Heaven [*Tian*]. Even though the virtue of Zhou wanes, Heaven [*Tian*]'s command has yet to change. Whether the cauldrons are important or unimportant is something that cannot yet be asked."

This passage claims that the longevity and duration of a dynasty and indeed the socio-political legitimacy with which that dynasty reigns is something that "is commanded by Heaven [*Tian*]." The exposition is prompted by the impressive cauldrons, symbols of socio-political authority, that the Zhou kings possess. Though intended to awe the attacking Prince of Chu into submission, the prince counters by commenting that the cauldrons are of no concern to him; rather, he values the moral quality of virtue. To the Prince of Chu these cauldrons are not a source of virtue but are, rather, a by-product of it, cast by the morally proper to instruct the people; though they may be large and impressive, in the hands of the immoral, they are not important. According to the Prince, socio-political authority is a reward by *Tian* to people of virtue, and as such this is what he respects. This exposition prompts the reader to understand that the Prince of Chu will not attack the Zhou, as they are still virtuous and rewarded by Heaven with socio-political power. From the perspective of extrahumans, this passage once again represents *Tian* in the idiom of punishment and reward. In terms of the historiography developed by these texts, one again can see a justification of the changing of dynasties through the representation of these agents as punishers and rewarders in this passage.

One could argue that given the proximity in time that these two texts have with the earlier *Shangshu* and *Shijing*, these idioms and representations could represent a Late Zhou/Early Warring States understanding of these extrahumans that changes in the middle and late Warring States. This would not hold with arguments in cognitive science that would argue for a greater, more temporally, and geographically blind set of religious paradigms and idioms, such as supernatural punishment theory, owing to basic human cognitive faculties.

Indeed, representations as punishers and rewarders can be observed throughout texts from the entire Warring States, as indicated through the roughly 3rd C BCE *Mozi*, *Mencius*, and *Xunzi* already discussed and by a text dated to the very close of the Warring States, the *Lüshi chunqiu*.

A huge compendium of a diverse array of topics and subjects, this text is representative of a world-building texts, what Mark Edward Lewis points out as the start of an "encyclopedic epoch" of writing, wherein a prescriptive microcosm of the world is constructed within the text, a genre that becomes dominant in the early Han (Lewis 1999b: 303–8). As such, extrahuman agents, such as the High Deities, are also represented in this microcosm constructed by the text and tend to appear often in sections devoted to socio-political and religious discourse.

Lüshi chunqiu 6:4

King Wen asked, "What steps do you suggest that I take to avert it?"

They replied, "Initiate projects and encourage the multitude to enlarge the city walls. Surely this could avert it!"

King Wen said, "No, I cannot permit that. Heaven [*Tian*] exhibits inauspicious signs when it intends to punish the guilty. I must certainly be guilty of something, and that is why Heaven [*Tian*] has done this—to punish me. Now were I to initiate projects and encourage the multitude to enlarge the city walls, that would simply multiply my guilt. No, I cannot permit it!"

They replied, "Alter your conduct and multiply your good deeds in order to avert it. Surely this could evade such consequences."

King Wen replied, "I, Chang, am requested to alter my conduct and multiply my good deeds in order to avert it".

(Knoblock and Riegel 2000: 164–5)

This passage explains proper socio-political behavior through the use of historical parables, a common trope in Warring States texts. The dialogue between King Wen of Zhou and his ministers is prompted by the occurrence of several earthquakes that occur after the King fell ill for five days. The ministers inform him that these are negative signs and urge him to "avert disaster."

This passage marks a change, in contrast to the *Shangshu*, from the expository speeches given by culture-heroes to a narrative in which culture-heroes ask the advice of their ministers, a trope seen in other Warring States texts like the *Mencius* and *Xunzi*. In terms of extrahuman representation, the idea that *Tian* is a punisher and does so for moral and socio-political reasons is still very much apparent in this passage. The King of Zhou argues that his illness and the earthquake, inauspicious signs, are punishments from *Tian*, something given only to the guilty. Although his ministers at first encourage him to urge on the masses, he states that as the faults are his, they are not the responsibility of the masses. The ministers then advise him to cultivate his own moral behavior to avert disaster, which in the remainder of the passage states the King of Wen did. According to proper moral behavior, which is associated with ritual, the reader is told the inauspicious signs disappeared and he reigned for fifty-one years.[33]

That inauspicious signs and calamities are punishment inflicted by *Tian* and *Shangdi* is emphasized elsewhere in this section, in 6:5 a list of ill omens is provided, often revolving around natural disasters, strange signs in the sky or oddities appearing in the countryside. The *Lüshi chunqiu*'s argument as to why this happens is again explicitly stated as:

Lüshi chunqiu 呂民春秋 **6:5**

If these anomalies appear in a state, but the ruler is not sufficiently alarmed to change his ways quickly, then the Supreme Sovereign [*Shangdi*] will send down misfortune, with catastrophes and disasters quickly following. The lord will cruelly perish and there will be no reprieve. The populace will flee, overwhelmed by starvation in less than a day.

(Knoblock and Riegel 2000: 170)

Furthermore, the idiom of extrahuman reward of the morally good is argued in other sections of the text. Consider *Lüshi chunqiu* 9:2 below, which depicts another didactic historical episode of another culture-hero, Tang 湯, the founder of the Shang, and whose rise to power over the Xia, as rewarded by *Tian*, was also recounted in the *Duofang* of the *Shangshu*.

Lüshi chunqiu 9:2

In the past, when Tang conquered the Xia and put the world aright, there had been great drought with no harvest for five years. Tang thereupon offered a prayer at Singling in which he offered his own body as the pledge, beseeching: "If I, the One Man, am guilty, let the punishment not reach the myriad peoples. If the myriad peoples are guilty, let it rest on me, the One Man. Do not let the One Man's lack of diligence cause the Supreme Sovereign [*Shangdi*] and the ghosts and spirits to harm the lives of the people." Thereupon, he cut his hair, put his hands in manacles, and had himself prepared in lieu of the usual animals as the offering in a sacrifice to beseech the blessings of the Supreme Sovereign [*Shangdi*]. The people were overjoyed, and the rains came as in a deluge. Thus, Tang influenced the transforming powers of the ghosts and spirits and the course of human events.

(Knoblock and Riegel 2000: 210)

Conclusion

These few examples vindicate supernatural punishment theory's expectation, even in China, of High Deities as punishers and rewarders. This is not an understanding isolated to specific texts, or portions of texts, that represent a particular genre of literature (say, "Confucian") or period of time within the Pre-Qin corpus, but rather representation that can be found throughout numerous different texts from the beginnings of Chinese literature, as seen in the *Shangshu* and *Shijing* to the end of the Warring States and the dawn of Imperial China in the *Lüshi chunqiu*. These representations manifest themselves in the earlier works of historiography as evidenced by the *Zuozhuan* and *Guoyu* and even in the intellectual discourses of the *Analects* (*Lunyu*), *Mozi*, and the *Zhuangzi*.

These examples are but a handful, though, of the more than 400 other instances throughout other texts where these extrahuman agents are observed to engage in punishing or rewarding others, as shown in Tables 1 and 2, and as such should only be taken to be the most representative of what is clearly a dominant understanding of these agents in Pre-Qin texts. The representation as punishers and rewarders is often coupled into an idiom where these extrahuman agents are also represented in moral terms in various capacities. In some instances they are the source of moral providence while in others they are its guardian or defender. Whatever the case, they have strategic information about the morality or the lack thereof in humans, and, based on this information, provide proper punishments and rewards, wherein they punish vice and reward virtue as would be expected from the understanding of High Deities in a large population as described by supernatural punishment theory.[34]

Contrary to arguments of a lack of theism in early China and Graham's assertion that idioms of moralizing High Deities who are punishers and rewarders are common only in certain works like the *Mozi*, it is clear that such ideas were surprisingly common throughout texts produced at this time, often forming cautionary tales and moralizing advice to these text's intended readers. Moreover, it is clear then that rather than being some small, ancillary realm dealt with by unpopular thinkers, or a vague enigmatic mess that cannot be understood, the realm of the extrahuman was an active area of engagement for many writers and thinkers in the Pre-Qin who felt no compunctions in evoking it when need be and no problems in engaging in discourse on it when they felt it necessary.

9

Lesser Gods of the Pre-imperial Era

The sovereign is the master of gods and aspirant of the people.
(*Zuozhuan* 1987: 1016)

The categorization of Heaven (*Tian* 天) and *Di/Shangdi* as High Deities implies a reciprocal category of extrahumans—lower or lesser deities. Lesser deities abound throughout pre-Qin texts, often in terse and offhand remarks that suggest that the readers of these texts were familiar with such extrahuman agents. Some texts, however, expand on these extrahumans, providing fascinating insights into how pre-Qin texts understood the extrahuman.

The above quote from the *Zuozhuan* 左傳 explicitly represents gods, a ubiquitous type of Lesser Deity (Winslett 2014: 948), in socio-political terms. It equates lesser deities with the people as equally subordinate to the sovereign. Socio-political relationships are also seen in representations of the High Deity, though its relationship to the sovereign tended to be one of superiority or authority over rather than subordination under. The depiction of lesser deities as involved in socio-political relationships is common in the *Zuozhuan* and in other texts from the pre-imperial period as well.

Gods, an expedient term for *shen* 神, are by far the most frequently found of the various agents that are understood as lesser deities in nineteen texts ascribed to the pre-imperial period; gods vastly outnumber the second most common agent, ghosts (*gui* 鬼), in almost all texts, except for the *Mozi* 墨子 where ghosts outnumber gods, four to one (Winslett 2014: 950–1). The two terms give rise to a coordinate compound *guishen* 鬼神 that maps onto the English term "deities," and in many texts is used as a collective noun for lesser deities and sometimes for high deities as well.

Although lesser deities are scattered amongst numerous texts, three texts stand out with the highest frequency of these terms—the *Zuozhuan*, *Guoyu*, and *Zhuangzi*. These three collectively include over half of all mentions of gods, with the *Zhuangzi* having the second highest mention of ghosts after the *Mozi* (Winslett 2014: 950–1). Since the matter of ghosts in the *Mozi* has been dealt with in previous research (see Wong and Loy 2004), this chapter will look at the representation of gods in the *Zuozhuan*, *Guoyu*, and *Zhuangzi*. Though dealing with different issues from different knowledge communities, common patterns of representation emerge among these texts that help shape our understanding of the lesser deities.

Zuozhuan 左傳

Zhao 昭20.6

The Marquess of Qi[1] came down with scabies followed by malaria, but after a year, he did not heal. There were many retainers of the Feudal Lords asking about the illness present. Liang Qiuju[2] and Yi Kuan said to the lord, "We have served the deities richly and have made additions for the previous lords. Now, our lord is ill which makes the Feudal Lords worry. This is the fault of the supplicators and scribes. The Feudal Lords do not know that they say we are not respectful. Why doesn't our lord order the executions of Supplicator Gu and Scribe Yin so as to dispense with the retainers." The lord was happy and told Yanzi.[3] Yanzi said, "In the days of the Covenant of Song (546 BCE), Qu Jian asked Zhao Wu[4] about the virtue of Fan Kuai.[5] Zhao Wu said, 'Of the houses of the princes that serve government, it is said about the state of Jin that it exhausts emotion and is without private concerns. When their supplicators and scribes perform sacrifices, they display sincerity and are not ashamed. The service of their houses is without suspicion and their supplicators and scribes did not pray.' Jian said this to King Kang.[6] King Kang said, 'Man and gods are without grievances because it is suitable that the light of the prince that assists the five sovereigns[7] be taken as the master of the Feudal Lords.'" The Lord said, 'Ju and Kuan say that if I am able to serve deities, then I should put to death the supplicator and scribe. You have said this. What is the reason?' He replied, "If the sovereign has virtue, then the outside and inside will not be abolished, the high and the low will not have grievances, and he will make effort without deviant services. His supplicators and scribes will put forward his sincerity without ashamed hearts. It is thus that when the deities are feasted in sacrifice and the state receives their good fortune, the scribes and the supplicators will participate in this. The reason that people have abundant good fortune and long life is because they are sincere to the sovereign's commands, and they will speak of loyalty and sincerity to the deities. If there is by chance a licentious sovereign, the outside and inside will be partisan and wicked, and the high and low will be angered and ill. Actions and works will be wrong and deviant, and indulgences and desires will be oppressive and selfish. They will raise platforms and dig pools, ring bells and set girls dancing. They will cut down the people's efforts and plunder from those that are assembled so as to complete their deviations and not consider those after them. If oppressive tyrants are licentious and indulgent and their wanton actions are without limit, they will not have any misgivings, ponder on the slanders and criticisms or fear the deities. If the gods are angry and the people suffering, and they are without repentance in their hearts, then when the supplicators and scribes put forward their sincerity, this will be speaking of wickedness. If they then for instance lose the numerous niceties, then this will be rectifying the accusations. If promotions and demotions are without retirement, then they will be empty and bring about toadying. Thereupon, when the deities are not feasted in sacrifice and their states are visited by calamities, the scribes and the supplicators will participate in this. The reason that people are greatly confused is because of being violent to the sovereign's commands, and they will speak of condescension and scorn to the deities."

(*Zuozhuan* 1987: 1415–18)

Though mentions of lesser deities abound in the *Zuozhuan*, they are, like the opening line of this chapter, usually casual mentions within larger narratives and so not the focus of the narratives themselves. Zhao 20:6, on the other hand, provides detailed and explicit representations of lesser deities. In this instance, the didactic begins with the Marquess of Qi falling ill and a critique of the actions of his supplicators and scribes. These officials have apparently been serving the deities in their own right to alleviate the Marquess' condition. Since their efforts are not working, they are recommended for execution. Yanzi, a revered minister, informs the Lord that execution is inappropriate. Yanzi initially cites historical precedent in the form of a conversation told by Zhao Wu to Qu Jian (who cites the example of the state of Jin). He explains the conversation as illustrating an idealized relationship between the sovereign, on the one hand, and the supplicators and scribes, on the other, in which they serve merely as mediums communicating the sovereign's virtue or lack thereof. The sovereign's illness is set aside to explain proper ritual order and the fundamental importance of virtue in governance.

In Yanzi's discussion, gods are represented as both subjects of the sovereign and objects of his actions. Yanzi is concerned with virtue and with the effects sovereigns with and without it have on their domains. Since Gods are expected to respond to the sovereign, when they are appeased in sacrifice, tyrannical rulers will not fear them and may even scorn them. Furthermore, gods are associated with people, "gods are angry and the people suffering"; lesser deities, like humans, are subjects under the control of and responding to the sovereign's virtue. Yanzi holds that gods have a specific role in serving the sovereign by giving him good fortune, which is in turn grounded in proper sacrifice and the virtue of the sovereign.

Guoyu 國語

Zhou 周 1:12

In the fifteenth year of King Hui (662 BCE), there was a god that descended to Shen. The King asked Royal Secretary Guo, "What is the reason for this? Has this really happened?" He responded, "It has. When a state is about to rise up, its sovereign is of a single mind, right and proper, clean and pure, generous and harmonious and his virtue is enough to proclaim his fragrant allure. His generosity is enough to be one with his people. The gods are provided for and the people listen. Man and gods have no complaints, thus brilliant gods descend to him, and when they observe his governance and virtue, they both present good fortune to him. When a state is about to perish, its sovereign is greedy and dangerous, wicked and deceitful, licentious and leisurely, wild and idle, course and dirty, volatile and tyrannical, his governance reeks and his fragrant allure does not ascend. His punishments are without reason and excessive. The common people hold duplicitous thoughts. The brilliant gods are not pure,[8] and the people have rebellious intentions. Man and gods are angry and in pain, and have nothing that could be relied on to return [to things as they were].[9] Thus gods also go to such a one, observe his tyranny and wickedness and send down calamities to him. Therefore some who see the gods are on the rise, yet some are also on the decline. In the past, when the Xia rose up, Rong[10] descended to Mt. Zong. When they went into decline, Huilu[11] lodged for two nights at Qinsui. When the Shang were on the rise, Taozhen[12] dwelt for more than two days at Mt. Pi. When they went into decline, an yiyang[13] was in Mu. When the Zhou were on the rise, a yuezhuo bird called at Mt. Zhi. When they were at the end, the Earl of Du[14] shot the King[15] at Hao These are all understood as ones that are showing the god's intention." The King said, "Who is this god now" He replied, "In the past, King Zhao[16] took a wife from Fang[17] and she was called Queen Fang. In actuality she was of questionable virtue and cavorted with Dan Zhu.[18] Dan Zhu had relied on a body[19] so as to be as a spouse to her and she gave birth to King Mu. These events then, were closely manifest in the descendants of Zhou and the good fortunes and calamities that befell them. The gods were one with them, not travelling far or moving. If we look over this then, is this perhaps the gods of Dan Zhu?" The King said, "Who has received him?" He replied, "He is on Guo's soil." The King said, "If this is correct, why?" He replied, "I have heard this: If one is with the Way and obtains a god, it is called welcoming good fortune. If one is licentious and obtains a gods, it is called coveting calamity. Now Guo has been lowly and wild. Will it be destroyed?" The King said, "What are we to do?" He replied, "Send the Grand Steward to lead the Li clan[20] as the supplicators and scribes and submit the sacrificial animals, vessels of grain and jade and silk sending and presenting them there. Do not have any prayers." The King said, "How long has Guo?" He replied, "In the past, Yao presided over the people for five years. Now, his descendant appears. When gods appear, they do not surpass this number. If we look upon all of this then, it does not surpass five years." The King sent Grand Steward Ji Fu to lead the Fu clan[21] and the Grand Supplicator and Grand Scribe in submitting the sacrificial animals, jade and wine and taking it as gifts to them. Royal Secretary Guo accompanied and arrived at the state of Guo. The Duke of Guo also sent a Grand Supplicator and Grand Scribe to seek territory there. The Royal Secretary Guo returned and told this to the King, "Guo will surely perish. They do not perform *yin* sacrifices[22] to the gods yet ask for good fortune from him. The gods will surely visit calamity on them. They are not close to their people but seek to employ them. The people will surely revolt against them. With pure intentions in sacrifice, this is performing a *yin* sacrifice. This protecting of the common people is being close to them. Now the Duke of Guo takes action without the hundred families in order to indulge in his deviance. He departs from the people and angers the gods, yet wants profit for this. Is this not calamity!" In the nineteenth year of King Hui (658 BCE), Jin took Guo.

(*Guoyu* 2002: 28–31)

Like the *Zuozhuan*, a common rhetorical technique of the *Guoyu* involves an individual, usually an official, who provides advice to the sovereign. While it is sometimes a remonstrance, in *Guoyu*'s Zhou 1:12 it is a series of questions. From a rhetorical perspective, the structure of the questions and answers—the first question regards the arrival of a god and leads to an explanation of proper sacrifice—is a tool to reinforce the linkage of these ideas in the reader's mind. Other rhetorical techniques commonly found in the oratory of the *Guoyu*, such as historical justification and the report of the actions of the state of Guo, also serve to convince its audience. Gods, in this passage, are evinced in a mythistorical narrative as seen in the *Zuozhuan*'s Zhao 20:6; they are represented not as mere observers or passive audience members of human sacrificial acts, but as active participants with roles and duties in sacrifice as well.

The concern for what lesser deities are is manifested in the questions and answers between the ruler and his minister. Guo explains that states that are on the rise witness the arrival of gods. Such states are on the rise because of the sagaciousness of their leader, thus reflecting his virtue. Leaders who lack virtue see their states decline and gods "observe his troublesome wickedness and send down calamities to him" (*Guoyu* 2002: 29). Thus, according to Guo, rather than being omens of good or bad fortune in themselves, gods are said to be attracted by a sovereign's virtue, metaphorically referred to as "a fragrant allure."

According to Guo, gods also appear to those without virtue; indeed, the god that prompts this discussion never appears to the virtuous. Since that god appears in territory controlled by the state of Guo, the ruler of Guo lacks virtue. A state's rising and falling are periods of change and transition that, within the framework of the ritual-informed order of the *Guoyu*, occur within a continuous cycle, with gods appearing at these transitions. Within the ritual-informed worldview of the *Guoyu*, the timely appearances of the gods tie them intimately to the virtue (or lack thereof) of the sovereign that determines these historic, socio-political changes.

Royal Secretary Guo insists that gods will visit calamities upon those without virtue; as such the state of Guo is the unlucky recipient of its ruler's actions. The Royal Secretary prescribes proper sacrifices, those involving the proper officials, proper offerings, and proper rites. The state of Guo is meant to participate as well but fails to perform the proper sacrifice; thus, the state of Guo will fall foul of the gods.

The text articulates that rulers who do not conform to the proper rituals are punished and dismissed. The allusion to historical sages and tyrant figures is standard *Guoyu* and *Zuozhuan* rhetoric—in this case, a series of named figures identified as gods that have visited the rise and fall of various rulers and dynasties. Dan Zhu, the god that descended to Guo, has the same name as the son of the sage-king Yao in the *Shiji* who is overlooked as the inheritor of the throne for Shun (*Shiji* 1963: 21). We read that Dan Zhu "relied on a body" to sire King Mu with Queen Fang. Although the details of this process are unclear, the commentary and Liu Zongyuan (in his critique of this passage in the *Fei Guoyu* 非國語) suggest that rather than creating a body, he took possession of one of the queen's attendants. Liu points out that this would be licentious and indicates that King Mu is the product of adultery (Liu 1979: 1272–3).

Although Dan Zhu takes possession of a human body for an immoral act, his immorality stems from neither robbing another person of their free-will nor the licentious affair. As Paul Goldin has pointed out, while adultery is considered licentious in the *Zuozhuan* (Goldin 2002: 26–33), the queen's affair is immoral only because of its connection to the rituals and sacrifice. Proper sacrifice is the goal of Guo and King Hui's exchanges.

Guo's answers locate gods within a sacrificial space replete with roles and duties determined by their relationships to the ruled. It is later reported that since the state of Guo does not perform the proper sacrifices, it will fall. The epilogue-like final clause—"In the nineteenth year of King Hui, (658 BCE) Jin took Guo"—informs us that the state of Guo does indeed fall within five years of Dan Zhu's coming. This provides the final proof of Guo's assertion and serves as the ultimate evidence of the links between virtue, sacrifice, and gods within a ritual paradigm.

Chu 楚 2:1

> King Zhao asked Guan Shefu, "With regard to what is said in the *Zhoushu* about Chong and Li causing Heaven and Earth not to meet, what is it? For if it were not correct, would people be able to ascend to Heaven?"
>
> Shefu replied, "This is not what is said. In the past, man and god didn't meet. There were some among the people who were insightful and not disloyal, and who were also able to be respectful and balanced. In their wisdom, they were able to follow the examples of the high and low. In their sagaciousness, they were able to illuminate the distant and proclaim their wisdom. In their understanding, they were able to illuminate and reveal it. In their keenness, they were able to listen through it. When a person was like this, then the spirits would descend to them. Those who were men were called *Xi*, and those who were women were called *Wu*. They arranged the sacrificial sites,[23] and they made them sacrificial tools and the appropriate clothing. Later, if there were those among the descendants of the first sages who were bright and knew the names of the mountains and rivers, the hierarchy of the temples, the duties of the ancestral shrines, the genealogy of fathers and sons, the efforts of decency and respect, the suitability of rituals and ceremonies, the standards of dignity, the adornments of appearance, the characteristics of loyalty and sincerity and the clothes of the *yin* sacrifices and cleansings, then those who were respectful and dutiful to the gods were taken as supplicators. If descendants of the old families knew the plantings of the four seasons, the animals of sacrifice, the types of jade and silk, the appearance of the colored clothes, the sizes of the sacrificial vessels, the order of the arrangements, the sites of importance and triviality, the locations of altars and clearings, the gods of the high and low, the origins of the clans and families, then those whose minds carried the old canons were taken as Family Unifiers. Thus there were officers for the types of things of man and gods of Heaven and Earth. These were called the Five Offices, and each governed over their own affairs, and they do not muddle with each other. People were therefore able to have loyalty and sincerity, and gods were therefore able to understand virtue.[24] Man and gods have different duties, they must be respected and not defiled, thus the gods blessed them with splendid crops, and man sacrificed to them with these things. Calamity and disaster did not befall them, and they never lacked for their wants and needs.
>
> At the decline of Shaohao, the Jiuli[25] brought chaos to this virtue. Man and gods intermingled and one could not distinguish them.[26] Everyone established

sacrifices and the households made their own mediums and officers. They did not have trust in their oaths. People were deficient in sacrifices and they did not know any of their good fortune. The sacrifices were without regulations and man and gods shared places. People disrespected the shared oaths and were without reverence and awe. The gods became accustomed to the rules of man and did not do their part. Excellent crops did not appear and there was nothing to be used in sacrifice. Calamities and disasters continued on and on and no one could exhaust their pneuma. Zhuanxu undertook this and then ordered the Superintendent of the South Chong to command Heaven so as to organise the gods, and the Superintendent of Fire Li to command the Earth so as to organise the people. This caused things to return to how they were in the past, and there were no more transgressions or contamination from either side. This is called the separating of the connections of Heaven and Earth.

Later, when the Sanmiao returned to the virtues of the Jiuli,[27] Yao again educated the descendants of Chong and Li to not disregard what was old and had them manage things again. From the Xia and the Shang, thus, Chong and Li's lines ordered Heaven and Earth and have divided their respective governors. Now in the Zhou, the Earl of Cheng and Xiu Fu are their descendants. At the time of King Xuan,[28] they eliminated their offices and made the Sima clan. They cherished the gods as their ancestors so as bring awe to the people, saying, "Chong raised up Heaven, and Li pushed down Earth." When we come to the disorder of the next generations, there were none who could stop it. This is incorrect; Heaven and Earth are fixed and do not change, how can they have interaction?".

(*Guoyu* 2002: 512–16)

Like the *Zuozhuan*'s Zhao 1:12, Chu 2:1 provides a mythistorical narrative prompted by questions between an advisor, Guan Shefu, and advisee, King Zhao.[29] Guan recounts an earlier, perfect world where everything and everyone perform as they are meant. This perfect world fell into disarray when the Jiuli brought disorder to the end of Shaohao's reign. Zhuanxu then ordered Chong and Li to restore the original order by separating Heaven and Earth. Guan then recounts how this incident was repeated by the Sanmiao, descendants of the Jiuli; it was rectified by Chong and Li's descendants under the authority of Yao, also a descendant of Zhuanxu (thus reinforcing appropriate filial ties).

The overarching concern of this story is the maintenance of the proper order between Heaven and Earth; lesser deities are represented as being a part of that proper order by not intermingling with humans. Guan's description of earlier times in the second paragraph constructs a properly ordered society in which those who are sagacious and wise are the ones to whom the gendered gods *xi* and *wu* descend.[30] The passage depicts them as establishing spaces for the proper sacrifices, alongside making tools and clothing. Two litanies of skills describe the descendants of the people who are eligible to become the two types of ritual specialists; Guan's explanation depicts the development of these ritual offices in terms of ancestral, meritocratic, and ethical development. Gods are represented in terms of their relationship with these agents, and this relationship is modulated by the agents' virtue—their proper conduct and abilities.

Guan argues that people and gods have "different duties" which must be respected; violations of the separation of duties lead to disorder and chaos, as is evident from the third paragraph. People have transgressed by mixing with the gods and performing their own rituals. As a result, their crops did not grow and calamities befell them. As in other passages of the *Guoyu* and the *Zuozhuan*, explicit depictions of lesser deities are present. In this instance, the gods give blessings when pleased (through bestowing good crops, an agricultural concern related to proper socio-political administration) and send down calamities when displeased.

Zhuangzi 莊子

The *Zhuangzi* does not offer the concerted narratives on extrahumans of the *Zuozhuan* or the *Guoyu*. Rather, extrahuman agents are scattered throughout its many sections alongside a panoply of other characters, such as animals and mythistorical culture heroes. On one level, this lack of explicit definitions comports well with the *Zhuangzi*'s eschewing of such modes of argumentation and, on the other, it offers implicit insight into how lesser deities are represented in its texts through their roles and performances in these diverse narratives.

Lesser Deities in the *Zhuangzi* are portrayed less as active agents than as passive referents embedded in a larger passages' performances. This is often seen in terms of using their representations as points of comparison or descriptive terms. This reflects the strong modes of wordplay found in the *Zhuangzi*. Passages in the *Zhuangzi* are notorious for repeating the same graph in a passage while employing its many different meanings, thus alluding to arguments in its *Qiwulun* and the *Yuyan* sections that argue for the fluidity and impermanence of words (Schwitzgebel 1996: 70–4).

Ying diwang 應帝王 (Excerpt)

There was a divine shaman called Li Xian in Zheng. He knew about the birth and death and existing and nonexisting of people, good fortune and calamity, longevity and dying early, and how to determine things through years, months, weeks and days like a god. When the people of Zheng saw him, they would all just abandon and flee from him. Liezi[31] met him and became intoxicated, he returned home to tell Huzi about it, "In the beginning, I took your way to be perfection, but there is also one whose is more perfect than yours."

(*Zhuangzi* 1961: 297)

In this brief excerpt from the *Ying diwang* 應帝王, the shaman is both "divine" and likened to a god. The overall passage depicts an event between master and disciple, Huzi and Liezi, respectively. Liezi encounters a magic man—the "divine shaman" Li Xian—who possessed the god-like abilities of knowledge of life and death, existence, lifespan, and astrological matters. These items of knowledge impress Liezi who becomes so "intoxicated" that he informs his master Huzi that he has discovered one whose way is superior to his. Though not translated in the above, Huzi meets with Li Xian on a number of occasions; rather than being impressed by him, he confounds Li Xian.

Understanding the Way plays within the larger *Ying diwang* passage; while the tale does not explicitly discount Li Xian's abilities, it emphasizes that Huzi's way is superior. Li Xian's abilities also represent what lesser deities are capable of by comparing the incredible skills of humans with those of lesser deities.

Dasheng 達生 (Excerpt)

Zai Qing carved wood to make a bell stand. When the bell stand was complete, those who saw it were shocked as it was akin to the deities. The Marquess of Lu saw this and asked about it, "What art have you made this into this?" He replied, "I am an artisan, what art have I? Although this may be so, I have one thing for you. When I go to make a bell stand, I have never dare to waste energy and am certain to fast in order to calm my mind. I fast for three days and do not dare to take upon myself congratulation, reward, rank or salary. I fast for five days and do not dare to take upon myself blame, slander, trickery or self-censure. I fast for seven days are always cast aside that I have four limbs and form and body. Right at this moment, I am refrain from public service to the court and my skill is at its most focused when the outside matters disappear. After this, I retreat into the mountains and forests, look upon Heavenly nature and see form and body to be perfect. After this, I successfully see the bell stand, and then I add my hand to this. If it is not so, then there is no more. For using Heaven to join with Heaven, there are those among the vessels that have the means to suspect the divine, is this not one?".

(*Zhuangzi* 1961: 658-9)

Qiwulun 齊物論 (Excerpt)

Ni Que said, "If you don't know what is beneficial or harmful, then does the perfect man certainly know what is beneficial and harmful?" Wang Ni said, "The perfect man is god-like. When there is a blazing conflagration, it is unable to make him hot. When the Yellow and Han rivers freeze over, it is unable to make him cold. When a flash of lightning shatters a mountain and the wind rocks the sea, it is unable to make him frightened. If there is one such as this, then he will ride the clouds and vapours, mount the sun and the moon and travel beyond the four seas.[32] Life and death will refrain from transforming him, what more the spectrum of benefit and harm!".

(Zhuangzi 1961: 96)

Like the earlier section from the *Ying diwang*, the matters in *Dasheng* and *Qiwulun* concerning lesser deities relate to the larger discourses of the passages, both of which are too complex to fully explore. In both passages, lesser deities are represented with uncanny abilities clearly contrasted with those typically associated with humans (though they are abilities humans can attain as well).[33] The first, from the *Dasheng*, describes a craftsman who displays uncanny skill in the crafting of a bell stand. While it is unclear if either he or the bell stand is "'like the deities,'" the passage describes the craftsman as following what is innate and heavenly. This story echoes other stories of the *Zhuangzi* in which a craftsman, through Heavenly innateness, crafts something perfect.[34] Perfection, though an indirect representation of lesser deities, is clearly correlated with them in these passages.

In the story from the *Qiwulun*, the character Ni Que asks Wang Ni about the "perfect man" and if he can deal with what is beneficial and harmful. Wang Ni replies that the perfect man is "god-like." Direct and poetic representations of what this means are provided—immunity to extreme temperatures, lack of fear and the ability to leave the bounds of the earth, traverse the cosmos, and even leave the bounds of the earth. Additionally, the perfect man is not affected by the vicissitudes of life and death and so, according to Wang Ni, is not concerned with benefits and harm. As in the other two stories, comparison of the human with the extrahuman offers explicit representation of lesser deities. Unlike the story from the *Ying diwang*, where lesser deity Li Xian suffered in comparison to Huzi, Wang Ni's description of a perfect man as a lesser deity seems positive and beneficial. But the *Zhuangzi* refrains from seeing humans with extrahuman qualities as noteworthy.

Exceptional humans are not the only agents that are compared to lesser deities in the *Zhuangzi*. Passages of the *Zhuangzi* are replete with evocative imagery in which non-human agents are compared to deities as well.

Waiwu 外物 (Excerpt)

Prince Ren made a large hook and long black line and took fifty bullocks to serve as bait. He then squatted on Kuaiji and cast his rod into the eastern sea, day after day, he fished, but in the space of a year he did not get a fish. After this, a large fish took the bait and pulled the long black line and hook under whilst diving down. It then flew upwards and beat its fins; the white waves looked like hills and the sea water surged and pulsated with a sound that equalled the deities that struck fear for a thousand *li*. When Prince Ren got this so-called fish, he cut it up and dried it. From the east of Zhihe and north of Cangwu, there were none who did not get their fill of this so-called fish.

(*Zhuangzi* 1961: 925)

Lesser deities not only manifest in natural contexts, we also find representations of lesser deities in socio-political contexts as well. The *Tiandi* section begins with a discussion of how the world works and role of the sovereign in it. The sovereigns of old are described as understanding the realities of governance, such as the way and virtue, in order to order the world. The closing lines of the opening passage recount:

Tiandi 天地 (Excerpt)

Thus it is said, "As for those among the ancients who tended to the realm, when they wanted nothing, the realm was satisfied, and when they did nothing, the myriad things transformed, when they abided in tranquillity, the people were settled." Records say, "When they connected in unity, then the myriad duties were completed, when they obtained without their hearts, the deities submitted".

(*Zhuangzi* 1961: 403)

Tiandi 天地 (Excerpt)

As for the person of kingly virtue, they search out through their travails and are demure in their connection with matters. They establish themselves in it and root themselves in the origin and are knowledgeable in their connection with the gods. Thus their virtue is vast and is what emerges from their hear for if there are things, they select properly from them.

(*Zhuangzi* 1961: 411)

Both of these statements endorse the gods' reciprocal relationships with rulers who engage in proper behavior: the first holds that the gods will submit to a virtuous ruler, and the second holds that a virtuous ruler will connect with the gods (a phrase found in the *Zuozhuan* and other pre-imperial texts). Through its representations of lesser deities in relation to the sovereign and proper order, the *Zhuangzi* reinforces socio-political concerns.

Conclusion

The *Zuozhuan* quote at the beginning of this chapter—*The sovereign is the master of gods and aspirant of the people*—asserts a powerful socio-political paradigm with the extrahuman alongside the human under the control of the virtuous sovereign. Liang Qichao argued that this is a defining feature of the text's attitude toward religion (Liang 1996). Socio-political representation is definitive of the *Zuozhuan*, the *Guoyu*, and *Zhuangzi* alike—gods as extrahuman agents are part of their socio-political world.

Lesser deities are also portrayed as "other" and nonhuman. The *Zuozhuan* and the *Guoyu* argue for a deep understanding of the difference between the human and the extrahuman. For example, *Guoyu* Chu 2:1 details a mythistoriographic account of the separation between the two and the construction of proper socio-political spaces for both. These socio-political spaces are also elucidated in Zhou 1:12 and the *Zuozhuan*'s Zhao 20:6 where the narratives also make use of mythistorical tales as rhetorical justification. While these tales represent lesser deities in socio-political spaces, Chu 2:1 defines those spaces as separate from humans but the latter two are more interested in the abilities the lesser deities have in these spaces. These passages represent them as being able to provide benefits and punishments in response to the virtue and propriety of the sovereign. Lesser deities are even capable of morally dubious actions and affairs, such as the adulterous affair between a household servant and the lady of a house in *Guoyu* Zhou 1:12.

The *Zhuangzi* likewise represents lesser deities in socio-political terms, albeit much less than the *Zuozhuan* or *Guoyu*. Further, where the *Zuozhuan* and *Guoyu* feature larger narratives and explicit accounts of lesser deities, the *Zhuangzi* represents them in less explicit ways. Their nature as extrahumans, in contrast to humans, is commonly evoked in the *Zhuangzi* to explain uncanny and incredible people and animals; it represents lesser deities as agents with inexplicable abilities and resplendent natures. Several passages in the *Zhuangzi* equate this with rulers or auspicious people, thus evoking yet another intersection between the incredible and the socio-political provided by the nature of lesser deities.

Appendix: The Curious Case of Dong Zhongshu

David Hall and Roger Ames reject the notion that the *Analects* grounds value in Heaven. They claim:

> The portrait of *t'ien* [Heaven] that emerges from an analysis of relevant passages in the *Analects* is one that clearly has some anthropomorphic characteristics. But it does not follow that, because of this, *t'ien* [Heaven] is equitable with the Western conception of the deity. On the contrary, any comparison that this similarity might encourage is blunted when measured against their profound differences. These differences center first on the contrast between the transcendence of the Western deity and *t'ien* as unqualifiedly immanent. A further important consideration in this disparity is the fact that the Confucian conception of 'person,' entailed by the seemingly shared characterization as "anthropomorphic," is in fact significantly different.
>
> (Hall and Ames 1987: 206)

Methodologically, Hall and Ames view Confucius through the lens of Dong Zhongshu.[1] They argue:

> Let us face a probable methodological criticism head-on. As an example, some sinologist is sure to ask how we can use a concept as it is defined by the text of Tung Chung-shu's [Dong Zhongshu] *Ch'un-ch'iu fan-lu* to elucidate its usage in the *Analects*. It would be equally irresponsible to say that the Confucian Tung Chung-shu (ca. 179-104 B.C.) is irrelevant as a resource for understanding classical Confucian vocabulary as it would be to accept his definition of these concepts uncritically. The problem, then, is to try to discover in Tung Chung-shu's presentation and elaboration of Confucian vocabulary that which is consistent with the *Analects* and that which deviates from it. This problem echoes a similar concern to distinguish a "process" reading of Confucius from a reading of Confucius where a process vocabulary is merely the most appropriate resource available to us to make Confucius clear to a Western reader. We are not presenting a Han dynasty interpretation of Confucius, but rather, are attempting to use Tung chung-shu's commentary critically where it sheds light on the idea being expressed in our record of Confucius.
>
> (Hall and Ames 1987: 42–3)

They concede: "There is in this approach certainly a playfulness, but it also acknowledges the profoundly organic nature of the Chinese language" (Hall and Ames 1987: 43). "A certain playfulness" indeed, but a careful assessment of Dong's views would support a transcendent, anthropomorphic Heaven in Confucius, not Hall and Ames' immanent, impersonal view of Heaven.

Dong presents us with an entirely different picture from that claimed by Hall and Ames. Dong consistently and insistently portrays Heaven as an agent with intentions, feelings, and purposes. And while Dong's syncretic philosophy includes portions of we might call Daoist thought (which is more amenable to Hall and Ames' process views), these views are subsidiary to Dong's more fundamental views of an anthropomorphic Heaven as ground of morality, government, and humanity.[2] It is beyond the scope of this appendix to exhaustively analyze Dong's thought. But since he is often claimed to be the author of Han Confucianism, hence the culmination of early Confucian thought, it would behoove us to pause and consider if Dong supports an anthropomorphic Heaven (or a naturalistic Heaven).

Consider just a few passages in which Dong discusses the nature of Heaven.

> Heaven has its own feelings of joy and anger, and a mind (which experiences) sadness or pleasure, analogous to those of man. Thus if a grouping is made according to kind, Heaven and man are one.

> The mind possesses the power of thinking, which corresponds to (Heaven's) power of deliberation and calculation.

> What produces (man) cannot (itself) be man, for the creator of man is Heaven. The fact that men are derives from Heaven. Heaven, indeed, is man's supreme ancestor. This is why man is to be classed with Heaven above. Man's physical body is given from through the transforming influence of the numerical (categories) of Heaven. Man's vigor is directed to love (*ren* 仁) through the transforming influence of Heaven's will. Man's virtuous conduct is expressed in righteousness through the transforming influence of Heaven's orderly principle. Man's likes and dislikes are influenced by Heaven's ordering principle. Man's likes and dislikes are influenced by Heaven's warmth and purity. Man's joy and anger are influenced by Heaven's cold and heat ... The duplicate of Heaven lies in man, and man's feelings and nature derive from Heaven.

The personal qualities of Heaven are unmistakable: just as humans deliberate, calculate, feel, and get angry, so, too, does Heaven. Or, rather vice versa: because a thinking and feeling Heaven created humans to be like Heaven, humans are thinking and feeling things. And the virtues which elevate humans above the other creatures are precisely the virtues that exalt Heaven above Earth. Humans both emerged from and are morally transformed by Heaven.

The famous and oft-cited claim that Heaven and humanity are one, according to Dong, precludes the view that Heaven is humanity idealized (and so has no reality above and beyond the human). Heaven and humanity are one in that both are above other creatures, because both are of the same stuff (mental, personal, etc.). Heaven is not reducible to humanity, according to Dong, because Heaven produced and stands in authority over humans (and not vice versa).

Dong sought to engineer a religious revolution in which cult was transferred from *Shangdi* and other/lesser deities, and even ancestors, to Heaven. He sought the reinstitution of the *jiao* sacrifice to Heaven, which he believed was instituted by the Son of Heaven at the beginning of the Zhou dynasty. Dong likewise held that Heaven is superior to and had authority over lesser deities. Rather than a sacrifice mediated by specialists, Dong contended that the Emperor should relate to Heaven as son to father and, like a filial son, should obey Heaven as father. Heaven, the universal father, was beseeched in the sacrifice to determine Heaven's will as a guide for the Emperor. The Emperor's filial and humble expression of the *jiao* sacrifice would restore the order of Heaven on earth.

Dong put Heaven to good political use. After seeing the abuses permitted and perhaps encouraged by legalism, where Law is created by the will of the Emperor, he sought a moral authority over the Emperor, to whom even the Emperor must bow. He argued that the Emperor, who should relate to Heaven as a son to his father, must obey Heaven's will.

Hu Shih argued that the Confucian revolution instituted by Dong was grounded in his trust in Heaven; in the *Chunqiu fanlu*, we learn that Han Confucianism involves "the subjection of the people to the ruler and of the ruler to God" (Hu 1929). Contra Hall and Ames: insofar as Dong can be used to interpret the *Analects*, appeals to Dong support an interpretation of Heaven as anthropomorphic.

Notes

Introduction

1. The transmitted texts include *Chuci* 楚辭, *Gongyang zhuan* 公羊傳, *Guanzi* 管子, *Guliang zhuan* 穀梁傳, *Erya* 爾邪, *Hanfeizi* 韓非子, *Laozi* 老子, *Analects* (*Lunyu*) 論語, *Lüshi chunqiu* 呂氏春秋, *Mengzi* 孟子, *Mozi* 墨子, *Shangshu* 尚書, *Shangjun shu* 商君書, *Shenzi* 慎子, *Shijing* 詩經, *Sunzi bingfa* 孫子兵法, *Wuzi* 吳子, *Xiaojing* 孝經, *Xunzi* 荀子, *Yanzi chunqiu* 晏子春秋, *Yijing* 易經, *Yinwenzi* 尹文子, *Zhouli* 周禮, *Zhuangzi* 莊子, and *Zuozhuan* 左傳.
2. The construction, "Confucianism," was meaningless in, say, 100 BCE. Nonetheless, representations of the High God(s) and the afterlife are prevalent in what came to be called, much later, the "Confucian" canon. I take the "Confucian" canon to refer to a mostly Song construction that included a shifting set of "canonical" texts that included, again not exclusively, the so-called "Four Books and Five Classics" (四書五經; *Sishu Wujing*). The Four Books included *The Analects* (論語 *Lunyu*), *The Mencius* (孟子 *Mengzi*), *The Great Learning* (大學 *Da Xue*), and *The Doctrine of the Mean* (中庸 *Zhongyong*). The Five Classics included The *Classic of Poetry* (诗经 *Shi Jing*; aka, the Odes), *The Classic of History* (书经 *Shu Jing*; aka the Documents), *The Classic of Rites* (礼记 *Liji*), *The Spring and Autumn Annals* (春秋 *Chunqiu*), and the *I Ching* (易經 *Yi Jing*).
3. You will note that this book refers to the High Gods in a variety of ways. Winslett prefers the locution, "High Deities," because it clearly differentiates the Chinese High Gods from Abrahamic monotheism. Moreover, Winslett takes seriously the possibility that the three names of the High Deities—*Di*, *Shangdi*, and *Tian*—refer to three different beings. Clark, on the other hand, takes the three names—*Di*, *Shangdi* and *Tian*—to refer to the same being. Clark follows Guo Moruo and Herlee Creel who argue that in the Zhou period, "*Shangdi*" and "*Tian*" were used interchangeably (Guo 1936 and Creel 1970). Clark, therefore, prefers the locution, "High God" to refer to that entity (recognizing that China's High God is not descriptively identical to the Abrahamic God). We have not regularized the name of the High Gods; we've decided to let the text live with our disagreement.

Chapter 1

1. We repeat this clarification from the Introduction: "You will note that this book refers to the High Gods in a variety of ways. Winslett prefers the locution, 'High Deities,' because it clearly differentiates China's High Gods from Abrahamic monotheism. Moreover, Winslett takes seriously the possibility that the three names of the High Deities—*Di*, *Shangdi* and *Tien*—refer to three different beings. Clark, on the other hand, takes the three names—*Di*, *Shangdi* and *Tien*—to refer to the same being. Clark, therefore prefers the locution, 'High God' to refer to that entity (all the while recognizing that China's High God is not descriptively identical to the Abrahamic God). We have not regularized the name of the High Gods; we've decided to let the text live with our disagreement."

2. Ping-ti Ho speculates that *Di* might be the First Ancestor who became the Shang tribal God, Diku 帝嚳 who was originally the ultimate/first progenitor of Shang people but then gradually became the God of the Shang (Ho 1975: 318–20). Even if this were the origin of *Shangdi*, by the time of the Shang dynasty the functions of and attitudes toward *Di* are qualitatively different from the functions generally performed by and attitudes toward ancestral spirits. Keightley argues that the primary function of ancestral spirits is to preserve the continuity of the dynastic lineage and power; *Shangdi*, however, orders disasters that harm the very existence of the dynasty. The following inscriptions from oracle bones confirm this interpretation: the "fang 方 (an enemy country) is harming and attacking [us]; it is *Di* who orders it to make disasters for us" (Keightley 1999: 253). In other inscriptions *Di* was credited as the cause of disasters to crucial Shang locations such as their cult center or various settlements. According to Keightley, even though Shang's ancestors could cause sickness, they "never struck at the dynasty in such vital spots, presumably because they lacked the power and motivation" (Keightley 1999: 253). Michael Puett, however, argues, "The most reasonable hypothesis is that *Di* was not recognized as part of the Shang ancestral line, and he was probably not an ancestor at all" (Puett 2002: 49). The model of the relationship of *Shangdi* to the heavenly beings and the rulers of the Shang is more suggestive of bureaucracy and hierarchy than blood kinship. Furthermore, various "creation" myths suggest that *Shangdi* is the creator of the world, thus preceding, not proceeding from, human beings.

3. Puett (2002) has raised an issue that has not been adequately addressed: are the lesser gods and ancestor spirits really part of a well-organized hierarchy (and do they have human well-being in mind)? There is textual evidence to support this, but also evidence to reject it as Puett points out. This speaks to the highly pluralistic nature of early Chinese texts.

4   The *Shangshu*, also known as the *Shujing* 書經 or the *Documents*, traditionally conceived, is a collection of official documents allegedly from three ancient Chinese dynasties: Xia, Shang, and Zhou. Scholars from antiquity to the present, however, have been critical of the authenticity of the documents. Although the traditional Chinese belief is that all of the chapters in the *Documents* are genuine and reliable, most contemporary scholars disagree. Edward Shaughnessy argues that "[a]mong the chapters of the *Shangshu* generally regarded as dating to the Western Zhou, I believe that the following can be used with considerable confidence: the five *gao* (Pronouncement) chapters (that is, 'Da Gao,' 'Kang Gao,' 'Jiu Gao,' 'Shao Gao,' and 'Luo Gao'), two of which ('Da Gao' and 'Jiu Gao') probably record the speeches of King Wu's son and successor, King Cheng (r. 1042/35–1006 BCE), two speeches of Zhou Gong … and one … a speech by Shao Gong Shi, Zhou Gong's half brother" (Shaughnessy 1999: 294). Virtually all contemporary scholars believe that the alleged Xia and Shang documents are forgeries from the Han or Jin dynasties (see also Shaughnessy 1993 and Nylan 2001). Lothar von Falkenhausen has argued that there is no archeological evidence of the exalted status of the early Zhou sages or the attendant ritual reforms to which the Zhou *Documents* attest until ca. 850 BCE; he argues: "Modern archaeology has revealed that such a view of the early Zhou is in large part a historical fiction—a projection of latter-day philosophical fantasy into a dimly and selectively remembered past" (von Falkenhausen 2006: 156, 2). We are not offering a historical reconstruction of the early Zhou dynasty, just how some of China's earliest texts represent the High Deities.

5   The use of both Legge's and Karlgren's translations of the *Shangshu* reflects their pervasiveness among numerous communities of readership, both the scholarly and the popular. Though one cannot question that their legacy speaks to the strong Sinological backgrounds of both translators, both translations come with heavy caveats—not least the accusations of a Christian lens in both, particularly Legge's. While how Christian Legge's translations are is a matter of some debate (see Redmond and Hon 2014), the most striking issue for the purposes of this chapter is the rendering of the terms for the High Deities, *Di* and *Shangdi* as God and God on High respectively while *Tian* is rendered as Heaven. But neither *Di*, *Shangdi* nor *Tian* is the Abrahamic God. That such conflation occurred, and with such ease, speaks to the need to better understand how these High Deities are actually represented in these texts.

6   Benjamin Schwartz argues that the Mandate of Heaven, as conceived in the *Documents* and the *Poetry,* is consciously concerned with human welfare (Schwartz 1985: 53).

7   He may have been only thirteen when his father, King Wu, died.

8   Divination using tortoise shells or cow scapulae was commonplace.

9   Yan Shigu, a commentator from the Tang dynasty, supported the notion that *shangdiming* is equivalent to *tianming* (see Bodde 1981: 309).

10   The fact that *Shangdi* and *Tian* are used interchangeably in these early Zhou documents suggests that the word *Tian* may have had such a connotation prior to the Zhou conquest. Recent archeological excavations have demonstrated more and deeper similarities among the ancient dynasties than previous thought. For example: "There is general agreement that the Hsia [Xia], the Shang, and the Chou [Zhou] shared the same culture, with differences only in detail … The Chou were located in the west, the Shang in the east, and the Hsia in the middle. Newly published carbon dates confirm the temporal overlap of these cultures in north China" (Hsu and Linduff 1988: 54–5). Feng Yulan concurs: "With the coming of the Hsia [Xia] and Shang dynasties, when the concept of 'Heaven' (*T'ien* [*Tian*]) and 'God' (Ti [*Di*]) arose, a monotheistic belief seems gradually to have gained influence, but at the same time there was no weakening of the old polytheism" (Feng 1952: 24).

11   Consider the sending down of calamities: "Nor shall I dare to restrain the majesty of Heaven in sending down its inflictions (on the criminals)." Legge's translation of *jiang* 降 as "sending down" suggests that *jiang* with its spatial/literal connotations communicates the origin of the order, as with *Shangdi*, from Heaven above. "Coming down from above" implies a particular authoritative act of Heaven only. This use of *jiang* is also found in the oracle bones from the Shang era to denote the act of *Shangdi* to send down calamities or other occurrences to the people on earth. *Wei yong* 威用, Legge's "majesty," can also be translated as the "fearsome/awful execution of." The whole sentence can be alternatively translated as follows: "I dare not restrain Heaven's fearsome punishment [on Shang]."

12   Puett cautions against taking these texts as definitive of the beliefs of those living in the Zhou era (Puett 2002: 60ff) (not least owing to the fact that these texts are multilayered and multithemed with many other views represented). Puett notes that there is textual evidence that suggests Heaven (as a transcendent place of the High Deities, lesser gods, and ancestors) is not harmonious; it seems that many deceased ancestors are disorderly and even malevolent. Moreover, in some texts it seems as though human sacrifices are required to order even *Di* himself (thus assuming an agonistic relationship between God and people). However, there are also many texts that represent *Tian* qua High God as the pattern for the world (one to which human communities ought to conform).

13   Hsu and Linduff write: "*Tian* was not considered extraordinary. In fact, the character *tian* was not distinguished from the character *da* 大, meaning great. The character that often signified sky, or heaven was *shang* 上 (up, above, upper) as opposed to *xia* 下 (down, below, lower)" (Hsu and Linduff 1988: 101).

14 Hsu and Linduff, for instance, write that "[i]n the 'Treatise on Sacrifices' and the 'Treatise on Geography' of the *Han-shu* virtually all the shrines or sacred sites for worship of a heavenly god, other than the official or imperial ones, are located in the provinces of Shanxi and Gansu. They seem to be associated with the area of the big, open sky" (Hsu and Linduff 1988: 102). And so, as standing over all, "Heaven was not tied to any nation as kin but was omnipresent. As such, *t'ien* [*tian*] acquired the status of an impartial judge who could transmit moral concerns to secular rulers" (Hsu and Linduff 1988: 108).

15 Feng concurs. According to Feng, *Tian*, in the ancient period, meant variously (1) the sky; (2) a Supreme, anthropomorphic Heavenly ruler; (3) fate (tianming); (4) Nature (a naturalistic force); and (5) the primordial moral Principle of the universe. He concludes: "The references to *T'ien* [*Tian*] in the *Shih Ching* [Shijing, the *Poetry*], *Shu Ching* [Shujing, the *Book of Documents*], *Tso Chuan* [Zuozhuan, the *Zuo Commentary on the* Spring and Autumn Annals] and *Kuo Yu* [Guoyu], excluding those to the purely physical sky of type one, seem generally to designate the ruling or presiding anthropomorphic *T'ien* of type two; which also seems to be the type of *T'ien* spoken of by Confucius in the *Lun Yu*" (Feng 1952: 31).

16 "It was seen and heard by God on High, and God favoured him" (Karlgren 1950).

17 This is suggested to refer to the five phases of Earth, Water, Fire, Wood, and Metal. Various metaphysical systems posit them in a dynamic cycle of victory over each other and destruction of each other.

18 See Durrant (1995), Hardy (1999), Lewis (1999: 50–80), and Puett (2002: 318–34).

19 Hayashi Minao, in his discussion of the depiction of deities in tombs from this period, does not mention any image as representing Heaven. Additionally, he mentions no motif or symbol that could arguably serve as a representation of Heaven (Hayashi 2002: 221–3).

20 Discussions of Heaven, and the High Deities in general, speak not only to the complex nature of these texts and the knowledge communities that produced them, but also, as will be discussed, how the modes of representation of these deities help further the arguments of the texts and subsume the nature of deities, particularly the High Deities into the didactic of their narratives.

21 This chapter takes "anthropomorphic" to mean something like being the physical that is depicted as human.

22 Allan 1991, p. 9.

23 Another name for Zichan 子產 (d. 522 BCE), a noted minister of the state of Zheng who piloted the small state through the turbulent political affairs of the Spring and Autumn period trying to see off annexation and dominion by larger, more powerful states, particularly the state of Jin 晉.

24 Another name for Di Ku 帝嚳, a mythistorical figure reported as a pre-Xia ruler in many texts. The *Shiji* recounts him as being the great grandson of the Huangdi (*Shiji*, 1:13). The details of his offspring as recounted by Zichan in this passage are found only in this text.

25 The Chinese constellation Shen 參 corresponds to only seven of the ten stars that make up the Western constellation Orion: α Orionis (Betelgeuse), γ Orionis (Bellatrix), ζ Orionis (Alnitak), ε Orionis (Alnilam), δ Orionis (Mintaka), κ Orionis (Saiph), and β Orionis (Rigel). Alnitak, Alnilam, and Mintaka are better known together as Orion's belt. Betelgeuse and Bellatrix and Saiph and Rigel make up the right and left shoulders and knees, respectively.

    How these figures are supposed "to be in charge of" these stars is unclear. However, a divine, supernatural understanding of this function is certainly possible. Yang Bojun suggests this refers to maintaining astronomical data on these constellations (*Zuozhuan*, Zhao 1.12.1218). This less supernatural way of reading points to Bodde's argument of reverse euhemerization, as mentioned in Chapter 1, and the ambiguity of actions in which *shen* are noted in many early Chinese texts.

26 This is not to be confused with Tang Shuyu, the first leader of the state of Jin, who is referred to here as Da Shu and why he has been given this name and the supernatural associations with it.

27 Another name for Shaohao 少皞. He is identified as Qingyang 青陽 and the son of the Huangdi in a text titled the *Shiben* 世本 (*Zuozhuan* Zhao 1.12.1218.). The *Shiji* reports Qingyang as the Huangdi's first son, with Di Ku as his second (*Shiji*, 1:10).

28 Four states that are within the state of Jin's territory.

29 Various characters are employed to name sacrifices and other rituals related to extrahumans throughout early Chinese texts. Details of how they are performed or differ from other sacrifices are often a matter of speculation from later commentators as even early ritual texts such as the *Liji* provide little clue. The *Shuowen jiezi* gives *yong* as "The using of prayers to the sun, moon, stars, mountains and rivers to avert wind and rain, snow and frost, floods and drought and pestilence and plague." (*Shuowen jiezi*, 1A.12B.6).

30 *Chunqiu zuozhuan zhu* (*Zuozhuan*), Zhao 1.12.1217–1221.

31 As suggested in the *Mao* commentary to the *Shijing*, that *mo* 莫 be understood as *ding* 定 is supported by a reading of lexical correlation with a graphic variant in the *Erya* 爾雅 (*Mao shijian*, p. 838).

32 The *Mao* commentaries suggest that both *jiu* 究 and *du* 度 can be understood as *mou* 謀 (*Mao shijian*, p. 839).

33 *Shijing*, p. 852.

34 Commentary purports Zhi to be a land 國 and not a person, though its relationship to Shang is unclear (*Mao*, p. 801).

35 He is given the name Ji Li 季歷 in the *Shiji*. Since King Wen overthrew the Zhou, King Ji posthumously gained the throne having been earlier enfoeffed as Lord Ji 公季 (*Shiji*, pp. 115–16).

36 *Shijing*, pp. 828–32.

37 *Lüshi Chunqiu*, pp. 144–5.

38 This is observed in other sections of the *Lüshi chunqiu* (Clark and Winslett 2011: 953–5).

39 *Guoyu*, pp. 329–30.
40 *Analects*, p. 273.
41 *Xunzi*, p. 59.
42 *Hanfeizi*, pp. 152–3.
43 *Lüshi chunqiu*, p. 42.
44 Ibid., p. 94.
45 For further discussion of creation myths, see Birrell (1993), Goldin (2008), and Ke (1978).
46 *Shijing*, pp. 922, 967.
47 *Mencius*, p. 758.
48 A mythistorical sage-king most often associated with stopping floods and founding the Xia dynasty.
49 *Lüshi chunqiu*, p. 555.
50 *Mozi*, p. 299.
51 *Zhuangzi*, p. 813.

Chapter 2

1 This construction of Confucius as a pupil in the *Zhuangzi* is explored more in depth by Wiebke Denecke (Denecke 2011: 262–5), who argues that it is a way to "dethrone" Confucius.
2 For a further discussion of the nature of characters in pre-imperial texts and the various Confuciuses, see Nylan and Wilson (2010).
3 Though commentary on the passage argues that this should be understood as the previously mentioned ears, eyes, nose, mouth, and form (*Xunzi* 1988: 309), which of course works well with the organic and human modes of representation, the term *wuguang* 五官 can also refer to official ministries furthering the intersection between these concepts.
4 Though not actively constructed in the macro/microcosm paradigms evinced by texts such as the *Huainanzi* or *Huangdi neijing*, the use of bodily terms alongside political discourse and notions of the extrahuman evoke such ideas and suggest that similar notions may be found within different texts. For discussions of such correlations in these texts, see Henderson (1984).
5 DeFoort and Standaert both note this as particularly marked by the paucity of the term *Tianzhi* in the three sections (DeFoort and Standaert 2013: 21).
6 Wiebke Denecke sees a distinction between the way in which the *Zhuangzi* employs some of these rhetorical techniques and how they are employed in the *Mozi*, ultimately arguing that the former is more subversive in its arguments (Denecke 2010: 237–8).

Chapter 3

1. Taeko Brooks argues to the contrary, based on the *Zuozhuan*'s use of Heaven, that "these passages imply different roles for Heaven in human affairs, and that the differences cannot be explained as differences in belief between states, or as evolution of ideas during the Spring and Autumn period, but are more likely compositional strata." (Brooks 2003/4: 51)
2. Pines' claims that this or that text is representative are problematic. As Barry B. Blakeley argues: "When making arguments about broad developments, there are often instances in which the *Zuo zhuan* contains so many examples that citing every one of them is not only unnecessary but also unduly cumbersome. But a representative sample should be offered. On the other hand, when relevant passages are limited in number, it is incumbent on the writer to point to all of them, simply to demonstrate that the example(s) cited are not unusual or unique. Pines can be faulted on both points" (Blakely 2004: 258).
3. Pines concedes that he's restricting his claims to those texts offered by statesmen who are concerned with the political consequences of religious thought.
4. I am not claiming that it supports a theistic view, either. There is a plethora of widely divergent voices and arguments in the *Zuozhuan*, which precludes favoring one view over the other.

Chapter 4

1. A strong case can be made that the received *Analects* is an accretional text with Han origins around the first century BCE (Makeham 1996; Csikszentmihalyi 2002; Hyun and Csikszentmihalyi 2014; Hunter 2012). Makeham argues that the *Analects* first appeared as a book around 150–140 BCE and that it was based on a number of earlier, inconsistent "sayings" of the Master. Successive "sayings" accumulated in response to changing social and political needs. Hyun and Csikszentmihalyi identify three different and competing versions of the *Analects* that were circulating in the first century BCE (Hyun and Csikszentmihalyi 2014: 23–4). Finally, they note that an excavated text of the fourth century BCE includes versions of some sayings of the *Analects* that vary substantially from the received text (32–3). The conclusion seems irresistible: the received *Analects* is a composite text of the Han dynasty which contains few, if any, identifiable sayings of the historical Confucius.
2. There is widespread disagreement about the *ippsissima verba* of Confucius. Traditionally scholars held that every word of the *Analects* derived from the mouth of Confucius (although written down later by his disciples). This view is scarcely

held by contemporary scholars. Brooks and Brooks (2001), at the other extreme, contend that very little of the *Analects* comes from Confucius. Although their views have been disputed (see Slingerland 2000), it is clear that Confucius is at best distantly related to the *Analects*. Nonetheless, I prescind from this debate and consider the "canonical" Confucius as found in the entire *Analects*.

3   *Analects* quotations are from Slingerland (2003) unless otherwise noted.

4   The concept of *Tianming* is one of the most significant concepts in Chinese thought and religion, but its meaning is not as simple as one might think. Wing-Tsit Chan, in his commentary, explains: "What *Tianming* is depends on one's own philosophy. In general, Confucianists before Tang dynasty (618–907) understood it to mean either the decree of God, which determines the course of one's life, or the rise and fall of the moral order, whereas Song's scholars, especially Zhu Xi, took it to mean 'the operation of Nature which is endowed in things and makes things be as they are.' This latter interpretation has prevailed. The concept of *Tianming* which can mean Mandate of Heaven, decree of God, personal destiny, and course of order, is extremely important in the history of Chinese thought. In religion it generally means fate or personal order of God, but in philosophy it is practically always understood as moral destiny, natural endowment, or moral order" (Chan 1963: 22–3). Chan's distinctions between pre-Tang and Song's conceptions of *Tianming* and between religious and philosophical senses of it are not completely correct. In the *Analects*, all of Chan's conceptions can be found in Confucius' words.

5   See Lai (1997: 32).

6   This reflects the belief that everything must return to its own extreme, in its own time. So everything that reaches its extreme point would naturally return to its opposing extreme.

7   See *Lunyu Zhushu* (1997: 44).

8   Lai (1997: 80).

9   See *Lunyu Zhushu* (1997: 44).

10 The Mandate of Heaven has a variety of meanings in the ancient texts. In the primary or focal instance, it means something like "divinely ordained political authority," but it can also mean something like fate. See, for example,

> Ssu-ma Niu, worrying, said, "All people have brothers but I have none." Tzu-hsia said, "I have heard (from Confucius) this saying: 'Life and death are the decree of Heaven; wealth and honor depend on Heaven. If a superior man is reverential (or serious) without fail, and is respectful in dealing with others and follows the rules of propriety, then all within the four seas (the world) are brothers.' What does the superior man have to worry about having no brothers?" (12:5)

Again, this sort of fate is allied with trust in Heaven's good will.

11 Although it is widely stated that "the Chinese have no creation myth," of the many we read in *Odes* #260: "Heaven gave birth to the multitude of people,/ They have

bodies, they have rules." This ode implies that Heaven is the creator of humanity and the source of human value. For a refutation of the claim that the Chinese have no creation myth, see Goldin (2008).
12 Ancient Chinese called the southwest corner of their house, *Ao*. They also believed that there was a god who resided there; this god (the god of the southwest corner) was also called *Ao*. Wangsun Gu used this as a covert reference to Nanzi (Nan means South, and Ao is the god of the southwest (*xinan*) corner), a favorite concubine of the ruler of Wei.
13 *Zao* literally means, "furnace." Ancient Chinese also called the god of the furnace/kitchen, *Zao*.
14 *Mengzi Zhengyi* (1987: 56).
15 Eno concurs: "As a prescriptive force, *T'ien* plays two major roles in the *Analects*. First, it provides a ground for the Ruist notion of transcendent wisdom, and legitimizes the Ruist claim that traditional ritual forms provide the path to attaining it. Second, it legitimizes Ruist political idealism and the rejection of practical politics" (Eno 1990a: 82).
16 Ivanhoe suggests how one might think Heaven is represented as an agent but not as a person. He writes: "There are a number of ways in which one might attribute agency but not personality to Heaven. One way would be to see Heaven as a kind of collective will—a conception that as noted earlier can be found in the early Zhou sources. A jury can make judgments and assign guilt without being a single person or being of any kind. At a minimum though, Kongzi and Mengzi did regard Heaven as what Daniel Dennett calls 'an intentional system.' This ambiguity concerning the nature of Heaven's agency echoes throughout the later Confucian tradition" (Ivanhoe 2007: 217). But noting this ambiguity is not sufficient to cast the textual weight in favor of impersonality. What would follow, strictly speaking, is not that the *Lunyu* represents Heaven as impersonal but rather that it is unclear whether the *Lunyu* represents Heaven as personal or impersonal; without textual evidence inclining the reader in one direction or the other, one should be agnostic about whether Heaven is personal or impersonal. My view, however, is that absent decisive considerations to the contrary, the reader should follow normal linguistic rules in understanding the term "Heaven." If Confucius uses "Heaven" as one would with a person and doesn't use the term as one would with a committee or a jury, then one should *prima facie* think Confucius represents Heaven as a person.
17 *guai* 怪 literally means "strange" and can apply to both supernatural phenomena and the abnormal, weird, or disturbingly bizarre daily occurrences in society. Many believed that strange phenomena are omens of Heaven's disapproval of an immoral ruler or wretched societal conditions. So, the text could mean that Confucius never discussed strange phenomena or disordered spiritual beings.
18 *li* 力 literally means "power, strength." Lai Kehong understands this as denoting violent behaviors (Lai 1997: 188). *Li* also includes physical arrogance, that is, people

who intimidate others by using or showing off their physical strength. Boasting through physical strength indicates an uncivilized or unlearned mind, and the presence of such tendencies in society, therefore, is a sign of civil and moral disorder (*luan* 亂).

19 *shen* 神 in modern Chinese can be used to refer to gods in general or *Shangdi* in particular. However, as used in this passage, *shen* likely means spirits. Hence, it is not correct to confuse Confucius' attitudes toward *shen* with Confucius' attitudes toward Heaven (in ancient Chinese, *shen* and Heaven/*Shangdi* were different words with different meanings). Feng Yulan, for instance, argued that Confucius was conservative toward the religious belief and practices of his time (which included the worships of *Shangdi* or Heaven and the ancestors), but had a more skeptical attitude toward spirits (Feng 1952: 58).

20 Historian Roel Sterckx notes this interpretation and then expresses his emphatic disagreement: "Generations of scholars, from *les philosophes* in the 17th and 18th centuries to Marxist-Leninist historiography in the 20th century, have quoted these statements, uncovering in Confucius an ally as a self-proclaimed agnostic. Yet nothing could be further from the truth than to claim that Confucius was indifferent to the spirit world at large. Ancestral spirits are a cornerstone in Confucius' moral program, which requires living descendants to perpetuate care and respect for the spirits of the deceased through sacrifice (*Analects* 2:24, 8:21)" (Sterckx 2007: 25).

21 The claim that Confucius is agnostic about spirits runs counter to other passages in the *Analects* where he prescribes or commends the proper ritual practices concerning spirits, evil spirits, and the spirits of deceased ancestors (2:24, 3:12, 8:21, 10:8, 10:15). His prescriptions and commendations assume the existence of spirits (see Sterckx 2007).

22 Dawson argues that Confucius believed in spirits and that proper sacrifice to them would keep them from adversely meddling in human affairs (Dawson 2008: 90).

23 Later ritual practice would include the subjection of spirits to *Shangdi*. In "Statutes of the Ming Dynasty" (1368–1642) addressed to the heavenly spirits, "the spirits of the Cloud-master, the Rain-master, the Lord of the Winds, and the Thunder-master," we read, "It is your office, O Spirits, to superintend the clouds and the rain, and to raise and send abroad the winds, as ministers assisting *Shang Ti*. All the people enjoying the benefits of your service." The spirits act from "Heaven-conferred powers, and nurturing influences" (Legge 1880: 18–19).

24 Many twentieth-century commentators decry the Christian influence on early translations of the *Analects*. Ironically, Legge's translation has given rise to the most complaints; yet, Legge himself believed that Confucius was both "unreligious" and "unspiritual," and that "he gave no impulse to religion."

25 While I argue that Confucius understands Heaven as a person, I do not believe that he affirmed a personal relationship with Heaven. In fact, most ordinary folks never

sought direct contact with Heaven. Religious rituals involved one's own ancestors, primarily, as well as lesser *gui* and *shen*. Except for the king, no one directly approached Heaven.

26 For a discussion of the history of interpretations of this enigmatic passage, see Ivanhoe (2002).

27 Including, in one passage, to Zigong. Confucius speaks to Zigong about Heaven and in a deeply anthropomorphic, almost confessional, manner:

> The Master said: "Alas! No one understands me."
> Zigong replied, "How can you say that no one understands you, Master?"
>
> "I am not bitter toward Heaven, nor do I blame others. I study what is below in order to comprehend what is above. If there is anyone who could understand me, perhaps it is Heaven" (*Analects* 14:35).

28 Consider Zhu Xi on Confucius' selective distribution of information to his disciples: "What Zengzi heard from the Master was not necessarily heard together with Yanzi. What Yanzi heard from the Master was not necessarily heard together with Zigong. Now, however, what each of them heard is combined in the book, the *Analects*. Are not students of later times fortunate?" (as quoted in Makeham 2003: 187).

29 Confucius' views on cosmological matters and human nature may be inferred from views he clearly states. On this I am in agreement with Hall and Ames: "Confucius' reticence about speculating on what he perceived to be problems beyond the purview of immediate concerns should not be interpreted to mean that his efforts to organize human experience with consistency and coherence are free of cosmological presuppositions. Although Confucius did not discuss speculative questions, there are tacit intuitions that underlie and serve as ground for his articulated philosophy. We may safely assume that the implicit cosmological vision of Confucius was equally tacit among his chief disciples" (Hall and Ames 1987: 198–9).

30 According to He Yan, a commentator from the Wei dynasty, Zigong said that Confucius' understanding of these topics was so profound it was simply beyond the ability of his disciples to understanding them. See *Lunyu Zhushu*, 61.

31 Eno interprets this passage in such a manner that it has no theistic connotations whatsoever: "If we look for the meaning of the passage in the balanced contrast between the two phrases, it appears to say something such as: 'Don't ask about theories of *T'ien* or man's nature; you will find all there is to know about these matters in the Master's program of self-stylization.' In other words, *T'ien*'s existence 'out there' does not matter; it gives us no clues as to what we are meant to be. For us, *T'ien* is manifest in and prescribes those behavioral forms that Confucius laid down as the basis for Ruist practice. If this interpretation is correct, then *A*:5:13 reassigns the considerable rhetorical force of the word '*t'ien*' from images of the heavens or of spirits to the everyday practice of ritual forms" (Eno 1990a: 85). This is a big "if" and not a very natural reading of the text.

32 For further evidence that Zigong lacks virtue and understanding, see *Analects* 3:17, 5:4, 5:9, 11:18, and 14:29; see also Slingerland's commentary on 5:4 (Slingerland 2003: 40).

33 Slingerland's translation is quite different: "The Master openly expressed his views on profit, the Heavenly Mandate, and Goodness" (see Slingerland 2003: 86).

34 Confucius discussed and sometimes bemoaned fate or destiny, which are granted by Heaven: "Anxiously, Sima Nu remarked, 'Everyone has brothers, I alone have none.' Zixia replied, 'I have heard it said, "Life and death are governed by fate, wealth and honor are determined by Heaven." A gentleman is respectful and free of errors. He is reverent and ritually proper in his dealings with others. In this way, everyone in the Four Seas is his brother. How could a gentleman be concerned about not having brothers?'" (*Analects* 12:5). And when Yan Hui died, he lamented, "Oh! Heaven has bereft me! Heaven has bereft me!" (*Analects* 11:9).

35 In de Bary and Bloom we find the following comment: "There has been much discussion about why, in [9.1], Confucius is said to have spoken 'little' about topics on which there are many recorded pronouncements. This is especially true in the case of humaneness, which is discussed at many points in the *Analects*. While there is no fully convincing answer to this, one possibility is that in many instances when Confucius discusses humaneness, he seems to have been responding to questions from disciples, and then guardedly, preferring to leave the question and its answer open-ended. For him humaneness knew no limit and could not be explicitly defined" (de Bary and Bloom 1999: 52).

36 With violence to this prima facie reading of this passage, Hall and Ames assert: "In this context, *t'ien* is not a preexisting creative principle which gives birth to and nurtures a world independent of itself. *T'ien* is rather a general designation for the phenomenal world as it emerges of its own accord. *T'ien* is wholly immanent, having no existence independent of the calculus of phenomena that constitute it. There is as much validity in asserting that phenomena 'create' *t'ien* as in saying that *t'ien* creates phenomena; the relationship between *t'ien* and phenomena, therefore, is one of interdependence" (Hall and Ames 1987: 207).

37 It would be curious indeed if Confucius sought to model himself on Heaven, as he does here, but Heaven be the human community, ritual activity, or some naturalistic force. Eno agrees that Heaven is the cosmic moral model: "There is a parallel between the action of the Sage, which is a function of his totalistic understanding, and the action of *T'ien*. *T'ien* itself—whether pictured as Nature or god—seems almost to be a cosmic version of the Ruist Sage" (Eno 1990a: 86). I'm arguing that it's more than "seems almost."

38 He writes: "My propositions serve as elucidations in the following way: anyone who understands me eventually recognizes them as nonsensical, when he has used them—as steps—to climb up beyond them. (He must, so to speak, throw away the ladder after he has climbed up it.) He must transcend these propositions, and then he will see the world aright" (Wittgenstein 1922: 6.54).

39 The entirety of *Analects* 10 is a showing—showing how Confucius, our moral model, carried himself in various circumstances.

Chapter 5

1 Eno (and the subsequent authors I consider) attributes views to Mencius, the character, while I following the concern in the opening paragraph, restrict my analysis to the *Mencius*.
2 We must be careful of claiming too much of these connections. Warring States texts were not as referential to each other as later texts were, and so all that can be said is that these two passages show a related intention.
3 Munro goes on to argue that we can and should remove all reference to the supernatural in Mencius and seek a reconstruction of Mencius' moral views along naturalistic, evolutionary lines.
4 http://www.iep.utm.edu/mencius/
5 I belabor the identification of *Tian* with *Shangdi* here to note that the *Mencius* does not represent *Tian* and *Shangdi* as distinct and different entities. Since *Tian* and *Shangdi* are identical, whatever is true of *Shangdi* is perforce true of *Tian*. The Shujing portrays *Shangdi* as an anthropomorphic extrahuman person. The claim that the *Mencius* does not represent *Tian* as an anthropomorphic extrahuman person would need to explain away the *Mencius*' affirmation of the tradition's identification of *Tian* with *Shangdi*.
6 While personhood is necessary for being a person, it may not be necessary for divinity given that many trees, stones, and animals are treated as extrahumans in many world cultures (the Chinese included). I leave to anthropologists the empirical question about whether or not such cultures personify such objects.
7 See Puett (2003). This passage permits another reading which does not belittle the nobility of Man in favor of the nobility of Heaven. According to this reading, the text may be suggesting that one should not be happy with one while lacking the other. Even so, the point remains—the nobility of Heaven involves the acquisition of personal virtues. Heaven serves as a human moral model because Heaven is a person with the highest personal attributes.

Chapter 6

1 Although Xunzi is widely taken today as the logical outcome of early Confucian thought, his influence on Chinese thought vanished by the middle of the Han dynasty (not to be recovered until the late twentieth century) (Goldin 2007: 135–6).

2   As Thomas Wilson argues, Confucian commentators understood canonical Confucianism in precisely this way: "An examination of classical commentaries and critical essays spanning no less than 1500 years divulges a remarkably consistent conception of spirits and the rites to venerate them. The history of Confucian discourse on ritual practice discloses subtle if important shifts in emphasis on what rites accomplish, yet the reverent sacrificing to the spirits never ceased to play a definitive role in the lives of men and women steeped in Confucian culture. The Confucian conception of spirits and the soul revolves around the basic assumptions that spirits linger after the death of the body and that they must be nurtured through pious feasting rites of cult sacrifice 祭祀. The Master and his later interpreters rarely spoke directly about the nature of spirits outside of the specific ritual contexts in which spirits and human agents interacted according to strict guidelines prescribed by the court. Imperial-era commentaries on the classics elaborated on the Master's description of two components of the soul—a *yang hun* 魂 (anima) spirit and a *yin po* 魄 ghost (corporeal soul)—and the rites, devised by the sages of remote antiquity, to venerate them properly. Classical commentaries well before the Tang and throughout the *longue duree* of Confucian ritual discourses on spirits and the soul stressed the moral effects on those who purify themselves and participate in such rites personally" (Wilson 2014: 186).

3   Anna Seidel (1982) rejects "journey models" of the afterlife, arguing instead that the tombs themselves were designed as permanent homes for the deceased. For purposes of this book, this debate is mostly beside the point: whether the tomb or paradise is the final destination, both concur: many early Chinese believed in an afterlife in which one's soul departs from one's body either to move freely around their well-appointed tomb or to fly off to paradise.

4   Poo Mu-chou argues that the elaborate tomb constructions and burial goods of the fourth- to third-century BCE imply that "the tombs were meant to be the houses of the dead in a realistic sense;" within the tombs, "the souls of the deceased were expected to move around" (Poo 2011: 16–17). See also Poo (1998), Pirazzoli-t'Serstevens (2009), and Erickson (2010).

5   In the *Chuci* chapter, "Summoning the Soul," which describes a soul-recalling ritual, the poet wrote: "O soul, Go not down to the City of Darkness, where the Lord Earth lies, nine-coiled, with dreadful horns on his forehead, and a great humped back and bloody thumbs, pursuing men, swift-footed: Three eyes he has in his tiger's head, and his body is like a bull's" (Poo 2011: 19). The underground was ruled by a wide variety of nefarious bureaucrats such as "The Assistant Magistrate of the Underworld" and the "Minister and Magistrate of Grave Mounds."

6   There is no evidence that the Chinese believed that souls live forever.

7   Since the *Mozi* uncontroversially defends the afterlife, we will set it aside for purposes of this chapter.
8   In Ji Fa, we read of the devolution of forgotten ancestors from ancestors into a "ghostly state" (*Liji*: Ji Fa).
9   I have selected a single, informative passage from several of the transmitted texts. I have omitted others within the selected texts and in other transmitted texts, some of which are equally informative. See, for example, Paul Goldin's discussion of the legion of references in the *Zuozhuan* 左傳 to people living in spirit after the destruction of their material bodies (Goldin 2015).
10 I am using Thomas Wilson's translation because it offers the strongest support for Confucius' skepticism about the afterlife (Wilson 2014: 4). Slingerland's translation is more benign.
11 Given the difficulties in ascertaining the views of the historical Confucius, as I proceed I will take "Confucius" to be synonymous with "Confucius the character as represented in the text named the *Analects*."
12 These prooftexts are also widely cited as evidence that Confucianism, the philosophy that uniquely represents the Chinese mind, rejects the afterlife. For example, Roger Ames writes: "Confucian religiousness is neither salvific nor eschatological" though it does entail "a transformation of the quality of human life in the ordinary business of the day that not only elevates and inspires our daily transactions, but further extends radially to enchant the world" (Ames 2011: 237). The Han Confucian revival of justice, compassion, and harmony is, according to this view, entirely this-worldly.
13 For example, Bryan Van Norden writes: "First and foremost, Confucius emphasized acting in and for this world, as opposed to being concerned with any supernatural realm or afterlife" (www.chinadaily.com.cn/epaper/html/cd/2000/200012/20001211/20001211006_2.html). Confident assertions about what Confucius said or believed are seldom if ever warranted. As argued in Chapter 4, we know very little about what the actual Confucius said or believed.
14 For a defense of the claim that the Chinese are material monists, see Zhang (2007). For another set of arguments against Chinese monism, see Slingerland (2011, 2013, 2017).
15 Goldin assumes, as I've argued, that Confucius' statements such as "To make sacrifices to a ghost that is not one's own is toadying" (Analects 2:24) show that "his ready acceptance of the existence of ghosts and spirits was unexceptional" (Goldin 2015: 60).
16 As an accretional text, we should expect to find differing views. And we do. So we read: "Zai Wo said, 'I have heard the names *Gui* and *Shen*, but I do not know what they mean.' The Master said, 'The (intelligent) spirit is of the *shen* nature, and shows that in fullest measure; the animal soul is of the *gui* nature, and shows that in fullest measure. It is the union of *gui* and *shen* that forms the highest exhibition

of doctrine. All the living must die, and dying, return to the ground; this is what is called *kwei*. The bones and flesh, moulder below, and, hidden away, become the earth of the fields. But the spirit issues forth, and is displayed on high in a condition of glorious brightness. The vapours and odours which produce a feeling of sadness, (and arise from the decay of their substance), are the subtle essences of all things, and (also) a manifestation of the *shan* nature. On the ground of these subtle essences of things, with an extreme decision and inventiveness, (the sages) framed distinctly (the names of) *kwei* and *shan*, to constitute a pattern for the black-haired race; and all the multitudes were filled with awe, and the myriads of the people constrained to submission'" (*Liji*: Ji Yi).

17 See Slingerland (2019) for a magisterial defense of early Chinese mind-body dualism.
18 Which, again, *prima facie* implies the belief that ancestors exist. As argued, the entire set of transmitted texts when allied with the tomb texts support an *ultima facie* case for the widespread belief that ancestors exist and deserve our continuing respect and honor.

Chapter 7

1 While there was a decided interest in Confucius, it was more for his alleged special relationship with Heaven than for teachings of the *Analects*. As Heaven's privileged emissary, "the Uncrowned King" was routinely invoked in order to rationalize various social and political views and regimes. Yet the "voice" of Confucius could be found in any number of texts including thousands of circulated sayings of the Master not included in the *Analects* (Hunter 2012) and the mutable four books and five classics. Some, for example, preferred *The Spring and Autumn Annals* because the former "was thought to have come from his own hand, and not from those of his disciples, as had the *Analects*" (Csikszentmihalyi 2002: 138). As such, during the Han dynasty, there were many versions of Confucius (Nylan 1999 and Nylan and Wilson 2010).
2 Again, I do not include the *Xunzi*, which would afford it a role in a narrative it didn't have until the twentieth century.
3 This discussion relates texts within socio-historical contexts that, as far as we know, were unrelated prior to, say, 200 BCE. Moreover, it associates texts based on ideas and schools (usually called "Confucian") which didn't exist prior to say 200 BCE (and likely didn't exist then). As such, this chapter offers a reconstruction of early, "canonical" "Confucianism" (see Introduction).
4 Unless noted, all *Analects* quotations are from Slingerland (2003).
5 While we focus on texts and their representations, historic Chinese cultic and ritual practices exemplified a robust understanding of the importance of proper human interactions with gods and postmortem ancestors. As Thomas Wilson writes, "In spite of their reputation for reticence on matters of spirits, Confucian officials

nonetheless performed sacrifices to spirits throughout imperial times until the early twentieth century. The emperor, court ministers, and civil officials followed a strict calendar of rites devoted to scores of gods and spirits at altars and temples in the capital and throughout the empire" (Wilson 2014: 185–6).

6   I will use Robert Eno's translation of *The Doctrine of the Mean* throughout. http://www.indiana.edu/%7Ep374/Daxue-Zhongyong.pdf

7   Strictly speaking, I mean, "Confucius the character as represented in the *Analects*." In the next sentence I mean, "Confucius the character as represented in *The Doctrine of the Mean*." Again, I have little idea about what Confucius the person, who may or may not have lived around 500 BC, believed or said.

8   Legge translates the character 敖 as "pride." While 敖 literally meant "strolling/roaming leisurely," it gained the meaning "pride." In terms of pronunciation, tone, and ideograph, 敖 is similar to another character for pride (傲). While some might argue that translating it "pride" is tendentious, reflecting Legge's Christian bias, modern Chinese people have come to understand it as pride as well; the text (敖不可长) has become a proverb which means, as Legge argues, "pride shouldn't be allowed to grow." According to the authoritative commentary "Liji Zhengyi (礼记正义)," by Zheng Xuan (郑玄) from the Eastern Han dynasty, and completed during Tang dynasty, 敖 here can be translated as pride. This commentator may be thinking that 敖 refers to the vestiges or the traces of one's prideful deeds or journey.

9   In the *Xiaogang* "The Influence of Filial Piety and the Response to It" 感應 we hear that the Son of Heaven requires "some whom he honors," in this case his august ancestors: "The Master said, 'Anciently, the intelligent kings served their fathers with filial piety, and therefore they served Heaven with intelligence. They served their mothers with filial piety, and therefore they served Earth with discrimination. They pursued the right course with reference to their (own) seniors and juniors, and therefore they secured the regulation of the relations between superiors and inferiors (throughout the kingdom). When Heaven and Earth were served with intelligence and discrimination, the spiritual intelligences displayed (their retributive power). *Therefore even the Son of Heaven must have some whom he honors;* that is, he has his uncles of his surname. He must have some to whom he concedes the precedence; that is, he has his cousins, who bear the same surname and are older than himself. In the ancestral temple he manifests the utmost reverence, showing that he does not forget his parents. He cultivates his person and is careful of his conduct, fearing lest he should disgrace his predecessors. When in the ancestral temple he exhibits the utmost reverence, the spirits of the departed manifest themselves. Perfect filial piety and fraternal duty reach to (and move) the spiritual intelligences and diffuse their light on all within the four seas. They penetrate everywhere'" (emphasis mine).

10 Recent social-scientific studies on awe suggest that experiences of awe make people more generous, harmonious, and happy. See Keltner and Haidt (2003), Valdesolo and Graham (2014), Valdesolo et al. (2016), Van Cappellen and Saroglou (2012), Piff et al. (2015), and Rudd et al. (2012).

11 The leader likely gets a power boost from his ancestors as well. Confucius' ritual veneration of his ancestors, Yao and Shun, and Wen and Wu, was doubly and triply transformative: their Daos, walking side by side, jointly combined to generate the powers of great and deeply transforming virtue (DM 30).

12 As Michael Puett puts it: "Thus, through these sets of rituals, an array of potentially antagonistic forces—Heaven, the ghost of a recently deceased ruler, the new ruler, his son, and the populace—come to have filial dispositions toward each other. As a result, the entire realm becomes, ritually speaking, a single family, linked through familial dispositions. Instead of interactions being dominated by dispositions like anger, jealousy, and resentment, the interactions within rituals are denied by the proper dispositions associated with the relations between particular roles in a patriarchal hierarchy: ancestor, father, son. Ritually speaking again, the world—including Heaven, ghosts, and living humans—comes to function as a perfect patriarchal lineage built up through father-son dyads" (Puett 2014: 220).

13 In "The Great Plan" of the *Documents*, the ruler is called to imitate Heaven's compassion and justice.

14 Roel Sterckx, in his study of *shen* (spirit) in early China, shows that the acquisition of such supernatural powers by sages was a prominent theme: "The potential to exert spirit-like powers was not solely reserved to ghosts and spirits; such powers could also be appropriated by humans, most notably sages, who, by extension, were associated with divinity, perspicacity and the ability to comprehend the changes and transformations that befall human fate, the natural world, and the cosmos at large" (Sterckx 2007: 24). It seems, from my analysis, that one gains such spirit powers from both Heaven and ancestors.

15 In addition to arguments and texts from previous chapters, see also: *Shangshu Zhonghui zhi Gao* 尚書 • 仲虺之誥: "To revere and honour the path prescribed by Heaven is the way ever to preserve the favouring appointment of Heaven" (欽崇天道, 永保天命。) (trans. James Legge). Again, this is not to deny that others, say Xunzi, who would later come to be identified as Confucian, reject this view: "The Way of which I speak is not the Way of Heaven or the Way of Earth, but rather the Way that guides the actions of mankind and is embodied in the conduct of the gentleman" *Xunzi* 8; trans. by John Knoblock in *Xunzi: A Translation and Study of the Complete Works*. Vol. II. Palo Alto, CA: Stanford University Press, 1990, p. 71.

16 See Chapter 2.

Chapter 8

1 The best case for bringing the insights of the social sciences into humanistic studies is Slingerland (2008).

2 See Johnson and Bering (2005, 2006), Johnson et al. (2005), Norenzayan and Shariff (2008), Norenzayan (2013), Norenzayan et al. (2016), and Sosis (2009).

3 Twenty-five transmitted texts identified from the Pre-Qin period are included in the database as of August 2010: the *Chuci* 楚辭, *Gongyang zhuan* 公羊傳, *Guanzi* 管子, *Guliang zhuan* 穀梁傳, *Erya* 爾邪, *Hanfeizi* 韓非子, *Laozi* 老子, *Analects* (*Lunyu*) 論語, *Lüshi chunqiu* 呂氏春秋, *Mengzi* 孟子, *Mozi* 墨子, *Shangshu* 尚書, *Shangjun shu* 商君書, *Shenzi* 慎子, *Shijing* 詩經, *Sunzi bingfa* 孫子兵法, *Wuzi* 吳子, *Xiaojing* 孝經, *Xunzi* 荀子, *Yanzi chunqiu* 晏子春秋, *Yijing* 易經, *Yinwenzi* 尹文子, *Zhouli* 周禮, *Zhuangzi* 莊子, and *Zuozhuan* 左傳. Searches were performed on all of these with only the *Shangjun, shu,* and *Shenzi* not yielding any results.

4 Since this chapter is primarily concerned with the interpretation of early Chinese texts, I will simply summarize some of the central claims of the cognitive science of religion as found in Lawson and McCauley (1990), Guthrie (1993), Boyer (1994), Atran (2002), Barrett (2004), Whitehouse and McCauley (2005), and McCauley (2011).

5 I will discuss this claim in more detail because of its China relevance. Cognitive science of religion suggests that common religious beliefs in purpose in the universe are undergirded by "the teleological bias," a human cognitive faculty that routinely ascribes purpose to natural events (Banerjee and Bloom 2014; Barrett 2012; Bering 2011; Bloom 2007; Kelemen 1999a, 2004; Kelemen, Rottman, and Seston 2013). While Deborah Kelemen's early studies focused on children (DiYanni and Kelemen 2005; Kelemen 1999b, 1999c, 2003; Kelemen and DiYanni 2005), she later turned to adults, often highly educated scientists who are taught to favor mechanistic explanations, to confirm to the ubiquity of the teleological bias (Kelemen, Rottman, and Seston 2013). Combined, the research suggests that humans have a robust tendency to default to teleological (i.e., purpose-based) explanations of natural phenomena (Evans and Curtis-Holmes 2005; Goldberg and Thompson-Schill 2009; Shtulman and Valcarcel 2012). However, like many psychological studies, the teleological bias was studied primarily among members of Western cultures—raising the concern that this "universal" cognitive faculty was merely a lingering cultural by-product of Western theological traditions. In 2013, I organized a team to assess the cross-cultural robustness of the teleological bias in mainland China, a country which (a) some allege is not religious and (b) whose political party stringently enforced forty years of institutional atheism. We conducted a study similar to Kelemen's work on Western adults and achieved similar results—Chinese adults manifest the same default to teleological thinking (Rottman et al. 2017).

6 Again, since this chapter is primarily concerned with Chinese textual representations of divinity, I will simply summarize some of the key claims of and support for supernatural punishment theory. The best single volume monograph on supernatural punishment theory is Norenzayan (2015).

7   While there are good evolutionary explanations of cooperation among kin and members of very small communities (where one can expect reciprocity for one's cooperative behavior), there are no good evolutionary explanations for large-scale group cooperative behavior (Johnson, Stopka, and Knights 2003: 911–12).
8   The term *di* also refers to a category of extrahumans that are not of immediate concern to this chapter. Many texts from this time talk about various *di* such as the Red *di* 赤帝 or Yellow *di* 黃帝 that exist in the sacrificial pantheon. Though the full relationship between these *di* and *Di/Shangdi* remains unstudied, when observed together, these other *di* are always beneath a greater agent that in some texts is *Di* and others *Tian* (Loewe 2005: 17).
9   *Guoyu* Zhou 1:6, Jin 4:33, and Yue 2:7 and *Shangshu, Shuoming. shang.* and *Hongfan*.
10 *Mozi Minggui xia, Shangshu Junyi*, and *Shijing Bigong*.
11 *Lüshi chunqiu Zhiyue, Mozi Minggui xia*, and *Shangshu Gaozong rongri*.
12 *Shangshu Taijia zhong, Xibo kanli, Dagao, Kanggao, Junyi*, and *Duofang*; *Shijing Tianbao*; *Zhuangzi Zaiyou* and *Zuozhuan* Xuan 3.
13 *Lüshi chunqiu Yingtong*.
14 *Guoyu* Jin 4:33 and *Zuozhuan* Huan 8.
15 *Lunyu* 9:6.
16 *Guoyu* Wu 3; *Shangshu Weizi*; *Shijing Jienanshan, Caiwei, Yunhan*, and *Shaomin*; *Xunzi Tianlun, Zuozhuan* Zhuang and Cheng 17.
17 *Guliang zhuan* Cheng 5 and Zhao 18; *Guoyu* Zhou 1:10, Jin 1:2, and Yue 1:1; *Lüshi chunqiu Shenshi*; *Shangshu Jinteng*; *Yijing Qian*; and *Zuozhuan* Xuan 15 and Ding 6.
18 *Shangshu Dagao*; *Shijing Shaomin*; and *Yanzi chunqiu* 1.1A.21.
19 *Guoyu* Zhou 2:24, Wu 1, 5, and 8; *Lüshi chunqiu Zhihua*; *Shangshu Xibo kanli* and *Duoshi* and *Zuozhuan* Xi 22, Xiang 20, 23, 27, and 29, Zhao 11 and 22.
20 *Gongyang zhuan* Xiang 29; *Mozi Minggui xia*; *Shangshu Gaozong rongri*; and *Hongfan* and *Shijing Huangniao*.
21 This does not mean that *Tian* is not represented as a moral agent in all of these texts; indeed, it is represented thus twice in the *Analects* (2:1 and 7:22) and ten times in the *Yijing* (*Kun* 坤, *Zhun* 屯, *Shi* 師, *Dayou* 大有, *Qian* 謙, *Lin* 臨, *Wuwang* 無妄, *Cui* 萃, *Ge* 革, and *Dui* 兌).
22 Nylan (2001: 2–5) and Schaberg (2001: 9, 308–9). For further discussion of "Confucians" at this time, see Cheng (2001).
23 Transliterations have been changed to Pinyin.
24 See Schaberg (2001) for an in-depth study of the rhetorical conventions employed by these texts.
25 *Xi* 襲 being taken as *ru* 入.
26 Rushou is a deity, identified here as a *shen*, whose depiction in early Chinese (and subsequent periods) primarily plays upon his association with the West and another deity, Shao Hao. The commentary to the *Guoyu* says that he is Shao Hao's son.

27. Zhou Zhiqiao is first mentioned here in the *Guoyu* and in the *Zuozhuan* as a minister of Guo who leaves to become a minister in Jin. In *Zuozhuan* Min 2:1 (660 BCE), he is said to have left Guo owing to its defeat at the hands of the Quan Rong at Chou. He claims the Lord of Guo had lost his virtue. He reappears in later passages of *Zuozhuan* Xi 28:2 and 6 during the great battle of Chengpu between Chu and Jin.
28. Being Jin.
29. 655 BCE. Winslett (2009: 67–8).
30. A location in modern Henan province.
31. A Zhou noble.
32. These are symbols of royal authority.
33. Extrahuman agents are often represented as being a part of ritual in pre-Qin texts. See Winslett (2009).
34. Though not a subject of this chapter that has merely looked at these terms as a unit, the High Deities, it is markedly clear that *Tian* is the more common of the three terms, and from Table 2 it is apparent that there are a far greater and more distributed instances of punishment and reward with *Tian* than with *Di* or *Shangdi*.

Chapter 9

1. This being Lord Jing of Qi 齊景公, Chu Xu 杵臼, who governed the state of Qi from 547 to 489 BCE.
2. Liang Qiuju is reported to be a favored official of Lord Jing of Qi.
3. Yanzi 晏子 (d. 500 BCE), Yan Ying 宴嬰, is well known for his many remonstrations to Lord Jing of Qi, particularly those collected in the *Yanzi chunqiu* 晏子春秋, of which the events in this passage do appear in *Jian shang* 諫上 of the *Nei pian* 內篇 in "*Jinggong bingjiu buyu yu zhu zhushi yi xie Yanzi jian* 景公病久不愈欲誅祝史以謝晏子諫" (*Yanzi yijian* (*Yanzi*) 晏子逸箋; Taipei: Taiwan Zhonghua shuju (1973), 1.21.34–9.), and in *Wai pian shang* 外篇上 as "*Jinggong you ji Liang Qiu ju Yi Kuan qing zhu zhushi Yanzi jian* 景公有疾梁丘據裔款請誅祝史晏子諫" (*Yanzi*, 7.7.399–404). The text of the *Wai pian*'s retelling is identical to the version held here in the *Zuozhuan*.
4. Qu Jian 屈建 (d. 545 BCE), also known as Zi Mu 子木, and Zhao Wu 范會 (d. 541 BCE), also known as Zhao Wenzi 趙文子 and Zhao Meng 趙孟, were ministers of the state of Chu and Jin respectively at the time of this covenant.
5. Fan Kuai, also known as Fan Wuzi 范武子 and Shi Kuai 士會, among others, was a minister of Lord Wen of Jin 晉文公 (r. 780–745 BCE).
6. King Kang of Chu 楚康王, also known as Zi Zhao 子昭, reigned 559–544 BCE.
7. According to Du Wei, these are meant to be the former Marquesses of Jin Wen 文 (r. 636–628 BCE), Xiang 襄 (r. 627–621 BCE), Ling 靈 (r. 620–609 BCE), Cheng 成 (r. 606–600 BCE), and Jing 景 (r. 599–581 BCE).

8. Xu Yuangao 徐元誥 reads *juan* 蠲 as *jie* 潔.
9. Xu also reads *huai* 懷 as *gui* 歸.
10. Wei Zhao annotates this Rong as Zhu Rong 祝融, a name often assigned to an entity identified as some type of deity in other texts and specifically as a god here.
11. Identified as a fire god in the commentary.
12. Held as a son of Zhuanxu in *Zuozhuan* Wen 18:7 (*Zuozhuan* 1987: 7636).
13. Wei Zhao identifies these both as a divine beast *shenshou* 神獸.
14. A mythistorical figure. The *Mozi* 墨子, in 'Minggui xia 明鬼下, recounts a tale of how the Earl of Du was killed by King Xuan of Zhou, and then took revenge by shooting him as a ghost to provide further evidence of the existence of ghosts. (*Mozi*, 31.331–2). In the *Fengshan shu* of the *Shiji*, sacrifices to a deity identified as Du, written as 社 but edited as 杜, were meant to occur in the state of Qin. He is identified as the Zhou Commander of the Right (*Shiji*, 28.1375).
15. Being King Xuan of Zhou (r. 827–781 BCE).
16. An historic king of the Western Zhou (ca. 11th BCE –771 BCE) who was preceded by King Kang 康王 and followed by King Mu as indicated in this passage; though it also recounts that Dan Zhu had a hand in his siring.
17. A state that is meant to be located in modern-day Zhuping 遂平 county in Henan. The *Zuozhuan*'s Zhao 13.5 reports that it was annexed by Chu (*Zuozhuan* 1987: 1360).
18. Like Zhu Rong, Dan Zhu is continually cited in other texts in the capacity of a deity or sometimes a mythistorical figure.
19. The commentary suggests that Dan Zhu relied on the body of one of her attendants.
20. Wei Zhao explains that the Li clan is made of the descendants of Dan Zhu (hence, King Mu), and that they must be present, as gods do not respond to those that are not their kin. This representation is also stated in Xi 10:3 (*Zuozhuan* 1987: 334).
21. The name the Li clan is known as in the Zhou.
22. The *Shuowen jiezi* gives the *yin* 禋 sacrifice as: "It is a cleansing sacrifice. One speaking pure intentions is a sacrificial ceremony taken as *yin*. 潔祀也。一曰精意以享爲禋。" (*Shuowen jiezi* 2006: 1A.6B.3).
23. Given here as resting sites for the gods.
24. Commentary indicates that this should be understood to mean that the *shen* will understand virtue and thus repay it with good fortune.
25. Wei Zhao suggests these are nine people.
26. This may suggest a notion of intermarriage.
27. That the term virtue *de* 德 is used here to refer to "virtues" antithetical to the proposal of the texts speaks to this term's lack of moral absolutism.
28. Presumably King Xuan of the Western Zhou. This is also the figure who was killed by the Earl of Du, as recounted earlier in Zhou 1:12.
29. The myth in question is also found in the *Dahuang xijing* 大荒西經 of the *Shanhai jing* (*Shanhai jing* 1985: 402) and the *Luxing* 呂刑 of the *Shangshu* (*Shangshu* 2007: 771–5).

30 Various terms have been used to translate the term *wu* 巫—medium, medicine-man, witch—however, "shaman" has enjoyed the most parlance, particularly within the discourse of the origin of Chinese religion as being shamanistic. Numerous scholars have argued that these figures and the rituals they practiced in pre-Zhou China would evolve into the religious and intellectual systems seen in the Warring States (Cheng 2001: 197–231). The authors of this passage, however, would seem to agree in some capacity with the former appraisal; though as Keightley in his analysis of this passage points out, this is not an exposition of history, but a justification of the religious order put forward in the *Guoyu*, just as the *Guoyu* is read in this chapter (Keightley 1998: 821–4). For a detailed analysis on the nature of the *wu* in the Zhou, see Boileau (2002: 350–78) and Michael (2015: 649–96).

31 Liezi is one of a diverse range of characters that appears in the *Zhuangzi*. Many are unique to the text, while others, such as Liezi, have iterations in other texts from the pre-Qin period. Many of these characters would come to have dominant iterations and historical narratives for them constructed in the imperial period, with Liezi being identified with Lie Yukou 列禦寇 and living in circa 4th C BCE. The transmitted text *Liezi* 列子 is identified with him.

32 The four seas is a metonym for the oecumene.

33 For more information on how the *Zhuangzi* conforms this, see Puett (2003: 122–32).

34 For a further discussion of the implications of skill, see (Barrett 2011) and Eno (1996).

Appendix

1 Dong's life is dated from ca. 179 to 104 BCE.

2 While Hall and Ames rely on these more typically Daoist concepts—especially Five Phases cosmology—in their interpretation of Confucius, Sarah Queen (1996) has convincingly argued that these Daoist elements are later accretions to the text and don't factor at all in Dong's moral and political argument.

Bibliography

Primary Texts

1984. *Lüshi chunqiu jiaodshi (Lüshi chunqiu)* 呂氏春秋校釋. Shanghai, China: Xuelin chubanshe.
1988. *Xunzi jijie (Xunzi)* 旬子集解. Beijing, China: Zhonghua shuju.
1990. *Chunqiu zuozhuan zhu (Zuozhuan)* 春秋左傳 注. Beijing, China: Zhonghua shuju.
2002. *Guoyu jijie (Guoyu)* 國語集解. Beijing, China: Zhonghua shuju.
2006a. *Lunyu zhengyi (Analects)* 論語正義. Beijing, China: Zhonghua shuju.
2006b. *Mozi jiaozhu (Mozi)* 墨子校注. Beijing, China: Zhonghua shuju.
2007a. *Mengzi zhengyi (Mencius)* 孟子正義. Beijing, China: Zhonghua shuju.
2007b. *Shangshu zhengyi (Shangshu)* 尚書正義. Shanghai, China: Shanghai guji chubenshe.
2007c. *Shijing yuanshi (Shijing)* 詩經原始. Beijing, China: Zhonghua shuju.

Allan, Sarah. 1991. *The Shape of the Turtle: Myth, Art, and Cosmos in Early China.* Albany, NY: SUNY Press.
Allan, Sarah. 2009. "Not the *Lun Yu*: The Chu Script Bamboo Slip Manuscript, *Zigao*, and the Nature of Early Confucianism." *Bulletin of the School of Oriental and African Studies* 72: 115–51.
Ames, Roger T. 2003. "Li and the A-theistic Religiousness of Classical Confucianism." In: Tu Weiming and Mary Evelyn Tucker (Eds.): *Confucian Spirituality*. New York: Crossroad.
Ames, Roger. 2011. *Confucian Role Ethics: A Vocabulary*. Hong Kong: The Chinese University of Hong Kong Press.
Ames, Roger and David Hall. 2001. *Focusing the Familiar: A Translation and Philosophical Interpretation of the Zhongyong*. Honolulu: University of Hawaii Press.
Atran, Scott. 2002. *In Gods We Trust: The Evolutionary Landscape of Religion*. Oxford: Oxford University Press.
Atran, Scott and Joseph Henrich. 2010. "The Evolution of Religion." *Biological Theory* 5(1): 18–30.
Banerjee, Konika and Paul Bloom. 2014. "Why Did This Happen to Me? Religious believers' and non-believers' teleological reasoning about life events." *Cognition* 133(1): 277–303. doi: 10.1016/j.cognition
Barrett, Justin L. 2004. *Why Would Anyone Believe in God?* Lanham, MD: Altamira Press.

Barrett, Justin. 2012. *Born Believers: The Science of Children's Religious Belief.* New York: Free Press.

Barrett, Nathaniel F. 2011. "'Wuwei' and Flow: Comparative Reflections on Spirituality, Transcendence, and Skill in the *Zhuangzi*." *Philosophy East and West* 61(4): 679–706.

Bateson, Melissa, Daniel Nettle and Gilbert Roberts 2006. "Cues of Being Watched Enhance Cooperation in a Real-World Setting." *Biology Letters* 2: 412–14.

Behuniak, James. 2005. *Mencius on Becoming Human.* Albany: State University of New York Press.

Behuniak, James. 2011. "Naturalizing Mencius." *Philosophy East & West* 61(3): 492–515.

Bering, Jesse M. 2002. "Intuitive Conceptions of Dead Agents' Minds: The Natural Foundations of Afterlife Beliefs as Phenomenological Boundary." *Journal of Cognition and Culture* 2(4): 263–308.

Bering, Jesse M. 2006. "The Folk Psychology of Souls." *Behavioral and Brain Sciences* 29: 453–462.

Bering, Jesse M. and David Bjorklund. 2004. "The Natural Emergence of Reasoning about the Afterlife as a Developmental Regularity." *Developmental Psychology* 40: 217–33.

Bering, Jesse M. 2011. *The Belief Instinct: The Psychology of Souls, Destiny, and the Meaning of Life.* New York: Norton.

Bering, Jesse M. and Dominic Johnson. 2005. "'O Lord... You Perceive My Thoughts from Afar.': Recursiveness and the Evolution of Supernatural Agency." *Journal of Cognition and Culture* 5(1–2): 118–42.

Bering, Jesse M. and Dominic Johnson. 2006. "Hand of God, Mind of Man: Punishment and Cognition in the Evolution of Cooperation." *Evolutionary Psychology* 4: 219–33.

Berkson, Mark. 1996. "Language: The Guest of Reality—Zhuangzi and Derrida on Language, Reality, and Skillfulness." In: Kuellberg, P. and Ivanhoe, P. (Eds.): *Essays on Skepticism, Relativism, and Ethics in the Zhuangzi.* Albany: State University of New York Press, 97–126.

Birrell, Anne. 1993. *Chinese Mythology: An Introduction.* Baltimore: John Hopkins University Press.

Blakeley, Barry B. 2004. "On the Authenticity and Nature of the *Zuo Zhuan* Revisited." *Early China* 29: 217–67.

Bloom, Paul. 2004. *Descartes' Baby.* New York: Basic Books.

Bloom, Paul. 2007. "Religion Is Natural." *Developmental Science* 10(1): 147–51. doi: 10.1111/j.1467-7687.2007.00577.x

Bodde, Derk. 1981. *Essays on Chinese Civilization.* Princeton: Princeton University Press.

Boileau, Gilles. 2002. "'Wu and Shaman.'" *Bulletin of the School of Oriental and African Studies* 65(2): 350–78.

Bokenkamp, Stephen R. 2007. *Ancestors and Anxiety: Daoism and the Birth of Rebirth in China.* Berkeley: University of California Press.

Boltz, William G. 2005. "The Composite Nature of Early Chinese Texts." In Martin Kern (Ed.): *Text and Ritual in Early China.* Seattle: University of Washington Press, 50–78.

Boyer, Pascal. 1994. *The Naturalness of Religious Ideas: A Cognitive Theory of Religion.* Berkeley, CA: University of California Press.
Boyer, Pascal. 2001. *Religion Explained: The Human Instincts That Fashion Gods, Spirits and Ancestors.* London, UK: Vintage.
Brashier, Kenneth. 1996. "Han Thanatology and the Division of 'Souls.'" *Early China* 21: 125–58.
Brashier, Kenneth. 2011. *Ancestral Memory in Early China.* Cambridge, MA and London: Harvard-Yenching Institute Monograph Series 72.
Brooks, E. Bruce and A. Taeko Brooks. 1998. *The Original Analects: Sayings of Confucius and His Successors.* New York: Columbia University Press.
Brooks, A. Taeko. 2003/04. "Heaven, 'Li', and the Formation of the 'Zuozhuan' 左傳" *Oriens Extremus.* Vol. 44 (2003/04), 51–100.
Bujard, Marianne. 2000. *Le sacrifice au Ciel dans la Chine ancienne: théorie et pratique sous les Han occidentaux.* Paris: École française d'Extrême-Orient.
Bujard, Marianne. 2009. "State and Local Cults in Han Religion." In: Lagerwey, John (Ed.): *Early Chinese Religion.* Leiden: Brill, 777–811.
Carr, Karen and Philip Ivanhoe. 2000. *The Sense of Anti-rationalism: The Religious Thought of Zhuangzi and Kierkegaard.* New York: Seven Bridges Press.
Carr, Michael. 2006. "The Shi 'Corpse/Personator' Ceremony in Early China." In Marcel Kuijste (Ed.): *Reflections on the Dawn of Consciousness: Julian Jaynes's Bicameral Mind Theory Revisited.* Henderson, NV: Julian Jaynes Society, 343–416.
Chan, Wing-Tsit. 1963. *A Source Book in Chinese Philosophy.* Princeton: Princeton University Press.
Chang, K. C. 1976. *Early Chinese Civilization: Anthropological Perspectives.* Cambridge, MA: Harvard University Press.
Chang, K. C. 1983. *Art, Myth, and Ritual: The Path to Political Authority in Ancient China.* Cambridge, MA: Harvard University Press.
Chang, K. C., ed. 1986. *Studies of Shang Archaeology: Selected Papers from the International Conference on Shang Civilization.* New Haven, CT: Yale University Press.
Chang, Ruth. 2000. "Understanding Di and Tian: Deity and Heaven from Shang to Tang Dynasties." *Sino-Platonic Papers* 108 September: 1–54.
Chen, Derong. 2009. "*Di* 帝 and *Tian* 天 in Ancient Chinese Thought: A Critical Analysis of Hegel's Views." *Dao* 8: 13–27.
Chen, Sanping. 2002. "Son of Heaven and Son of God: Interactions among Ancient Asiatic Cultures Regarding Sacral Kingship and Theophoric Names." *Journal of the Royal Asiatic Society* 12(3): 289–325.
Cheng, Anne. 2001. "What Did It Mean to Be a Ru in Han Times?." *Asia Major* XIV(2): 101–18.
Chin, Annping. 2007. *The Authentic Confucius.* New York: Scribner.
Ching, Julia. 1977. *Confucianism and Christianity.* New York: Harper and Row Publishers.

Ch'u Tz'u. 1962. *The Songs of the South (楚辭): An Ancient Chinese Anthology*. Hawkes, David, trans. Boston: Beacon Press.

Clark, Kelly James. 2005. "The Gods of Abraham, Isaiah, and Confucius." *Dao: A Journal of Comparative Philosophy* 5: 109–36.

Clark, Kelly James. 2009. "Tradition and Transcendence in Masters Kong and Rorty." In Yong Huang (Ed.): *Rorty, Pragmatism, and Confucianism*. Albany: State University of New York Press, 227–54.

Clark, Kelly James and Justin Winslett. 2011. "The Evolutionary Psychology of Chinese Religion." *Journal of the American Academy of Religion* 79(4): 928–60.

Cline, Erin. 2014. "Religious Thought and Practice in the *Analects*." In: Olberding, Amy, (Ed.): *Dao Companion to the Analects*, vol 4. New York: Springer, 259–91.

Cook, Constance A. 2006. *Death in Ancient China: The Tale of One Man's Journey*. Leiden: Brill.

Creel, Herrlee Glessner. 1932. "Was Confucius Agnostic?" *T'oung Pao* 29(1): 55.

Creel, Herrlee Glessner. 1970. *The Origins of Statecraft in China*. Vol. 1. Chicago, IL: University of Chicago Press.

Csikszentmihalyi, Mark. 2002. "Confucius and the *Analects* in the Han." In Van Norden, Bryan (Ed.): *Confucius and the Analects*. New York: Oxford University Press. 134–62.

Csikszentmihalyi, Mark and Michael Nylan. 2003. "Constructing Lineages and Inventing Traditions through Exemplary Figures in Early China." *T'oung Pao* 89(1): 59–99

Dawson, Raymond. 2008. *The Analects*. Oxford: Oxford University Press.

de Bary, Theodore Wm. 1996. *The Trouble with Confucianism*. Cambridge, MA: Harvard University Press.

de Bary, Theodore and Irene Bloom. 1999. *Sources of Chinese Tradition*, 1. Second Edition. New York: Columbia University Press.

Defoort, Carine and Nicolas Standaert. 2013. *The Mozi as an Evolving Text: Different Voices in Early Chinese Thought*. Leiden: Brill.

de Groot, J. J. M. 1910. *The Religious System of China: Its Ancient Forms, Evolution, History and Present Aspect, Manners, Customs and Social Institutions Connected Therewith*. Leiden: E.J. Brill.

Denecke, Wiebke. 2010. *The Dynamics of Masters Literature: Early Chinese Thought from Confucius to Han Feizi*. Cambridge: Harvard University Press.

DiYanni, Cara and Deborah Kelemen. 2005. "Time to Get a New Mountain? The Role of Function in Children's Conceptions of Natural Kinds." *Cognition* 97(3): 327–35. doi: 10.1016/j.cognition.2004.10.002

Durkheim, Émile. [1915] 1965. *The Elementary Forms of Religious Life*. J. W. Swain, trans. New York: Free Press.

Durrant, Stephen. 1995. *The Cloudy Mirror: Tension and Conflict in the Writings of Sima Qian*. New York: SUNY Press.

Eno, Robert. 1990a. *The Confucian Creation of Heaven*. Albany: State University of New York Press.

Eno, Robert. 1990b. "Was There a High God *Ti* in Shang Religion?" *Early China* 15: 1–26.

Eno, Robert. 1996. "Cook Ding's Dao and the Limits of Philosophy." In: Paul Kuellberg and Philip Ivanhoe (Eds.): *Essays on Skepticism, Relativism, and Ethics in the Zhuangzi*. Albany: State University of New York Press, 127–51.

Eno, Robert. 2009. "Shang State Religion and the Pantheon of the Oracle Texts." Kalinowski and Lagerwey 2009: 41–102.

Erickson, Susan. 2010. "Han Dynasty Tomb Structures and Contents." In: Michael Nylan and Michael Loewe (Eds.): *China's Early Empires: A Re-appraisal*. Cambridge: Cambridge University Press, 13–82.

Evans, J. St. B. T. and J. Curtis-Holmes. 2005. "Rapid Responding Increases Belief Bias: Evidence for the Dual-process Theory of Reasoning." *Thinking & Reasoning* 11(4): 382–89. doi: 10.1080/13546780542000005

Falkenhausen, Lothar von. 1994. "Sources of Taoism: Reflections on Archaeological Indicators of Religious Change in Eastern Zhou China." *Taoist Resources* 5(2): 1–2.

Falkenhausen, Lothar von. 2006. *Chinese Society in the Age of Confucius (1000–250 BC): The Archaeological Evidence*. Los Angeles: Cotsen Institute of Archaeology, UCLA.

Falkenhausen, Lothar von. 2008. "Archaeological Perspectives on the Philosophicization of Royal Zhou Ritual." In: Dieter Kuhn and Helga Stahl (Eds.): *Perceptions of Antiquity in Chinese Civilization*. Heidelberg: Forum, 135–75.

Feng, YuLan. 1952. *A History of Chinese Philosophy*. Second Edition. Princeton: Princeton University Press.

Fibiger Bang, Peter and Karen Turner. 2015. "Kingship and Elite Formation." In: Walter Scheidel (Ed.): *State Power in Ancient Rome and China*. Oxford: Oxford University Press, 11–38.

Fingarette, Herbert. 1972. *Confucius: The Secular as Sacred*. New York: Harper Torchbooks.

Flanagan, Owen and Stephen Geiz. 2015. "Confucian Moral Sources." In: Brian Bruya (Ed.): *The Philosophical Challenge from China*. Cambridge, MA: MIT Press, 205–28.

Fu, Charles Wei-hsun. 1978. "Fingarette and Munro on Early Confucianism: A Methodological Examination." *Philosophy East and West* 28(2): 181–8.

Gernet, Jacques. 1985a. *A History of Chinese Civilization*. J. R. Foster, trans. Cambridge: Cambridge University Press.

Gernet, Jacques. 1985b. *China and the Christian Impact: A Conflict of Cultures*. Janet Lloyd, trans. Cambridge: Cambridge University Press.

Goldberg, Robert and Sharon Thompson-Schill. 2009. "Developmental 'Roots' in Mature Biological Knowledge." *Psychological Science* 20(4): 480–7. doi: 10.1111/j.1467-9280.2009.02320.x

Goldin, Paul. 2002. *The Culture of Sex in Ancient China*. Honolulu: University of Hawai'i Press.
Goldin, Paul. 2007. "Xunzi and Early Han Philosophy." *Harvard Journal of Asiatic Studies* 67(1) (Jun): 135–66.
Goldin, Paul. 2008. "The Myth That China Has No Creation Myth." *Monumenta Serica* 56: 1–22.
Goldin, Paul. 2015. "The Consciousness of the Dead as a Philosophical Problem in Ancient China." In R. A. H. King (Ed.): *The Good Life and Conceptions of Life in Early China and Graeco-Roman Antiquity*. Berlin: De Gruyter, 59–92.
Graham, A. C. 1978. *Later Mohist Logic, Ethics and Science*. Hong Kong: Chinese University Press.
Graham, A. C. 1989. *Disputers of the Tao*. La Salle, IL: Open Court.
Graham, Jesse and Jonathan Haidt. 2010. "Beyond Beliefs: Religions Bind Individuals into Moral Communities." *Personality and Social Psychology Review* 14(1): 140–50.
Granet, Marcel. 1934. *La Pensee Chinoise*. Paris: Albin Michel.
Guo, Jue. 2011. "Concepts of Death and the Afterlife in Newly Discovered Tomb Objects and Texts from Han China." In: Amy Olberding and P. J. Ivanhoe (Eds.): *Mortality in Traditional Chinese Thought*. Albany: State University of New York Press, 85–116.
Guo, Moruo. 1936. *Xian-Qin tiandao guan zhi jinzhan*. Shanghai: Shangwu, 1–18.
Guo, Moruo. 1982. *Complete Works of Guo Moruo*. Beijing: People's Publishing House.
Guthrie, Stewart. 1993. *Faces in the Clouds*. Oxford, UK: Oxford University Press.
Hall, David L. and Roger T. Ames. 1987. *Thinking through Confucius*. Albany: State University of New York Press.
Hardy, Grant. 1999. *Bamboo and Bronze: Sima Qian's Conquest of History*. New York: Columbia University Press.
Harper, Donald. 1994. "Resurrection in Warring States Popular Religion." *Taoist Resources* 5(2): 13–28.
Harper, Donald. 1999. "Warring States Natural Philosophy and Occult Thought." In Michael Loewe and Edward Shaughnessy (Eds.): *The Cambridge History of Ancient China: From the Origins of Civilization to 221 B.C.* Cambridge: Cambridge University Press, 813–84.
Harper, Donald. 2004. "Contracts with the Spirit World in Han Common Religion: The Xuning Prayer and Sacrifice Documents of A.D. 79." *Cahiers d'Extrême-Asie* 14: 227–67.
Hayashi, Minao. 2002. 林巳奈夫 *Chūgoku kodai no kamigami* 中国古代の神がみ. Tokyo: Yoshikawa Kōbunkan.
He Yan 何晏. 2000. *Lunyu zhushu* 論語注疏. Beijing: Peking University Press.
Henderson, John B. 1984. *The Development and Decline of Chinese Cosmology*. New York: Columbia University Press.
Henderson, John B. 1991. *Scripture, Canon, and Commentary: A Comparison of Confucian and Western Exegesis*. Princeton: Princeton University Press.

Henrich, Joseph. 2009. "The Evolution of Costly Displays, Cooperation and Religion: Credibility Enhancing Displays and Their Implications for Cultural Evolution." *Evolution and Human Behavior* 30: 244–60.

Ho, Ping-ti. 1975. *The Cradle of the East*. Hongkong: The Chinese University Pub. Office and Chicago: The University of Chicago Press.

Hsu Cho-Yun and Katheryn Linduff. 1988. *Western Chou Civilization*. New Haven, CT: Yale University Press.

Hu Shih. 1929. "The Establishment of Confucianism as a State Religion during the Han Dynasty." *Journal of the North-China Branch of the Royal Asiatic Society* LX: 20–41.

Hunter, Michael Justin. 2012. *Sayings of Confucius, Deselected*. PhD dissertation, Princeton University.

Hunter, Michael Justin. 2017. *Confucius Beyond the Analects*. Leiden: Brill.

Ivanhoe, Philip J. 1988. "A Question of Faith: A New Interpretation of Mencius 2B.13." *Early China* 13(321): 153–65.

Ivanhoe, Philip J. 1991. "Thinking through Confucius" by David L. Hall and Roger T. Ames. *Philosophy East and West* 41(2): 241–54.

Ivanhoe, Philip J. 2007. "Heaven as a Source for Ethical Warrant in Early Confucianism." *Dao* 6(3): 211–20.

Ivanhoe, Philip J. 2011. "Death and Dying in the *Analects*." In: Amy Olberding and Philip J. Ivanhoe (Eds.): *Mortality in Traditional Chinese Thought*. Albany: SUNY Press, 137–51.

Jensen, Lionel M. 1998. *Manufacturing Confucianism*. Durham: Duke University Press.

Johnson, Dominic. 2005. "God's Punishment and Public Goods: A Test of the Supernatural Punishment Hypothesis in 186 World Cultures." *Human Nature* 16: 410–46.

Johnson, Dominic. 2011. "Why God Is the Best Punisher." *Religion, Brain and Behavior* 1: 77–84.

Johnson, Dominic, Stephen Knights, and Pavel Stopka. 2003. "The Puzzle of Human Cooperation." *Nature* 421: 911–12.

Kalinowski, Marc and John Lagerwey, eds. 2009. *Early Chinese Religion, Part One: Shang through Han (1250 BC–220 AD)*. Leiden, UK: Brill.

Karlgren, Bernhard. 1950. *The Book of Odes*. Stockholm: Museum of Far Eastern Antiquities.

Keightley, David. 1978a. "Religious Commitment: Shang Theology and the Genesis of Chinese Political Culture." *History of Religions* 17: 211–25.

Keightley, David. 1978b. *Sources of Shang History: The Oracle-Bone Inscriptions of Bronze Age China*. Berkeley: University of California Press.

Keightley, David. 1984. "Late Shang Divination: The Magico-Religious Legacy." *Journal of the American Academy of Religion Thematic Studies* 50(2): 11–34.

Keightley, David. 1988. "Shang Divination and Metaphysics." *Philosophy East & West* 38: 367–97.

Keightley, David. 1996. "The Shang: China's First Historical Dynasty." In: Michael Loewe and Edward Shaughnessy (Ed.): *The Cambridge History of Ancient China: From the Origins of Civilization to 221 B.C.* Cambridge, UK: Cambridge University Press, 232–91.

Keightley, David. 1998. "Shamanism, Death, and the Ancestors." *Asiatische Studien* LII/3: 821–4.

Keightley, David. 1999. "The Shang: China's First Historical Dynasty." In Michael Loewe and Edward L. Shaughnessy (Eds.): *The Cambridge History of Ancient China: From the Origins of Civilization to 221 B.C.* New York: Cambridge University Press, 232–91.

Keightley, David. 2000. *The Ancestral Landscape: Time, Space, and Community in Late Shang China.* Berkeley, CA: Institute of East Asian Studies.

Kelemen, Deborah. 1999a. "Beliefs about Purpose: On the Origins of Teleological Thought." In M. Corballis and S. Lea (Eds.): *The Descent of Mind.* Oxford: Oxford University Press, 278–94.

Kelemen, Deborah. 1999b. "The Scope of Teleological Thinking in Preschool Children." *Cognition* 70: 241–72.

Kelemen, Deborah. 1999c. "Why Are Rocks Pointy? Children's Preference for Teleological Explanations of the Natural World." *Developmental Psychology* 35(6): 1440–52.

Kelemen, Deborah. 2003. "British and American Children's Preferences for Teleofunctional Explanations of the Natural World." *Cognition* 88(2): 201–21. doi:10.1016/S0010-0277(03)00024-6

Kelemen, Deborah. 2004. "Are Children "Intuitive Theists?" Reasoning About Purpose and Design in Nature." *Psychological Science* 15(5): 295–301. doi: 10.1111/j.0956-7976.2004.00672.x

Kelemen, Deborah. 2012. "Teleological Minds: How Natural Intuitions about Agency and Purpose Influence Learning about Evolution." In: Karl S. Rosengren, Sara K. Brem, E. Margaret Evans, and Gale M. Sinatra (Eds.): *Evolution Challenges: Integrating Research and Practice in Teaching and Learning about Evolution.* Oxford, England: Oxford University Press, 66–92.

Kelemen, Deborah and Cara DiYanni. 2005. "Intuitions about Origins: Purpose and Intelligent Design in Children's Reasoning about Nature." *Journal of Cognition and Development* 6(1): 3–31. doi: 10.1207/s15327647jcd0601_2

Kelemen, Deborah. and Evelyn Rosset. 2009. "The Human Function Compunction: Teleological Explanation in Adults." *Cognition* 111(1): 138–43. doi: 10.1016/j.cognition.2009.01.001

Kelemen, Deborah, Josh Rottman and Rebecca Seston. 2013. "Professional Physical Scientists Display Tenacious Teleological Tendencies: Purpose-based Reasoning as a Cognitive Default." *Journal of Experimental Psychology: General* 142(4): 1074–83. doi: 10.1037/a0030399

Keltner, Dacher and Jonathan Haidt. 2003. "Approaching Awe, a Moral, Spiritual, and Aesthetic Emotion." *Cognition and Emotion* 17(2): 297–314.

Kern, Martin. 2005. "Introduction: The Ritual Texture of Early China." In: Martin Kern (Ed.): *Text and Ritual in Early China*. Seattle: University of Washington Press, vii–xxvii.

Kern, Martin. 2009. "Bronze Inscriptions, the Shijing and the Shangshu: The Evolution of the Ancestral Sacrifice during the Western Zhou." In: John Lagerwey and Marc Kalinowski (Eds.): *Early Chinese Religion, Part I*. Leiden: Brill, 143–200.

Kim, Tae Hyun and Mark Csikszentmihalyi. 2014. "History and Formation of the *Analects*." Olberding 2014: 21–36.

Klein, Esther and Colin Klein. 2012. "Did the Chinese Have a Change of Heart?" *Cognitive Science* 36: 179–82.

Knoblock, John and Jeffrey Riegel. 2000. *The Annals of Lü Buwei*. Stanford: Stanford University Press.

Kunio, Shima 島邦男. 1967. *Inkyo bokuji sōrui* 殷墟卜辭綜類. Tokyo: Daian.

Lagerwey, John and Marc Kalinowski, eds. 2009. *Early Chinese Religion, Part One: Shang through Han (1250 BC–220 AD)*. Vol. II. Leiden and Boston: Brill.

Lai Guolong. 2002. "Lighting the Way in the Afterlife: Bronze Lamps in Warring States Period Tombs." *Orientations* 4: 20–8.

Lai Guolong. 2005. "Death and the Otherworldly Journey in Early China as Seen through Tomb Texts, Travel Paraphernalia, and Road Rituals." *Asia Major* 3rd ser, 18(1): 1–44.

Lai Guolong. 2015. *Excavating the Afterlife: The Archaeology of Early Chinese Religion*. Seattle: University of Washington Press.

Lai Kehong 來可泓. ed. 2000. *Lunyu zhijie* 論語直接. Shanghai: Fudan University Press.

Lau, D. C., trans. 1970. *Mencius*. London, UK: Penguin Books.

Lawson, E. Thomas and Robert N. McCauley. 1990. *Rethinking Religion: Connecting Cognition and Culture*. Cambridge: Cambridge University Press.

Leeming, David. 2001. *A Dictionary of Asian Mythology*. Oxford: Oxford University Press.

Legge, James. 1852. *The Notions of the Chinese Concerning God and Spirits*. Hong Kong: Hong Kong Register Office.

Legge, James. 1865. *The Chinese Classics. Vol. III: The Shoo King*. London: Trübner Co.

Legge, James. 1880. *Religions of China*. London: Hodder and Stoughton.

Legge, James. 2000a. *The Sacred Books of the East. Vol. III*. Repr. Oxford, UK: Clarendon Press.

Legge, James. 2000b. *The Chinese Classics* IV. Taibei: SMC Publishing.

Lewis, Mark Edward. 1999a. "The Feng and Shan Sacrifices of Emperor Wu of Han." In: Joseph P. McDermott (Ed.): *State and Court Ritual in China*. Cambridge: Cambridge University Press, 81–111.

Lewis, Mark Edward. 1999b. "Warring States Political History." In: Michael Loewe and Edward Shaughnessy (Eds.): *The Cambridge History of Ancient China: From the Origins of Civilization to 221 B.C.* Cambridge, UK: Cambridge University Press, 587–650.

Lewis, Mark Edward. 1999c. *Writing and Authority in Early China.* Albany: State University of New York Press.

Leys, Simon. 1997. *The Analects of Confucius.* New York: W. W. Norton.

Li, Xueqin 李學群. 1998. *Inquiry on Chinese Ancient Civilization and the Formation of the State* 《中國古代文明與國家形成研究》. Kunming 昆明: Yunnan Renmin Chubanshe 雲南人民出版社.

Li, Xueqin 李學勤. 2000. "The Confucian Texts From Guodian Tomb Number One: Their Date and Significance." In: Sarah Allan and Crispin Williams (Eds.): *The Guodian Laozi: Proceedings of the International Conference, Dartmouth College, May 1998.* Berkeley, CA: Society for the Study of Early China and Institute of East Asian Studies, 107–11.

Liang, Qichao. 1996. 梁啟超 *Xianqin zhengzhi sixiang shi* 先秦政治思想史. Beijing, China: Donfang shuju, 33–44.

Liu, Zongyuan. 1979. *Fei Guoyu* 非國語 in *Liu Zongyuan ji* 柳宗元集. Beijing: China Zhonghua shuju, 1265–329.

Loewe, Michael. 1979. *Ways to Paradise: The Chinese Quest for Immortality.* London: George Allen & Unwin.

Loewe, Michael. 1986. "The Former Han Dynasty." In: Denis Crispin Twitchett and John King Fairbank.(Eds.): *The Cambridge History of China, Volume I: The Ch'in and Han Empires, 221 B.C.—A.D. 220.* Cambridge: Cambridge University Press, 193–222.

Loewe, Michael. 1993. "Shih Ching 詩經." In: Michael Loewe (Ed.): *In Early Chinese Texts: A Bibliographic Guide.* Berkeley, CA: The Society for the Study of Early China, 415–23.

Loewe, Michael. 2005 reprint. *Faith, Myth and Reason in Han China.* Indianapolis: Hackett Publishing Company.

Loewe, Michael. 2011. *Dong Zhongshu, a "Confucian" Heritage and the Chunqiu fanlu.* Leiden: Brill Academic Publishers.

Loewe, Michael. 2012. "'Confucian' Values and Practices in Han China." *T'oung Pao* 98: 1–30.

Louden, Robert. 2002. "'What Does Heaven Say?': Christian Wolff and Western Interpretations of Confucian Ethics." In: Bryan W. Van Norden (Ed.): *Confucius and the Analects: New Essays.* New York: Oxford University Press, 73–93.

Machle, Edward. 1993. *Nature and Heaven in the Xunzi.* New York: SUNY Press.

McCauley, Robert N. 2011. *Why Religion Is Natural and Science Is Not.* Oxford University Press.

Makeham, John. 1996. "On the Formation of *Lunyu* as a Book." *Monumenta Serica* 44: 1–24.

Makeham, John. 2003. *Transmitters and Creators*. Cambridge, MA and London: Harvard University Asia Center.

Makeham, John. 2009. "In Quest of the Authentic Confucius." *China Heritage Quarterly* 18.

Makeham, John. 2011. "A Critical Overview of Some Contemporary Chinese Perspectives on the Composition and Date of *Lunyu*." A paper presented at "The *Analects*: A Western Han Text?", a conference held at Princeton University, November 4–5, 2011.

Michael, Thomas. 2015. "Shamanism Theory and the Early Chinese *Wu*." *Journal of the American Academy of Religion* 83(3), September: 649–96.

Mote, Frederick. 1972. "The Cosmological Gulf between China and the West." In: David C. Buxbaum and Frederick W. Mote (Eds.): *Transition and Permanence: Chinese History and Culture*. Hong Kong Cathay Press, 1972, 3–21.

Mou, Zhongjian 牟宗鑒 and Zhang Jian 張踐. 2003. *General History of Chinese Religion* 《中國宗教通史》. Vol. 1. Beijing 北京: Shehui Kexue Wenxian Chubanshe 社會科學文獻出版社.

Mueller, Charles, translator. 2003. *The Doctrine of the Mean (Zhongyong)*. www.hm.tyg.jp/~acmuller/contao/docofmean.htm

Mungello, David. 1974. *Curious Land: Jesuit Accommodation and the Origins of Sinology*. Stuttgart: Franz Steiner Verlag Wiesbaden.

Munro, Donald J. 2002. "Mencius and an Ethics of the New Century." In: Alan K. L. Chan (Ed.): *Mencius: Contexts and Interpretations*. Honolulu: University of Hawai'i Press, 305–16.

Needham, Joseph. 1974. *Science and Civilisation in China*. Cambridge: Cambridge University.

Ni, Peimin. 2017. *Understanding the Analects of Confucius*. New York: SUNY Press.

Nivison, David Shepherd. 1999. "The Classical Philosophical Writings." In Michael Loewe and Edward L. Shaughnessy (Eds.): *The Cambridge History of Ancient China: From the Origins of Civilization to 221 B.C.* Cambridge: Cambridge University Press, 745–812.

Norenzayan, Ara and Azim Shariff. 2008. "The Origin and Evolution of Religious Prosociality." *Science* 322: 58–62.

Norenzayan, Ara. 2013. *Big Gods: How Religion Transformed Cooperation and Conflict*. Princeton: Princeton University Press.

Norenzayan, Ara, Azim Shariff, Will Gervais, Aiyana Willard, Rita McNamara, Edward Slingerland and Joseph Henrich. 2016. "The Cultural Evolution of Prosocial Religions." *Behavioral and Brain Sciences* 39, E1.

Nylan, Michael. 1999. "A Problematic Model: The Han 'Orthodox Synthesis,' Then and Now." In: Kai-Wing ChowOn-Cho Ng and John B. Henderson (Eds.): *Imagining Boundaries: Changing Confucian Doctrines, Texts, and Hermeneutics*. Albany: SUNY Press, 17–56.

Nylan, Michael. 2001. *The Five "Confucian" Classics*. New Haven, CT: Yale University Press.

Nylan, Michael. 2016. "Xunzi: An Early Reception History, Han Through Tang." In: Eric L. Hutton (Ed.): *Dao Companion to the Philosophy of Xunzi*. New York: Springer.

Nylan, Michael and Thomas Wilson. 2010. *Lives of Confucius*. New Haven, CT: Yale University Press, 395–433.

Olberding, Amy ed. 2014. *Dao Companion to the Analects*. Dordrecht, The Netherlands: Springer.

Olberding, Amy and Philip Ivanhoe, eds. 2011. *Mortality in Traditional Chinese Thought*. Edited by SUNY series in Chinese Philosophy and Culture, Roger T. Ames, editor. Albany: State University of New York Press.

Overmeyer, Daniel. 1995. "Chinese Religions: the State of the Field." *Journal of Asian Studies* 54(1), February: 124–60.

Pankenier, David. 1995. "Astrological Origins of Chinese Dynastic Ideology." *Vistas in Astronomy* 39(4): 503–16.

Paper, Jordan. *The Spirits Are Drunk: Comparative Approaches to Chinese Religion*. Albany, NY: State University of New York Press, 1995.

Perkins, Franklin. 2014a. *Heaven and Earth Are Not Humane: The Problem of Evil in Classical Chinese Philosophy*. Bloomington: Indiana University Press.

Perkins, Franklin. 2014b. "The *Mozi* and the *Daodejing*." *Journal of Chinese Philosophy* 41(1–2), March–June: 18–32.

Pfister, Lauren. 1999. "Discovering Monotheistic Metaphysics: The Exegetical Reflections of James Legge (1815–1897) and Lo Chung-fan (d. circa 1850)." In Ng On-cho, et. al. (Eds.): *Imagining Boundaries: Changing Confucian Doctrines, Texts and Hermeneutics*. Albany: SUNY Press, 213–54.

Piff, Paul, et al. 2015. "Awe, the Small Self, and Prosocial Behavior." *Journal of Personality and Social Psychology* 108(6): 883–99.

Pines, Yuri. 2002. *Foundations of Confucian Thought: Intellectual Life in the Chunqiu Period, 722–453 B.C.E.* Honolulu: University of Hawaii Press.

Pirazzoli-t'Serstevens, Michele. 2009. "Death and the Dead: Practices and Images in the Qin and Han." In: John Lagerwey and Marc Kalinowski (Eds.): *Early Chinese Religion: Part One: Shang through Han (1250 BC–220 AD)*, vol. 2, Handbuch der Orientalistik 21–22. Leiden: Bril), 949–1026.

Poo, Mu-Chou. 1998. *In Search of Personal Welfare: A View of Ancient Chinese Religion*. Albany: State University of New York Press.

Poo, Mu-Chou. 2004. "The Concept of Ghost in Ancient Chinese Religion." In: John Lagerwey (Ed.): *Religion and Chinese Society*. Paris: École française d'Extrême-Orient, 173–92.

Poo, Mu-Chou. 2009. "Ritual and Ritual Texts in Early China." In: John Lagerwey and Mark Kalinowski (Eds.): *Early Chinese Religion*, vol 1, 281–313.

Poo, Mu-Chou. 2011. "Preparation for the Afterlife in Ancient China." In: Amy Olberding and Philip Ivanhoe (Eds.): *Mortality in Traditional Chinese Thought*. Albany: State University of New York Press, 13–36.

Puett, Michael. 1997. "Nature and Artifice: Debates in Late Warring States China Concerning the Creation of Culture." *Harvard Journal of Asiatic Studies* 57(2), December: 471–518.

Puett, Michael. 2003. *To Become a God: Cosmology, Sacrifice, and Self-divination in Early China*. Cambridge: Harvard University Asia Center.

Puett, Michael. 2009. "Combining the Ghosts and Spirits, Centering the Realm: Mortuary Ritual and Political Organization in the Ritual Compendia of Early China." Lagerwey and Kalinowski 2009: 695-720.

Puett, Michael. 2014. "Ritual Disjunctions: Ghosts, Philosophy, and Anthropology." In: Veena Das, et. al. (Eds.): *The Ground between: Anthropologists Engage Philosophy*. Durham: Duke University Press, 218-33.

Puett, Michael. 2011. "Sages, the Past, and the Dead." In: Amy Olberding and Philip J. Ivanhoe (Eds.): *Mortality in Traditional Chinese Thought*. Albany: State University of New York Press, 225-48.

Queen, Sarah. 1996. *From Chronicle to Canon: The Hermeneutics of the Spring and Autumn, According to Tung Chung-shu*. Cambridge: Cambridge University Press.

Raphals, Lisa. 2013. *Divination and Prediction in Early China and Ancient Greece*. Cambridge: Cambridge University Press.

Rawson, Jessica. 1998. "Chinese Burial Patterns: Sources of Information on Thought and Belief." In: Colin Renfrew and Chris Scarre (Eds.): *Cognition and Material Culture: The Archaeology of Symbolic Storage*. Cambridge, England: McDonald Institute for Archaeological Research, 107-33.

Rawson, Jessica. 1999a. "Ancient Chinese Ritual as Seen in the Material Record." In: Joseph P. McDermott (Ed.): *State and Court Ritual in China*. Cambridge: Cambridge University Press, 20-49.

Rawson, Jessica. 1999b. "The Eternal Palaces of the Western Han: A New View of the Universe." *Artibus Asiae* 59(1–2): 5-58.

Redmond, Geoffrey and Tze-Ki Hon. 2014. *Teaching the I Ching*. Oxford: Oxford University Press.

Richert, Rebekah and Paul Harris. 2008. "Dualism Revisited: Body vs. Mind vs. Soul." *Journal of Cognition & Culture* 8: 99-115.

Rorty, Richard. 1982. *Consequences of Pragmatism*. Minneapolis, MN: University of Minnesota Press, 90-109.

Rorty, Richard. 1998. "The Historiography of Philosophy: Four Genres." In *Truth and Progress: Philosophical Papers Volume 3*. Cambridge: Cambridge University Press, 1998, 247-73.

Rottman, Joshua, Zhu Liqi, Wang Wen, Rebecca Schillaci, Kelly James Clark and Deborah Keleman. 2017. "Cultural Influences on the Teleological Stance: Evidence from China." *Religion, Brain & Behavior*, 7(1), 17– 26. doi:10.1080/2153599X.2015.1118402

Rudd, Melanie, et al. 2012. "Awe Expands People's Perception of Time, Alters Decision Making, and Enhances Well-being." *Psychological Science* 23(10): 1130–1136.

Santangelo, Paolo. 2007. "Emotions and Perception of Inner Reality: Chinese and European." *Journal of Chinese Philosophy* 34(2): 289–308.

Schaberg, David. 2001. *A Patterned Past: Form and Thought in Early Chinese Historiography*. Cambridge, MA: Harvard Asia Center.

Schwartz, Benjamin. 1985. *The World of Thought in Ancient China*. Cambridge, MA: The Belknap Press of the Harvard University Press.

Schwitzgebel, Eric. 1996. "Zhuangzi's Attitude toward Language and His Skepticism." In: P. Kjellberg and Philip J. Ivanhoe (Eds.): *Essays on Skepticism, Relativism, and Ethics in the Zhuangzi*. Albany: Suny Press, 68–96.

Seidel, Anna. 1982. "Tokens of Immortality in Han Graves." *Numen* 29(1): 79–122.

Seidel, Anna. 1987. "Traces of Han Religion in Funeral Texts Found in Tombs." In: Akizuki Kan'ei 秋月観英 (Ed.): *Dōkyō to shūkyō bunka* 道教と宗教文化. Tokyo: Hirakawa shuppansha, 714–78.

Shahar, Meir and Robert Weller. 1996. *Unruly Gods: Divinity and Society in China*. Honolulu: University of Hawaii Press, 1996.

Shaughnessy, Edward. 1992. *Sources of Western Zhou History: Inscribed Bronze Vessels*. Berkeley: University of California Press.

Shaughnessy, Edward. 1993. "Shangshu." In: Michael Lowe (Ed.): *Early Chinese Texts: A Bibliographical Guide*. Berkeley: The Society for the Study of Early China and The Institute of East Asian Studies, 376–89.

Shaughnessy, Edward. 1999. "Western Zhou History." In: Edward Shaughnessy and Michaele Lowe (Eds.): *The Cambridge History of Ancient China*. New York: Cambridge University Press, 292–351.

Shaughnessy, Edward L. 1993. "*Shang shu* 尚書 (*Shu ching* 書經)." In: Michael Loewe (Ed.): *Early Chinese Texts: A Bibliographic Guide*. Berkeley, CA: The Society for the Study of Early China, 376–89.

Shun, Kwong-loi. 1993. "*Jen* and *Li* in the *Analects*." *Philosophy East and West* 43(3): 457–79.

Shiji 史記. 2006. Beijing: Zhonghua shuju.

Shtulman, Andrew and Joshua Valcarcel. 2012. "Scientific Knowledge Suppresses but Does Not Supplant Earlier Intuitions." *Cognition* 124(2): 209–15. doi: 10.1016/j.cognition.2012.04.005

Sima Qian 司馬遷, ed. 1963. *Shiji* 史記. Beijing: Zhonghua shuju.

Slingerland, Edward. 2000. "Why Philosophy Is Not 'Extra' in Understanding the *Analects*, a Review of Brooks and Brooks, *The Original Analects*." *Philosophy East and West* 50(1): 137–41, 146–7.

Slingerland, Edward, trans. 2003. *Confucius: Analects: With Selections from Traditional Commentaries*. Indianapolis: Hackett Publishing, 62.

Slingerland, Edward, trans. 2008. *What Science Offers the Humanities: Integrating Body & Culture*. Cambridge: Cambridge University Press.

Slingerland, Edward, trans. 2013. "Body and Mind in Early China: An Integrated Humanities-Science Approach." *Journal of the American Academy of Religion* 81(1): 6–55.

Slingerland, Edward, trans. 2019. *Mind and Body in Early China: Beyond Orientalism and the Myth of Holism*. Oxford: Oxford University Press.

Slingerland, Edward and Maciej Chudek. 2011. "The Prevalence of Mind–Body Dualism in Early China." *Cognitive Science* 35: 997–1007.

Slingerland, Edward and Maciej Chudek. 2017. "China as the Radical 'Other': Lessons for the Cognitive Science of Religion." In: Ryan G. Hornbeck, Justin L. Barrett and Madeleine Kang (Eds.): *Is Religion Natural? The Chinese Challenge*. New York: Springer, 55–76.

Smith, Kidder and Sima Tan. 2003. "Sima Tan and the Invention of Daoism, 'Legalism,' et cetera." *The Journal of Asian Studies* 62(1): 129–56.

Sosis, Richard. 2009. "The Adaptationist-Byproduct Debate on the Evolution of Religion: Five Misunderstandings of the Adaptationist Program." *Journal of Cognition and Culture* 9: 315–32.

Sosis, Richard and Bradley Ruffle. 2003. "Religious Ritual and Cooperation: Testing for a Relationship on Israeli Religious and Secular Kibbutzim." *Current Anthropology* 44: 713–22.

Sterckx, Roel. 2007. "Searching for Spirit: Shen and Sacrifice in Warring States and Han Philosophy and Ritual." *Extrême-Orient, Extrême-Occident* 29: 23–54.

Sterckx, Roel. 2010. "Religious Practices in Qin and Han." In: Michael Loewe and Michael Nylan (Eds.): *In China's Early Empires, a Re-appraisal*. Cambridge, UK: Cambridge University Press, 415–29.

Sterckx, Roel. 2011. *Food, Sacrifice, and Sagehood in Early China*. Cambridge: Cambridge University Press.

Tu, Weiming. 2002. "Transcendent and Yet Immanent: The Unique Features of Confucian Spirituality." In *Collected Works of Tu Weiming*, vol. 1. Wuhan, China: Wuhan Press.

Tuan, Yi-Fu. 1999. *Cosmos & Hearth*. Ann Arbor: University of Minnesota Press.

Valdesolo, Piercarlo and Jesse Graham. 2014. "Awe, Uncertainty, and Agency Detection." *Psychological Science* 25(1): 170–8.

Valdesolo, Piercarlo, et al. 2016. "Awe and Scientific Explanation." *Emotion* 16(7): 937–40.

Van Cappellen, Patty and Vassilis Saroglou. 2012. "Awe Activates Religious and Spiritual Feelings and Behavioral Intentions." *Psychology of Religion and Spirituality* 4(3): 223–36.

van Els, Paul. 2012a. "Confucius' Sayings Entombed: On Two Han Dynasty Bamboo *Analects* Manuscript." In Michael Hunter, Martin Kern, and Oliver Weingarten (Eds.): *The "Analects" Revisited: New Perspectives on the Dating of a Classic*. Leiden: Brill, 152–86.

van Els, Paul. 2012b. "Tilting Vessels and Collapsing Walls–On the Rhetorical Function of Anecdotes in Early Chinese Texts." *Extrême-Orient Extrême-Occident*, 34(2): 141–66.

Van Norden, Bryan, ed. 2002. *Confucius and the Analects*. New York: Oxford University Press.

Waley, Arthur. 1938, 1996 (rev). *The Book of Songs*. New York: Grove Press.

Wang, Bo. 2012. "Religion and Belief in the Shang and Zhou Dynasties." In: Yuan Xingpei, et al. (Eds.): *The History of Chinese Civilization*. Cambridge: Cambridge University Press, 443–76.

Wang, Zhongjiang. 2016. *Order in Early Chinese Excavated Texts: Natural, Supernatural and Legal Approaches*. Misha Tadd, trans. New York: Palgrave-Macmillan.

Wawrytko, Sandra. 2000. "Kong Zi as Feminist: Confucian Self-cultivation in a Contemporary Context." *Journal of Chinese Philosophy* 27(2): 171–86.

Wen, Nicole, et al. 2016. "Ritual Increases Children's Affiliation with In-group Members." *Evolution and Human Behavior* 37(1): 54–60.

Whitehouse, Harvey and Robert McCauley. 2005. *Mind and Religion: Psychological and Cognitive Foundations of Religiosity*. Lanham, MD: Rowman Altamira.

Wilson, Thomas. 2014. "Spirits and the Soul in Confucian Ritual Discourse." *Journal of Chinese Religions* 42(2): 185–212.

Wiltermuth, Scott and Chip Heath. 2009. "Synchrony and Cooperation." *Psychological Science* 20(1): 1–5.

Winslett, Justin. 2009. *Form or Function: The Representation of Deities in Early Chinese Texts*. Oxford: Doctoral Thesis

Winslett, Justin. 2014. "Deities and the Extrahuman in Pre-Qin China: Lesser Deities in the *Zuozhuan* and the *Guoyu*." *Journal of the American Academy of Religion* 82(4), December 1: 938–69.

Wittgenstein, Ludwig. 1922. *Tractatus Logico-Philosophicus*. D. F. Pears and B. F. McGuinness, trans. London: Routledge and Kegan Paul.

Wittgenstein, Ludwig. 1953. *Philosophical Investigations*. New York: Macmillan Publishing Company.

Wong, Benjamin and Hui-chieh Loy. 2004. "War and Ghosts in Mozi's Political Philosophy." *Philosophy East and West* 54(3): 343–63.

Wu, Hung. 1998. "Where Are They Going? Where Did They Come From? Hearse and 'Soul Carriage' in Han Dynasty Tomb Art." *Orientations* 29(6): 22.

Xu, Shen. 2002. *Shuowen Jiezi*, Beijing: Zhonghua Shuju. 许慎, 说文解字, 卷一. 上 北京: 中华书局.

Yü Chün-fang. 2007. "Eye on Religion: Miracles in the Chinese Buddhist Tradition." *Southern Medical Journal* 100(12): 1243–5.

Yü Ying-Shih. 1981. "'O Soul, Come Back!' A Study in the Changing Conceptions of the Soul and Afterlife in Pre-Buddhist China." *Harvard Journal of Asiatic Studies* 47(2): 363–95.

Yü Ying-Shih. 2016. "New Evidence of the Early Chinese Conception of Afterlife." In Josephine Chiu-Duke, and Michael S. Duke (Eds.): *Chinese History and Culture, volume 1: Sixth Century B.C.E. to Seventeenth Century*. New York: Columbia University Press, 85–90.

Yuan Ke 袁珂. 1978. "*Shanhai jing* xiezuo de shidai ji pianmu kao 山海經寫作的時代及篇目考" in *Zhonghua wenshi luncong 7* 中華文史論叢 7 ies 65(2); (2002): 350–78.

Zhang Xuezhi. 2007. "Several Modalities of the Body-Mind Relationship in Traditional Chinese Philosophy." *Frontiers of Philosophy in China* 2(3): 379–401.

Zhao Zhenxin. 1961. "*Lunyu* jiujing shi shuei bianzuan de" 《論語》究竟是誰編纂的, *Beijing shifan daxue xuebao* 4: 16–20.

Index

A
a-theistic, atheistic 47, 204
Abraham, Abrahamic 1, 2, 8, 180–2, 207
afterlife 3, 4, 5, 6, 7, 9, 52, 69, 87–115, 134, 136, 180, 194–5, 205, 209, 212, 215, 219
agency-detecting device 140–1
agnostic, agnosticism 62–4, 66–7, 69, 104, 189–90, 207
Allan, Sarah 22, 27 184, 204
Ames, Roger 45, 63, 177–9, 195, 203–4, 209–10, 215
Analects Lunyu 論語 5–7, 26, 30, 45, 48, 51, 55–6, 58–70, 82, 88, 95, 98, 104–8, 113, 115–16, 122–1, 126–7, 129, 146–7, 149–50, 161, 177, 179–80, 186, 188–91, 193, 195–7, 199–200, 204, 206–7, 209–10, 212–19
ancestor 3, 5, 9, 13, 20, 22, 41, 88, 90, 94, 97–100, 102–9, 111, 113–14, 116–17, 119, 126–9, 131–6, 141, 143, 170, 178–9, 181, 183, 190, 195–8, 205–6, 211
"Announcement of Merits" 94
"Announcement to the Prince of Kang" 17–19, 121
anthropomorphism, anthropomorphic 4, 13–17, 19, 21–2, 25, 27–8, 33–4, 36, 38–9, 42, 45, 52, 60, 62, 65, 71, 82, 90, 98, 115, 144, 148, 154, 177–9, 184, 193
Azim, Shariff 214

B
Banerjee, Konika 199, 204
Baonan, Liu 106
Baoshan tomb 93
Barrett, Justin 140–1, 199, 203–5, 218
Barrett, Nathaniel 41, 205
de Bary, Theodore 13–14, 20, 59, 207
de Bary, Theodore and Bloom, Irene 192, 207

Bateson, Melissa 142, 205
Behuniak, James 82, 205
benevolence, benevolent (*ren*) *See* humaneness
Bering, Jesse 141, 199, 205
Berkson, Mark 40, 205
Birrell, Anne 186, 205
Blakeley, Barry 187, 205
Bodde, Derk 183, 185, 205
Boileau, Gilles 203, 205
Bokenkamp, Stephen 205
Boltz, William 30, 205
Boyer, Pascal 2, 199, 206
Boyou, ghost of 109, 110
Brashier, Kenneth 95–6, 103–4, 206
Brooks, A. Taeko 49–50, 206
Brooks, E. Bruce and Brooks, A. Taeko 55–6, 104, 187–8, 206
Buddhism, Buddhist 65, 87, 89, 109, 216
Bujard, Marianne 94, 206

C
Chan, Wing-Tsit 188, 206
Chang, K. C. 143, 206
Chang, Sarah 4, 206
Chen Derong 4, 15, 206
Cheng, Ann 200, 203, 206
Cheng, King 15–16, 19, 23, 158, 182
Ching, Julia 206
Chuci, *Odes* 111–12
Chuci 楚辭 (Songs of the South)112, 146–8, 180, 194, 199
Chunqiu fanlu 春秋繁露 177, 179, 213
Clark, Kelly James 3–4, 6–7, 28, 143, 150, 180, 181, 185, 207, 216
Confucian, Confucianism 5, 7, 30–1, 45, 47, 52, 55, 59, 61–3, 66, 75, 82, 88, 91, 94–6, 98, 100, 104, 107–9, 113, 115–17, 119, 121–8, 134–6, 149–50, 161, 177–80, 188–9, 193–6, 200, 204, 206–10, 213, 215, 218–19

Confucius (*Kongzi*) 4–5, 7, 29–31, 40, 47, 49, 55–70, 78, 81–2, 88, 102, 104–9, 113, 116, 119, 122–4, 126–7, 129, 131, 149–50, 177–8, 184, 186–93, 195–8, 203, 206–10, 213–15, 217–18
Cook, Constance 93, 110, 208
creator 1–2, 26, 62, 78, 87, 178, 181, 189
Creel, Herlee Glessner 63–4, 143, 180, 207
Csikszentmihalyi, Mark 30, 187, 196, 207, 212

D
Dahuang xijing 大荒西經 202
Daming 大明 24–6
Dang 蕩 26
Dao, Daoism, Daoist 7, 30, 31, 40, 51, 117, 131, 135, 151, 178, 198, 203, 205, 208, 209, 215, 218
Daodejing 215
Dawson, Raymond 67, 190, 207
de Groot, Jan 110–11, 207
DeFoort, Carine 34–5, 186, 207
demonic, demons 105, 157
Denecke, Webke 35, 71, 186, 207
depersonalization of *Tian* 6, 45–7, 50–1
Di 帝 (the Sovereign on High) 4, 13, 21–4, 41, 94, 98, 115–16, 140, 142–6, 148, 151–2, 156–7, 163, 180–3, 200–1, 206
divination 16–17, 94, 158, 182, 210, 216
DiYanni, Cara 199, 207, 211
The Doctrine of the Mean Zhongyong 中庸 70, 98, 102, 115, 117, 128, 133, 180, 197, 204, 214
Documents, Classic of See *Shangshu*
Dong Zhongshu (Tung Chung-shu) 177–9, 203, 213, 216
dualism, mind-body 5, 87, 97, 109–14, 196, 216, 218
Duke of Zhou 17–18, 102, 128, 151–2
Duofang 多方, *Shangshu* 151, 160, 200
Duoshi 多士, *Shangshu* 151, 200
Durkheim, Emile 135, 207
Durrant, Stephen 184, 208

E
Eno, Robert 21–2, 24, 32, 71–7, 83, 143, 150, 189, 191, 193, 203, 208
Erickson 194, 208

Erya 爾邪 180, 185, 199
Evans, J. St. B. T. 199, 208
extrahuman 4–5, 8–9, 20–3, 25, 32, 62, 71, 89, 140, 142–52, 155, 159–61, 163, 171, 173, 175, 186, 193, 201, 219

F
Falkenhausen, Lothar von 89, 182, 208
Fei Guoyu 非國語 168, 213
Feng Yulan 7, 105, 183–4, 190, 208
Fengshan shu 封禪書, *Shiji* 20, 202
Fibiger Bang, Peter 23, 208
Filial Piety, Classic of, xiaojing 孝治 98, 100–1, 126, 146–7, 180, 199
filial piety, filial, filiality, *xiao* 孝 88, 95–6, 100–3, 106, 108, 111–12, 114, 127–31, 134, 170, 179, 197–8
Fingarette, Herbert 208

G
Gao 誥 (Pronouncements) 15, 182, 198
gentleman (*junzi* 君子) 35, 40, 95, 118, 123–4, 126, 128, 129, 130–1, 133, 192, 198
Gernet, Jacques 2, 148–9, 208
ghosts (gui 鬼) 5–6, 9, 37–8, 41, 67, 88, 103–6, 109–10, 113, 119, 141, 148, 160, 163–4, 194–5, 198, 202, 215–16, 219
ghosts and spirits (*guishen* 鬼神) 67, 163
god, deity 1–2, 4, 6–8, 13, 19, 17, 37, 51, 53, 65, 68–9, 76–7, 87, 96–7, 115–17, 128–36, 139, 151, 155, 166–9, 172, 179–84, 188–9, 202, 204–6, 208, 210, 216
  See also *Di*, *Shangdi Tian*
  High Gods, High Deities, Lord-on-High 1, 4–9, 13–28, 31, 33, 37, 42, 47, 50–1, 61, 71, 78, 80–1, 88, 94, 97–8, 103, 115–17, 128–9, 133–6, 139, 140–5, 148, 150–5, 157, 159, 161, 163, 180–4, 183, 201, 208
  Lesser Gods, Lesser Deities 9, 13, 20, 49, 61, 103, 142, 163–75, 181, 183, 219
Goldberg, Robert 199, 208
Goldin, Paul Rakita 5–6, 109–10, 168, 186, 189, 193, 195, 209

Gongyang zhuan 公羊傳 147, 180, 199, 200
govern, government 22-3, 32-3, 36, 39, 42, 73, 95, 98-100, 103, 116-17, 123, 125, 131-3, 144, 155, 164-6, 169-70, 174, 178
Graham, A. C. 6-7, 87-8, 109, 148-9, 152, 155-6, 161, 197, 209
Granet, Marcel 1-2, 4, 209
Guanzi 管子 146-7, 180, 199
gui 鬼 See ghosts
guishen 鬼神 See ghosts and spirits
Guliang zhuan 穀梁傳 146-7, 180, 199-200
Guo Moruo 郭沫若 4, 14, 180, 209
Guoyu 國語 25, 50, 146-8, 156-7, 161, 163-4, 166-8, 170-1, 175, 184, 186, 200-1, 203-4, 213, 219
Guthrie, Stewart 21, 199, 209

H
Haidt, Jonathan 135, 197, 209, 211
Hall, David 45, 63, 177-9, 191-2, 203-4, 209-10
Hanfeizi 韓非子 26, 147, 180, 186, 199
Hardy, Grant 184, 209
harmony 和 *he* 18, 41-2, 51, 59, 63-4, 70, 75, 78, 91, 97, 100-3, 105-6, 108, 117-29, 131-2, 134-5, 158, 166, 183, 195, 197
Harper, Donald 209
Hayashi, Minao 184, 209
Heaven 天 (*tian*, *t'ien*) 1-2, 4, 6-8, 13-29, 31-52, 55-83, 87, 91-4, 96-8, 100-1, 103, 106, 100-18, 120-2, 126-7, 129-31, 133, 136-7, 148-51, 153-4, 156, 158-9, 163, 169-70, 172, 177-9, 182-4, 187-93, 196-8, 206, 208, 213, 215
hell 93
Henderson, John 186, 209, 214
Henrich, Joseph 136, 204, 210, 214
Ho, Ping-ti 181, 210
Hon, Tze Ki 182, 216
Hsu, Cho-Yun 183-4, 210
Huainanzi 淮南子 186
Huan Tui 59, 129
humaneness, benevolence *ren* 仁 40, 59, 63, 67, 73, 79, 116-17, 123-35, 178, 182, 192

humanism, humanist 6, 45, 47, 63, 91, 93, 104-5
hun 魂, *hunpo* 魂魄 (soul) 91-2, 96, 110-14
Hunter, Michael 55, 187, 196, 210, 218

I
immortality 87, 93-4, 141, 213, 217
Ivanhoe, Philip 62, 82-3, 107-8, 189, 191, 205-6, 208-10, 215

J
Jensen, Lionel 210
jiang 降 (sending down) 183
jiao 郊 sacrifice 179
Johnson, Dominic 142, 199-200, 205, 210
junzi 君子 See gentleman

K
Kalinowski, Marc 2, 210
Karlgren, Bernhard 15-16, 182, 184, 210
Keightley, David 13, 143, 181, 203, 210-11
Kelemen, Deborah 199, 207, 211, 216
Keltner, Dacher 197, 211
Kern, Martin 30, 205, 212
King Wen See Wen, King
Knights, Stephen 200, 210
Knoblock, John 159-60, 198, 212
Kongzi 孔子 See Confucius 55, 113, 113, 114, 195
Kunio, Shima 22, 212

L
Lagerwey, John 2, 206, 208, 210, 212, 221, 215-16
Lady Dai 92
Lai Guolong 90, 93, 212
Lai Kehong 188-9, 212
Laozi 老子 30-1, 146-7, 180, 199, 213
Lau, D. C. 150, 212
Lawson, E. Thomas 199, 212
Leeming, David 4, 212
legalism 179, 218
Legge, James 1, 3, 14-19, 99-101, 121-2, 151, 153-5, 182-3, 190, 197-8, 212, 215
Lewis, Mark 22, 92-3, 144, 159, 184, 212-13

Leys, Simon 69, 213
Liang Qichao 175, 213
Liezi 172, 203
Liji 禮記 See *Rites, Classic of*
Linduff, Katheryn 183-4, 210
Liu Zongyuan 168, 213
Loewe, Michael 2, 48-9, 92, 148, 142, 153, 200, 208-9, 211, 213-14, 217-18
Louden, Robert 65, 213
Lunyu 論語 See *Analects*
Lunyu Zhengyi 論語正義 61, 204
Lüshi Chunqiu 呂氏春秋 See *Spring and Autumn Annals*

M

Makeham, John 187, 191, 213-14
Mandate of Heaven *Tianming* 天命 15-19, 25, 27, 47, 56, 58, 61-2, 73-5, 80-1, 94, 120, 129, 182-4, 188, 192
McCauley, Robert 199, 212-13, 219
Mencius *Mengzi* 孟子 7-8, 26, 31, 51, 64, 71-83, 115, 128, 146-7, 149, 150, 156, 159, 180, 186, 189, 193, 199, 204-5, 210, 212, 214
Minggui xia 明鬼下 Mozi (understanding ghosts) 148, 200, 202
Mohist 6, 31, 150, 209
monotheism 180-1, 183, 215
Mote, Frederick 1, 214
Mozi 墨子 6-7, 27, 31, 34-41, 51, 82, 115, 146-50, 152, 155-6, 159, 161, 163-4, 180, 186, 195, 199-200, 202, 204, 207, 215, 219
Mueller, Charles 102-3, 214
Mungello, David 220
Munro, Donald 77, 193, 208, 214

N

naturalism, naturalistic 32, 36, 51, 56, 65, 80, 91, 93, 178, 184, 193
naturalizing narrative 6-8, 51, 83
Needham, Joseph 87-8, 214
Nettle, Daniel 146, 205
Ni Peimin 7, 214
Nivison, David 214
Norenzayan, Ara 136, 199, 214
Nylan, Michael 30-1, 182, 186, 196, 200, 207-8, 214-15, 218

O

Odes, Classic of, Poetry, Songs, Book of Songs, Shijing 詩經 5, 23-6, 28, 50, 65, 80, 95, 97-8, 102, 107, 111-12, 114-16, 120, 128, 130, 146-8, 150, 153-6, 158, 161, 180, 182, 184-6, 188, 199-201, 204, 210, 212, 218
oracle bones 13, 22, 24, 94, 181, 183, 208, 210
Overmeyer, Daniel 2, 215

P

Pan Geng 98-9, 132
Pankenier 17, 215
paradise 92-4, 200, 213
pattern of Heaven 22, 27, 59-60, 68, 81, 100, 122, 129, 131, 134, 183
peace *ning* 寧 16, 18, 75, 78, 81-2, 108
personator 206
Pfister, Lauren 215
Pines, Yuri 46-52, 187, 215
Pirazzoli-t'Serstevens, Michele 91, 94, 194, 215
po 魄, soul 91, 110-11, 113, 196
Poetry, Classic of See *Odes, Classic of*
Poo, Mu-chou 2, 94, 103, 194, 215
Prince Feng 121-2
Puett, Michael 2, 4, 14, 59, 68, 181, 183-4, 193, 198, 203, 216
punishment 6-7, 19, 25, 28, 29, 38, 60, 98, 99, 103, 107, 117, 121-4, 127, 132, 134-6, 166, 168, 175, 183, 201
punishment theory, supernatural 8, 139-61, 199

Q

Qiwulun 齊物論, *Zhuangzi* 171-3

R

Raphals, Lisa 23, 216
Rawson, Jessica 89, 216
Records of the Grand Historian See *Shiji*
Redmond, Geoffrey 182, 216
ren 仁 See humaneness
respect, respectful 2, 22, 62-4, 75, 94, 96, 99-102, 106, 108, 114, 121, 125-8, 130-2, 134, 135, 139, 151, 156, 166, 169, 188, 190, 192, 200

reverence 17, 19, 30, 37, 56, 63, 80–1, 88, 96, 100–1, 117, 122, 125–9, 131, 132, 134–5, 170, 188, 192, 194, 196
reward 7–8, 19, 25, 28, 38, 98, 107–8, 112, 123, 131, 140–1, 143–55, 157–61, 172, 201
Riegel, Jeffrey 159–60, 212
righteous, righteousness *yi* 義 8, 16, 35–6, 38–9, 80, 98, 102–3, 124–5, 128, 130, 133, 135, 145, 150, 178
Rites, Classic of Liji 禮記 7, 16, 98–100, 109, 111–12, 116, 124–5, 127–8, 130, 132–3, 135, 180, 185,195–7
rites, ritual *li* 禮 2–3, 5, 7–8, 17–18, 20, 32, 46–7, 51, 59, 63–4, 88–91, 93–100, 102–3, 107–9, 111–19, 122–6, 142, 149, 153, 160, 165, 168–9, 171, 180, 182, 185, 189–92, 194, 196–8, 201, 203, 205–6, 208, 210, 212, 215–16, 218–19
Roberts, Gilbert 142, 205
Rorty, Richard 207, 216
Rottman, Josh 199, 211, 216
Rudd, Melanie 197, 216
ruist 95, 189, 191–2
Rushou 156–7, 200

S

sacrifice 5, 7, 13, 14, 19–20, 23, 37–8, 64, 80–1, 90, 93, 96, 98, 100–4, 106–7, 111, 115–21, 123, 125, 126–31, 138, 135, 144, 149, 151, 160, 164–70, 179, 183, 184, 185, 190, 194, 197, 202, 206, 209, 212, 216, 218
sage 18, 21, 27, 33, 41, 50, 52, 58, 41–2, 56, 59, 71, 116, 138, 182, 192, 194, 196, 212, 216
sage-king 34, 59, 100, 106, 162, 168, 186
Santangelo, Paolo 87, 217
Saroglou, Vassilis 197, 218
Schaberg, David 50, 200, 217
schools *jia* 家 5, 29–31, 51, 121, 196
Schwartz, Benjamin 6–7, 14, 58–9, 83, 182, 217
Schwitzgebel, Eric 171, 217
Seidel, Anna 194, 217
shaman, shamanism 171–2, 203, 205, 211, 214

Shangdi 上帝 1, 4, 13, 21–4, 29, 31, 61, 71, 73, 78, 80, 94, 98, 115–16, 140, 142–6, 148, 154–5, 160, 163, 179–83, 190, 193, 200–1
Shangshu 尚書, *Shujing* 書經, Documents 14–16 25, 28, 65, 78, 98, 107, 115–17, 121–2, 132, 146–8, 150–3, 155–156, 158–61, 165, 180, 182–4, 186, 193, 198–200, 202, 204, 212, 217
Shao Tuo's Tomb 92–3, 182
Shaughnessy, Edward 21, 157, 188, 215, 217, 219, 220, 223
shen 神, spirit, soul, spiritual being 41, 61–2, 91–2, 98–9, 110–11, 113, 142, 156–7, 163, 166, 185, 190, 195, 198, 200, 202, 218
Shenzi 慎子 180, 199
Shiji 史記 Records of the Grand Historian, the Historical Records 19–21, 31, 168, 184–5, 202, 217
Shijing 詩經 See *Odes, Classic of*
Shou, King 117, 121
Shtulman, Andrew 199, 217
Shujing 書經 See *Shangshu*
Shun, King 24, 34, 73–4, 76, 79, 81, 121, 124–5, 149–50, 168, 198
Shuowen jiezi 說文解字 185, 202, 219
Sima Hou 47–8
Sima Qian 司馬遷 208–9, 217
Sima Tan 司馬談 30, 218
skill, skillfulness 27, 39, 171–3, 203, 205
Slingerland, Edward 150, 188, 192, 195–6, 198, 214, 217–18
Smith, Kidder 30, 218
Songs, Book of Songs See *Odes, Classic of*
Songs of the South See *Chuci* 楚辭
Sosis, Richard 142, 199, 218
soul, summoning, recalling 111–13, 194, 219
soul 41, 87–88, 90–3, 96–7, 109–13, 194–5, 216, 219
    see also *shen, po, hun*
Spring and Autumn Annals, Lushi Chunqiu 呂氏春秋 25–8, 146–8, 159–61, 180, 185–6, 199–200, 204
Standaert, Nicolas 34–5, 186, 207
Sterckx, Roel 65, 142, 190, 198, 218

T

Sunzi bingfa 孫子兵法 147, 180, 199
superknower, superknowing 8, 45 61–2, 141

T
Tang 湯, first King of Shang 99, 151–2, 160
Tanggao 湯誥 151
Tangshi 湯誓 157
Tao, Taoism, Taoist *See* Dao, Daoism, Daoist
teleological 199, 204, 211, 216
theodicy 77, 81
Thompson-Schill, Sharon 199, 208
Tian, T'ien 天 *See* Heaven
Tianbao 天保, *Shijing* 153–4, 200
Tiandao 天道, *Zhuangzi* 31, 40, 42, 209
Tiandi 天地, *Zhuangzi* 31, 40, 42, 174
Tianlun 天論, *Xunzi* 31–2, 200
Tianming 天命 *See* Mandate of Heaven
Tianzhi 天志 of the *Mozi* 33, 37, 154, 192
Toeless Shushan 29, 30
Tractatus Logico-Philosophicus 68–9, 219
Tung Chung-shu, *See* Dong Zhongshu
Turner, Karen 23, 208

U
underworld 91–2, 94, 96–7, 194
  see also, Yellow Spring

V
Valcarcel, Joshua 199, 217
Valdesolo, Piercarlo 197, 218
van Els, Paul 34, 218
Van Norden, Bryan 65, 195, 218
virtue, de 德 15, 17–19, 24, 26–7, 29, 38–42, 50, 58–61, 69, 73–4, 79–80, 94–6, 99–100, 104, 108, 111, 114, 116, 119, 122–35, 141, 143, 145, 148, 150, 152–3, 157–8, 161, 164–71, 174–5, 178–9, 193, 198, 201–2

W
Waley, Arthur 55, 97, 218
Wang Ni 172–3
Wang Zhongjiang 7, 219
Wangsun Gu 60–1, 189
Wawrytko, Sandra 219
Weiming, Tu 218

Wen, King 16, 24, 25, 50–51, 60, 97–98, 117, 121, 152, 159, 160–160, 185, 198
Wen 文, culture 47, 51, 59–60, 152, 159–160, 171, 183, 194
Whitehouse, Harvey 199, 209
Wilson, Thomas 5, 88, 105–106, 109, 186, 194–197, 215, 219
Wiltermuth, Scott 136, 219
Winslett, Justin 3–4, 8, 21, 28, 163–164, 180–181, 185, 201, 207, 219
Wittgenstein, Ludwig 68–69, 89, 192, 219
wuwei 無為 41, 205
Wuzi 吳子 147, 180, 199

X
xiao 孝 *See* filial piety
Xiaojing 孝治 *See* Filial Piety, Classic of
Xunzi 荀況, Xun Kuang 6, 26, 29, 31–4, 40–1, 47, 51, 83, 91, 146–7, 150, 156, 159, 180, 186, 193, 196, 198–200, 204, 209, 213, 215

Y
Yan Shigu 183
Yanzi chunqiu 晏子春秋 146, 180, 199–201
Yao 堯 34, 58–9, 73, 76, 78–9, 81, 124–5, 129, 149–50, 167–8, 170, 198
Yellow Spring, Dark City 91, 94
Yü Chün-fang 1, 219

Z
Zhanguo 戰國 51–2
Zhongyong 中庸 *See The Doctrine of the Mean*
Zhouli 周禮 98, 103, 146–7, 180, 199
Zhuangzi 莊子 6, 27, 29–31, 39–42, 83, 146–7, 161, 163–4, 171–5, 180, 186, 199–200, 203, 205–6, 208, 217
Zigong 61, 65–8, 105, 191–2
Zilu 60, 104–6, 149–50
zu-sacrifice 99
Zuozhuan 左傳, *Zuo Commentary on the Spring and Autumn Annals* 22, 24, 46–52, 109–11, 146–7, 156–8, 161, 163–5, 167–8, 170–1, 174–5, 180, 184–5, 187, 195–6, 199, 199–204, 219

www.ingramcontent.com/pod-product-compliance
Lightning Source LLC
Chambersburg PA
CBHW062220300426
44115CB00012BA/2143